Bt 4.85

P9-AOK-332

BEN JONSON
AND THE LANGUAGE
OF PROSE COMEDY

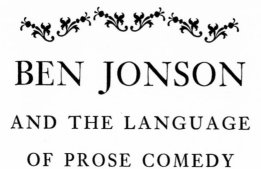

BEN JONSON

AND THE LANGUAGE

OF PROSE COMEDY

Jonas A. Barish

HARVARD UNIVERSITY PRESS

Cambridge, Massachusetts

1 9 6 0

Publication of this book has been aided by
a grant from the Ford Foundation

Distributed in Great Britain by Oxford University Press, London

✲

Typography and Design by Burton J Jones

Printed in the U.S.A. by Harvard University Printing Office

Bound by Stanhope Bindery, Inc., Boston

✲

Library of Congress Catalog Card Number 60–7987

TO HARRY LEVIN

Acknowledgments

If the good will of others sufficed to make books excellent, the present study would automatically qualify as a masterpiece: it has been blessed beyond its deserts by friendly counsel, and the number of those who at one time or another durings its preparation have rescued my fainting spirits from despair is legion. Happily, such debts become pleasures when it is possible to acknowledge them. To John J. Enck I owe not only the suggestion of the subject in the first place, and more than one lynx-eyed perusal of the text, but scores of inspiriting conversations, over the years, about Jonson and about literature. Lowry Nelson, Jr., read the earliest version of the manuscript as it came formless into the world, and with criticism both forthright and gentle helped lick it into preliminary shape. At a later date, in a foreign city, R. W. Flint gamely read through a semilegible typescript and enabled me to view it through the eyes of an impassioned and insightful, but nonacademic, critic of literature. Latest of all, Stanley Cavell turned a gaze of the utmost beneficence, wisdom, and penetration on the final draft, illuminating its dark corners and helping to dispel some cobwebs.

My most continuous and unpayable debt is to Harry Levin, under whose surveillance the present study was begun long ago, and to whom it is affectionately dedicated. If I may do so without temerity, I shall beg leave to borrow Jonson's phrase for himself when he inscribed *Cynthia's Revels* for Camden: "alumnus olim, aeternum amicus."

I should like to thank Elizabeth Walser and Sherna Steinberg for help in readying the manuscript for the press.

ACKNOWLEDGMENTS

An earlier version of part of Chapter II appeared in *PMLA*, in June 1958, under the title "Baroque Prose in the Theater: Ben Jonson." A portion of Chapter V was published in *Modern Language Quarterly* of March 1959, under the title "*Bartholomew Fair* and its Puppets." To the editors of both these journals, my thanks for permission to reprint.

Berkeley, California
February 23, 1960

CONTENTS

BEN JONSON

AND THE LANGUAGE
OF PROSE COMEDY

I

Antecedents

Prose has for so long now been the normal language of comedy that one tends to think of it, perhaps, as the "natural" language of the genre. When critics describe a contemporary playwright, like Giraudoux, as "poetic," they do not mean that he is writing in verse. When, on the other hand, a playwright like Christopher Fry chooses to write comedies in verse, he stamps himself immediately as an experimenter. In the sixteenth century, needless to say, it was otherwise. Verse was the norm, and prose the exotic intruder. As a language for explicitly literary works of art, the latter had barely intruded with Malory. In the hands of sixteenth-century writers, it underwent a series of strenuous trials and errors, in which its possibilities as a literary medium were explored by the importing into it of techniques associated with poetry, medieval pulpit rhetoric, and classic oratory. Fostered by such champions of style as Roger Ascham, these explorations culminated in the scrollwork of *Euphues* and the *Arcadia,* and in the massive sonorities of Hooker's *Laws,* each a triumph of style that tended to shun, rather than court, resemblance to ordinary speech. But before this cycle had run its course a countercycle was in motion that aimed at the exact opposite, at the repudiation of "curiosity" and a return to "naturalness."

I

Tentatively, first, in the cony-catching pamphlets of Greene and others, and then, more self-consciously, in the pamphlet skirmishes between Nashe and Harvey, the Ciceronianism of Ascham and the ornateness of Lyly were arraigned, condemned, and replaced with a licentious style that affected to dispense with all artifice. The first wave of experiment tended to make prose the rival of verse. The second tended to give it a character as distinct as possible from that of verse, and (in principle) as close as possible to the spoken word.[1]

More sporadically, an analogous process was taking place in the theater. Lyly, writing for the court, converted his own Euphuism into a mannered stage prose from which realism was severely barred, while the writers for the public playhouses, with little assistance from formal rhetoric, began clumsily to transfer live speech into the mouths of clowns and rustics. The two currents converge in the prose of Shakespeare and Jonson, who have in common, if nothing else, a style that can pass without effort from the most vibrant solemnity to the most loose-jointed colloquial chatter, a style firmly grounded in a conscious rhetoric and at the same time able to absorb large quantities of realistic material. Shakespeare belongs, on the whole, to the older school of rhetorical ornament, Jonson to the newer school of antirhetorical naturalness. Shakespeare uses a syntax derived from Lyly, in which artful symmetry plays a cardinal role. In Jonson, syntactic effects are equally studied, but with a different purpose: to dislocate symmetry and thus create the illusion of the absence of rhetoric. In Jonson, with his mimetic bias, obvious rhetorical patterning is often associated with insincerity or affectation in a character. In Shakespeare, it may only imply heightened feeling or witty playfulness. Shakespeare gradually discovers the possibilities of realism within the formal syntactic frame, Jonson achieves realism by disrupting such formality from the outset.

It would be, if not impossible, at least very difficult to write a connected history of comic prose before Jonson. Prior to 1590 especially, the plays survive haphazardly, often in mangled texts, of uncertain date and conjectural authorship. One finds prose used now throughout, now in scattered scenes, now not at all. Often it absents itself from comedy and makes desultory intrusions into tragedy. Now it seems to be the object of the author's loving care, now an object of no care whatever. Sometimes it represents revision by a later hand; sometimes it is merely tumbling measure or blank verse misprinted; sometimes it is masked as blank verse by the reverse kind of misprinting. The number of interlocking variables is intimidatingly large. Instead of attempting a connected history, therefore, the present chapter will glance selectively at a few landmarks of prose comedy between 1566 and 1597, in order to map out roughly the terrain Jonson entered when he began his career in the theater.

The chief instrument of survey in the present chapter, and almost the sole one in Chapter II, will be study of syntax, the arrangements of words whereby an artist urges his material into form more continuously and perhaps at a deeper level than by the conscious employment of stylistic devices. Not that one can divorce syntax from other stylistic categories. Many of the formal rhetorical schemes (asyndeton, anaphora, and the like) belong explicitly to the domain of syntax; they are methods of arranging words, and are so labeled by traditional analysts. A metaphor, any image, must assume *some* syntactic embodiment. Vocabulary itself not merely conforms to syntactic patterns, it often dictates them; and concern with syntax will on occasion prove identical with concern for grammar. Nevertheless, to read for syntax is to alert oneself to something distinct: the ways an author yokes his phrases together or splits them apart; the size, shape, and texture of the phrases themselves; the kinds he shuns as well as those he prefers; the degrees of likeness or unlikeness among them. And all of this, as in any stylistic study, to get the feel of the style, to take its pulse, and then to relate that pulse to the larger currents of meaning that inform the author's imaginative world.

I

The alliance between comic prose and realism begins to form at least as early as 1566, when George Gascoigne translated Ariosto's *I suppositi* into English under the title of *Supposes*. The fact that Gascoigne was free to choose between alternate versions of his original, one in verse, one in prose — and that, indeed, he worked simultaneously from both texts [2] — perhaps lends some significance to his choice of prose for his own version. Prose, in any case, makes its entry into English drama in a city-comedy rich in potentialities for realism, and the first thing we notice when we compare *Supposes* with *I suppositi* is that Gascoigne has infused into the language a good many realistic touches for which Ariosto supplies no authority. Gascoigne tends to particularize: instead of "eggs," he will say "twenty eggs"; instead of "money," he will specify sums and name coins. He interpolates native proverbs into the dialogue, giving the speech of his characters a strong local flavor, and he indulges in the colloquial habit of multiplying abusive epithets, Ariosto's "malefica vecchia" (I, 124),[3] for example, becoming "old scabbed queane" (III.iv.67), and "questo tisico / Vecchio" (I.iii.384–385), "this olde doting doctor, this buzard, this bribing villaine" (I.iii.100–101). In fact, though he worked with his Ariosto at both elbows, and thus committed himself to reproducing the chief rhetorical features of the original — the soliloquies, exhortations, and

4

apostrophes — it is fair to say that both the merits and defects of style in *Supposes* are his own.

The chief stylistic virtue is the increased picturesqueness of the language. The most obvious defect is Gascoigne's relentless hunt for the letter, which produces a lumpy, thudding, spasmodic rhythm. If Ariosto says:

Né ti bastava avermi gittato questo laccio ne' piedi, se ancora non facevi l'amorosa trama del giovane Erostrato insiememente discoperta riuscire? Tu l'hai tenuta giá dua anni sino a questa ora occulta, per riserbarti a questo scelerato giorno a rivelarla,   (I, 146)

Gascoigne translates:

Neither art thou content to entangle me alone in thy ruinous ropes; but thou must also catch the right Erostrato in thy crooked clawes, to reward us both with open shame and rebuke. Two yeeres hast thou kept secrete our subtill supposes, even this day to discipher them with a sorowfull successe.   (V.iii.24–30)

"Ruinous ropes" is more specific than "laccio," and "crooked clawes" is certainly more vivid than "trama," yet Gascoigne's version deforms the original in more than one way. It not only throws excessive emphasis on the alliterated pairs, but it spoils the continuity of Ariosto's metaphor. Fortune, in Ariosto's version, throws a snare about Dulipo's feet and at the same time reveals the "amorous net" it has woven for Erostrato. In Gascoigne, it throws ruinous ropes, and then, like a harpy, sets to work with its claws, producing the gratuitously specified miseries of "open shame and rebuke." The link between Ariosto's two sentences, through "amorosa trama," is broken by Gascoigne, who abandons the metaphor in search of new alliterative discoveries, and these new combinations, "subtill supposes," "sorowfull successe," absorb all the weight of the second sentence and bleed the emphasis out of the sequence that in Ariosto comes to a climax with "scelerato giorno."

Gascoigne is, himself, ensnared in the ruinous ropes of a penchant for "poetical" embellishments, chiefly Petrarchan similes, and caught in the crooked claws of a northern Protestant passion for moralizing. The Petrarchan ornaments tend to be pasted on without much concern for decorum or for the texture of the language as a whole; the moralizing habit results in the expansion of ethical maxims, and, in at least one instance, in a full-scale homily.

Each of these traits — the excessive alliteration, the Petrarchizing, the sermonizing — tends to counteract the realism in the dialogue and produce a sense of unreality, of meaningless emphasis and intermittent "fine" writing. The instability of texture, perhaps, is the only stable thing about the style. Just beneath the violent alliteration and the exclamatory outbursts one discovers a prevailing diffuseness. Gascoigne is often merely prolix, heaping up little expletive phrases that clog the forward movement of the dialogue. Where Ariosto's old man laments "se io venissi a morte et egli non vi si trovassi, me ne morrei disperato" (I, 131), Gascoigne interpolates two pleonastic phrases: "I am olde nowe, and if God shoulde call mee in his absence, *I promise you I thinke* it woulde drive me into disperation" (IV.iii.69–72, my italics). Even when aiming for economy, Gascoigne often manages to produce a wordy or diluted version of the original. Where Ariosto says, "Amar li figliuoli è cosa umana, ma averne tanta tenerezza è feminile" (I, 131), Gascoigne translates, "It is commendable in a man to love his children, but to be so tender over them is more womanlike" (IV.iii.73–75). Ariosto's maxim is hardly a model of epigrammatic compression, but it has a certain compactness, which Gascoigne manages to smudge in several ways at once. By altering the order of object and subject in the first clause, he destroys the symmetry between the two halves of the statement; he blurs the opposition between "cosa

6

umana" and "feminile" into a feeble contrast between "commendable" and "womanlike"; and by inserting the weak little adverb "more" before "womanlike," he undermines the antithetic feel of the whole statement almost beyond repair.

At the root of the trouble lies the fact that Gascoigne does not work with a very flexible syntax. The tendency to load down his sentences with heaps of little words would matter less if it were not linked to a persistent preference for clumsy connectives, unwieldy constructions involving auxiliary clauses, and in general a preference for a roundabout rather than a direct way of stating a thing. Conjunctions like "to the end that," "in such sort that," "by the means that" are not only awkward in themselves, they are the cause of further awkwardness in the clauses that must follow them. Gascoigne's habit of multiplying subordinate clauses to do the work of modifiers occasionally can be traced to the effort to convey a sentence accurately into English, but his English, with its weak modal auxiliaries, is no match for the panoply of precise subordinate tenses and moods available to Ariosto. "Venivo per vedere se io trovavo Pasifilo, che io lo menassi a desinar meco" (I, 110) bristles with dependent verbs, but it seems concise next to Gascoigne's rendering, which actually uses fewer words: "I come to seeke Pasiphilo, to the ende he may dine with mee" (II.iv.5–6).

Uncertain handling of syntax appears most strikingly in Gascoigne's odd addiction to a negative rather than a positive form of statement. Instead of saying, "I think thus and so," Gascoigne will say, "I do not think but that thus and so"; instead of "This has begun well" (Ariosto: "Il principio è assai buono" [I, 109]), he will say "This geare hath had no evill beginning" (II.iii.1–2); instead of "Who would have believed such a thing of her?" ("Chi averia di lei cosí creduto?" [I, 123]), "Who wold have beleeved the contrary but that she

7

had bin a virgin?" (III.iv.53–54). When he expands on Ariosto, it is often to add some kind of negative affirmation, as in the following examples, where the additions are represented in brackets.

I met, at the foote of the hill, a gentleman riding with two or three men: [and as me thought by his habite and his lookes, he should be none of the wisest].   (II.i.92–95)

[. . . yet all this while I thought not that anye body had heard me, but it befell cleane contrarye;] for my maister was on the other side of the wall . . .   (III.v.28–31)

Gascoigne, in short, instead of confronting a statement directly, prefers to sidle around it like a crab. The result is to turn even a simple statement into a winding, circuitous syntactic journey.

Obviously the roundabout connective, the pleonasm, the negative assertion, contain expressive possibilities. They do not constitute stylistic faults per se. But Gascoigne seems fettered to them. He repeatedly finds himself in awkward syntactic situations from which he can extricate himself only by further awkwardness. Hence the pervasive sense of ineffectuality about the prose of *Supposes*. It needs its joints tightened. The alliteration, instead of acting as a discreet binder, merely ties the language into clumsy knots, and thus further hampers it in its task of knitting together the action.

The point, which will have to be made again, is simply that a fluid, unobtrusive syntax — not to speak of a vigorous or eloquent one — is by no means the birthright of a dramatic author, even though he may, like Monsieur Jourdain, have been speaking prose all his life. The first problem, and it was acute in the sixteenth century, was to find a rhetoric that could accomplish the basic business of stage dialogue clearly and economically. The second requirement was a rhetoric with enough potency of its own to do the subtler things for which language exists in the theater — to convey gradations of feeling, to establish atmosphere, and to suggest complexity of motivation.

2

Whether or not *Supposes* exercised any influence on subsequent comedy is a matter of conjecture. More important, probably, was Italian precedent in general, to which Elizabethan authors were prone to submit in every sphere of literary activity.[4] But we seem to owe the first genuine comic prose in English to a fluke, to the fact that the most gifted court playwright under Elizabeth — John Lyly — was also the author of *Euphues* and *Euphues and his England*, two romances whose fabulous virtuosity of style made anything that had been written before seem crude and barbarous. By taking his models in art rather than life, by manipulating words in as many intricate ways as he could devise, by burnishing his phrases like a goldsmith working on precious metals, Lyly had hammered out a style that had made him famous overnight. And when he came to adapt this style for the theater,[5] he had the tact to recognize that it would lend itself better to fantasy than to realism.

Accordingly, he invented a dramatic world for which his jeweler's prose seemed the only normal language, a world governed by its own laws, which disdained all kinship with ordinary affairs. It was a world, as he urged his auditors to remember, composed of *"fictions," "pastimes,"* and *"fancies"* (III, 21);[6] "a Labyrinth of conceites," a "daunce of a Farie in a circle" (II, 416), and *"a tale of the Man in the Moone"* (III, 21); images of things seen "in a deepe dreame" (II, 372), and "shadowes" (II, 317); "a Gallimaufrey," *"a mingle-mangle," "an Hodge-podge"* (III, 115), concocted without reference to the laws of geometry or physics, a never-never land of gods and shepherds in which the courtly spectators might see their own desires transfigured. In Lyly's world, villains can blaspheme without grossness; witches can cast their enchantments without ugliness; pages can bandy off-color jests without seeming indecent, and complain of their toothaches and their empty stomachs without persuading us that they have ever suffered from either. The perpetual embarkation for Cythera that takes place in Lyly's comedies assumes a certain Watteauesque poignancy, perhaps, from the hard facts of court life and their author's own embittered career, but nothing ever mars the translucent surface: no blood stains the garments of his soldiers, the monster never comes to eat the virgin, and lust and greed are always mysteriously transmuted into an aspiration after beauty. Every earthly emotion emerges purified in the delicate tracery of the prose, which acts as chief agent of transformation. The glitter of the antitheses and similitudes, the mock logic and combats of wit, become an appropriately radiant music for the cloud-cuckoo land, turning the festive weddings and allegorical triumphs and ritual reconciliations into air and fire.

The signal quality of Lyly's prose may be described as its logicality,[7] the analytic syntax that passes every idea and sentiment through a prism, so as to dissect its hidden contradictions. In the plays the colors of the spectrum begin to melt into each other. The paromoiotic devices that articulate the bands so rigidly in *Euphues* and *Euphues and his England* begin to diminish. Certain stiff syntactic formulas used to frame antithetic statements — "by how much the more . . . by so much the more," for example — gradually disappear. The analytic disposition of the syntax continues to mirror the symmetries of the plots, but there is a softening of outline, a lifting of the heavy beat and thump of like sounds coming at predictable intervals. The style undulates instead of goose-stepping. This modification in technique accompanies an advance in quality. Looking at two passages on a similar theme, one can see how the brash smartness of the early style modulates into the genuine elegance of the later one. In the first instance, Euphues is urging his feminine acquaintances not to forget the passage of time:

When the blacke crowes foote shall appeare in theyr eye, or the blacke Oxe treade on their foote, when their beautie shall be lyke the blasted Rose, theyr wealth wasted, their bodies worne, theyr faces wrinckled, their fyngers crooked, who will lyke of them in their age, who loued none in their youth? If you will be cherished when you be olde, be curteous while you be young, if you looke for comfort in your hoary haires, be not coye when you haue your golden lockes, if you would be embraced in the wayning of your brauery, be not squeymish in the waxing of your beautie, if you desyre to be kept lyke the Roses when they haue loste theyr coulour, smell sweete as the Rose doth in the bud, if you would be tasted for olde wyne, be in the mouth a pleasant Grape, so shall you be cherished for your curtesie, comforted for your honestie, embraced for your amitie, so shall you be preserued with the sweete Rose, and droncke with the pleasant wyne.   (I, 203)

Despite a certain melancholy gracefulness in this passage, especially in the opening lines, one can scarcely help feeling that the great Elizabethan theme of mortality has rarely been handled with less conviction. The first sentence, with its well-worn proverbs and its listless enumeration of wealth, bodies, faces, and fingers, limps to a conclusion so predictable as to border on banality. The alliterated pairs that follow, "cherished" and "curteous," "comfort" and "coye," and so on, strike one as proceeding chiefly from the desire to alliterate; "hoary haires" must have provoked a yawn even from Euphues' listeners. The antithesis between "wayning of your brauery" and "waxing of your beautie" suffers badly from the fact that while "wayning" and "waxing" are genuine oppositions, "brauery" and "beautie" are merely synonymous. As for the vegetable persuasions of the peroration, how a rose while young can avoid smelling sweet, or how a grape tasted in the mouth can then survive to be turned into old wine, the hastily spun figures do not trouble to explain. Throughout, the claims to logicality implied by the syntax are defeated, or weakened, by the semantic pattern itself.[8]

It may possibly be objected that Lyly is here deliberately suggesting sophistry — the perversion of Euphues' wit [9] — but the same sophistry creeps into the speeches of Eubulus, whose wit is not perverse, and is absent from the spell of the wicked crone Dipsas of *Endimion* as she casts the hero into his enchanted sleep:

Thou that laist downe with golden lockes, shalt not awake vntill they bee turned to siluer haires; and that chin, on which scarcely appeareth soft downe, shalbe filled with brissels as hard as broome: thou shalt sleep out thy youth and flowring time, and become dry hay before thou knowest thy selfe greene grasse, & ready by age to step into the graue when thou wakest, that was youthfull in the Courte when thou laidst thee downe to sleepe.

(II.iii.29–36)

Here Lyly reviews the great commonplaces with a meditative lyricism that any of the song writers might have envied. The jealousy of Tellus is purified into a pensive regret. Endimion's enchanted sleep is transmuted into a symbol of the dreamlike passage of life. The symmetrical clarity of the syntax, slightly muted by the departures from strict parison, serves not as excuse for verbal jingles but to articulate a fresh vision of the transition from youth to age. The familiar metaphor of the withering plant evolves so that Endimion gradually becomes associated with nature; he is not mechanically coupled to it as are the ladies to the grapes and roses of the earlier passage. The "siluer haires" (not "hoary haires," as in the clinking doublet of *Euphues*) suggest a precious residue that survives after the first gold has faded. The "brissels as hard as broome" begin to emphasize the process of change that Endimion shares with the rest of nature, and the process reaches an affecting climax in the contrast between "dry hay" and "greene grasse," where the unexpected reversal of the normal chronological order produces a poignant effect of compression, suggestive of the brevity of life that is the theme of the passage. The same reversal prevails in the next and final antithesis, so that whereas at first we looked forward with the speaker into Endimion's old age, we now at the end of the passage find ourselves gazing back into the vanished flowering time of his youth. All is done with the thrust and counterthrust of matched phrases, yet there is no egregious straining after chiming sounds. The movement of the antitheses themselves conveys the pathos of an existence that collapses into the space of a moment, of a lifetime that melts from youth to age within the span of a single clause.

Again, the difference between the Petrarchan simile as it appears in *Supposes* and its counterpart in *Endimion* is that Gascoigne's conceit on the whole lacks genuine relevance to character or situation: it has the air of a decorative patch stuck on because the author could not bear to leave it out, and it jars in the prevailingly rowdy context of new comedy, whereas in Lyly the conceit merely crystallizes the qualities of the prose in which it is embedded, like a jewel set in a brocaded mantle, let us say, instead of one fastened clumsily to leather britches.

I will see if I can beguile my selfe with sleep, & if no slumber will take hold in my eyes, yet will I imbrace the golden thoughts in my head, and wish to melt by musing: that as Ebone, which no fire can scorch, is yet consumed with sweet sauours; so my heart which cannot bee bent by the hardnes of fortune, may be brused by amorous desires. (II.iii.4–9)

Endimion's comparisons well up freshly from the mood of the play: "imbrace the golden thoughts in my head" and "melt by musing" were found in no Petrarchan lexicon of fine figures. If the analogy of the ebony lacks exactness, it still projects the langorous bewitchment of Endimion's plight, and the aura of magic that clings to everything in the play. The fact that Lyly has allowed himself to be maneuvered by his own logical syntax into an illogical position is mitigated, in this case, at least, by the fact that even the pseudologic reinforces the poetic atmosphere.

When we move from the love-dreams of gods and shepherds to the japes of the pages, we move one step from the dream world toward the waking world, and the prose becomes correspondingly less precious, more colloquial in manner. But it is a tiny step, only enough to differentiate the Euphuistic ardors of the protagonists from the burlesque raptures and more humdrum concerns of their attendants. We remain well within the charmed circle. The elegant pavanes are interrupted by jigs and corantoes, but the dance goes on: a whirl of comic definitions, schoolboy logic applied and misapplied, grammar parodied, puns batted back and forth like tennis balls, mock eulogies, and travestied similitudes. The page Epiton proclaims himself "an absolute Microcosmus," "a pettie worlde" in himself, and proves it: "my library is my heade, for I haue no other bookes but my braines: my wardrope on my backe, for I haue no more apparrell then is on my body; my armorie at my fingers ends, for I vse no other Artillarie then my nailes; my treasure in my purse. *Sic omnia mea mecum porto*" (IV.ii.36–41). Epiton's mock-heroics thus wittily reduce the portentous concept of the microcosm to a metaphor for the self-sufficiency of the needy scholar. Sir Tophas, probably the most innocent and endearing *miles gloriosus* that ever slew mouse, parodies Endimion's rapture on Cynthia with an account of his own feminine ideal:

What a sight would it be to embrace one whose hayre were as orient as the pearle! whose teeth shal be so pure a watchet, that they shall staine the truest Turkis! whose nose shall throwe more beames from it then the fierie Carbuncle! whose eyes shall be enuirond about with rednesse exceeding the deepest Corall! And whose lippes might compare with siluer for the palenesse!

(V.ii.95–100)

The burlesque catalogue, in which subjects and adjuncts are scrambled like the letters of alphabet soup, betrays the self-conscious logician even more patently than the symmetry of the phrasing. Here, as elsewhere in the comic subplots, Lyly achieves a semblance of farce by purely verbal means — without drunkenness, without beatings, without horseplay, with nothing but the precocious chatter of the lapwing pages and the nightingale roar of an occasional gull like Sir Tophas. Low comedy almost rarefies itself into high comedy.

The language, with its artful patterning, thus keeps its distance from realism, as Lyly meant it to when he designed it for the treble voices of the chapel children. The balanced structure, the wheels within wheels of parisonic symmetry, demand stylized declamation as absolutely as Marlovian blank verse, and as well for the quaintly pedantic prattle of the pages as for the lyric eloquence of the principals. Lyly reaches a high-water mark of preciosity from which subsequent experiments were to ebb back toward the humbler levels of realism. With Shakespeare, Euphuism begins at once to transform itself into a more versatile instrument, adapting itself to colloquial rhythms and common concerns, while verse — as in *A Midsummer Night's Dream* and *Love's Labour's Lost* —

reassumes its ancient empire over the province of the courtly, the fabulous, and the mythic.

3

While Lyly was perfecting the filigree of his own prose for courtly audiences, another kind of prose was beginning to be heard in the popular theater, a rough-and-tumble language spoken by the clowns in chronicle plays, mythological comedies, or romances. The clowns perform a strictly limited set of gestures. They make clownish love, and so burlesque the poetical raptures of the principals, or they resist conscription into the army and so afford a scurrilously skeptical view of great affairs of state, or they quarrel with their shrewish wives after the manner of Noah and his wife in the guild plays, or they impede the intrigues of their masters by their clumsiness or drive them to distraction by pointlessly "witty" repartee when executing orders. The repertory of themes is exceedingly small, and the thing that strikes one about the language of such scenes, especially among the anonymous playwrights of the eighties and nineties, is its poverty of resource.

The Famous Victories of Henry V provides a good demonstration piece because it contains not only the comic scenes but also a serious main plot in prose, evidently before Marlowe's example had established verse as the staple vehicle for heroic action. The language divides itself into two chief modes: the boisterous idiom of the prince and his companions, the soldiers, thieves, and townsmen, and the more operatic style of the episodes at court. The chief quirk of the low style is its addiction to a few epithets like "villain" and a few oaths like "Gogs wounds" and "Gogs blood" and their variants,[10] used so often and so promiscuously that they almost cease to register on the ear. The chief structural feature of both styles is syntactic primitiveness: sentences, clauses, and phrases alike spliced together by a few rude connectives such as "and," "but," and "for." Sometimes one or another of these particles will suddenly start multiplying at an abnormal rate.

. . . but heres such adoo now a-dayes, heres prisoning, heres hanging, whipping, and the diuel and all: but I tel you sirs, when I am king, we will haue no such things, but my lads, if the old king my father were dead, we would be all kings. . . . But *Ned*, so soone as I am king, the first thing I wil do, shal be to put my Lord chief Iustice out of office, And thou shalt be my Lord chiefe Iustice of England.[11]   (Sig. C)

The "but" here not only grows monotonous through repetition; it tends to shed its logical force and dwindle into a meaningless steppingstone between clauses. The same thing happens elsewhere with "if" and "and": by a kind of leveling process they merge into each other. The author reaches into his box of connectives, pulls out a "but" or an "and," and without bothering to read the label, uses it to pin two clauses together. In the following lines, the "and," momentarily in the ascendant, becomes a pleonastic bleat rather than a genuine compounding word.

> Most soueraign Lord, and welbeloued father,
> I came into your Chamber to comfort the melancholy
> Soule of your bodie, and finding you at that time
> Past all recouerie, and dead to my thinking,
> God is my witnesse: and what should I doo,
> But with weeping tears lament the death of you my father,
> And after that, seeing the Crowne, I took it:
> And tel me my father, who might better take it then I,
> After your death?   (Sig. C4v)

The elaborate locutions of address here ("Most soueraign Lord, and welbeloued father"), the absurd redundancies ("melancholy / Soule of your bodie," "weeping tears"), and the exclamatory tone suggest the kind of heightening at which

the author of *The Famous Victories* aimed when he wished
to convey the emotions proper to dying monarchs and repent-
ant princes, a heightening that the printer believed in enough
to print the passage as verse. The king, musing on his son's
follies, laments in loud soliloquy, "Ah *Harry*, *Harry*, now
thrice accursed *Harry*, / That hath gotten a sonne, which with
greefe / Will end his fathers dayes" (Sig. B2). The prince,
answering his father's reproaches, borrows the Ciceronian
device of breaking off suddenly and correcting himself, as
evidence of intense feeling: "know my beloued father, far
be the thoughts of your sonne, sonne said I, an vnworthie
sonne for so good a father"; begs forgiveness three times with
the phrase "Pardon sweete father: pardon" (Sig. C3); berates
himself thrice as "thrice vnhappie Harry" (Sigs. C3, C4);
curses the day of his birth and the hour of his begetting; and
vows to retire to a solitary place where with more "weeping
tears" he can lament his sins and die the miserable death he
deserves. That the author has by this time exhausted his rhetorical resources we may judge not only by the repetitions in
the scene in question, but by the fact that when the prince, as
Henry V, later falls in love with Katherine of France, he can
find no other way to express this new sentiment than by the
already abused self-apostrophe: "Ah *Harry*, thrice vnhappie
Harry. / Hast thou now conquered the French king, / And
begins a fresh supply with his daughter" (Sig. F3v).

The rather stilted posturing in the language of these scenes
suggests an effort on the part of the anonymous playwright to
stiffen his style so that it might deal worthily with noble
sentiments. But unable to coerce his shapeless idiom into order,
and uninventive in the use of formal rhetorical devices, he falls
back on the wearisome repetition of a few heavy gestures.
Marlowe's success in any case decreed that henceforth such
scenes would be written in verse. The comic sequences, which

suffer from related faults — redundancy and inconsequence, rather mindless iteration of epithets, and a good deal of simply fatuous repetition — have at least this much importance: they represent an early attempt to create for the stage a colloquial, nonliterary prose, based, insofar as literary language ever can be, directly on the language of the street, and virtually innocent of rhetorical artifice. It matters little whether these scenes, and clown scenes in other plays, are regarded as a deliberate fresh start in the unfamiliar element of prose or as the final disintegration of tumbling verse.[12] In either case the result is the same: a rambling, ramshackle style, clumsily hitched together with "and's," "but's," and "for's" and eked out with oaths and expletives, a style often engagingly hearty, but incapable of effects other than simple heartiness or rowdiness. The problem for more sophisticated playwrights was to assimilate this raw speech into an organized style that would lend itself to more complex uses without, in the process, losing its vitality and its close kinship with the spoken word.

That the problem was chiefly a theatrical as opposed to a literary one, we may judge from the fact that Thomas Deloney, the "popular" writer par excellence, handles dialogue with much greater sureness than most of his theatrical colleagues. In the opening scene of *Jack of Newbury*, for instance, we find Jack's friends teasing him on his courtship of the widow.

Doubtlesse (quoth one) I thinke some female spirit hath inchaunted *Iacke* to his treadles, and coniured him within the compasse of his Loome, that he can stirre no further.

You say true (quoth *Iacke*) and if you haue the leasure to stay till the Charme be done, the space of six dayes and fiue nights, you shall finde me ready to put on my holy-day-apparell, and on Sunday morning for your paines I will giue you a pot of Ale ouer against the Maypole.

Nay (quoth another) Ile lay my life, that as the Salamander

cannot liue without the fire, so *Iack* cannot liue without the smel of his Dames smock.

And I maruell (quoth *Iacke*) that you being of the nature of a Herring (which so soon as he is taken out of the Sea, presently dyes) can liue so long with your nose out of the pot.[13]

Anyone who thinks that Deloney is a naive or artless writer should look twice at this passage, which has not only a metaphorical vitality lacking in *The Famous Victories*, and a lithe handling of syntax missing from *Supposes*, but an ironic smoothness that no mere primitive could have approached. The "Omphale archetype," to borrow a term from Northrop Frye,[14] crops up briefly but tellingly in the opening gibe, to which Jack replies not with the fleering frump or the privy nip but with the retort suave, in which the friend is offered, after a moment's deliberate suspense, not a box on the ear but a pint of ale. The whimsical parody of Euphuism in the second friend's salamander simile is then capped by Jack's retaliatory figure of the herring, with its far from unnatural natural history hastily improvised for the occasion. The same spirited comedy continues in the dialogues between Jack and the widow, where the workaday surroundings and the bourgeois status of the lovers produce a continuous flicker of comic incongruity as they woo each other in Euphuistic symmetries. Or if one is seeking more clownish, more rustical effects, one can find them expertly handled in the *Arcadia*, in the garrulous old wives' talk of Miso or the hoydenish gabble of Mopsa.[15] And Lodge's own dialogue in the *Alarum against Usurers* has a dozen times the vivacity of its counterpart in *A Looking Glass for London and England*. But the language that seemed to come so effortlessly on the page had to struggle to articulate itself in the theater, perhaps because playwrights were still wrestling with the more basic problems of an unfamiliar stagecraft.

Turning from *The Famous Victories* to a more academic play, Lodge and Greene's *Looking Glass for London and England*, one finds, in the comic episodes, a prose slightly more incisive, slightly less gluey with "and's" and "but's," but addicted in its own right to the still primitive conjunctions "for" and "therefore." "For," which supplies reasons for something already affirmed, or a cause for some effect already described, marks a step in a logical sequence, and when a writer habitually links his statements together with it, we are entitled to describe his language as logical, even if the logic remains on a rudimentary level. The clown scenes in *A Looking Glass*, usually ascribed to Lodge,[16] swarm with "for's," often coupled together in a semiautomatic fashion that drains them of their full connective force.

Nay then gentlemen stay me, for my ch[oller] begins to rise against him, for marke the words a paltry S[mith]. (225–226)

[No]w sir I haue a feate aboue all the Smythes in *Niniuie*, for sir [I] am a Philosopher that can dispute of the nature of Ale, for [ma]rke you sir, a pot of Ale consists of foure parts . . .
(258–260)

I tell you sir, when the slaue vttered this word no Cow, it strooke to my heart, for my wife shall neuer haue so fit for her turne againe, for indeed sir, she is a woman that hath her twidling strings broke. (385–389)

"Therefore," a word that ushers in some kind of conclusion or draws some kind of inference, is a natural companion of "for," and it accordingly occasions no surprise to find Lodge almost as enamored of the one as he is of the other, sometimes (though not in the examples below) making the two bear almost all the weight of syntactic connection.

Alasse poore man, thy matter is out of my head, and therefore I pray thee tell it thy selfe. (724–725)

Well sirrha, I must be short, and therefore say on. (729)

I haue paid you *18.* pence a weeke, & therefore there is reason I should haue my Cow. (366–367)

I would not be disgracst in this action, therefore here is twentie angels say nothing in the matter, and what you say, say to no purpose, for the Iudge is my friend. (656–658)

Needless to say, "for" is a more sophisticated conjunction than the "and's" and "but's" that clutter the speeches of *The Famous Victories.* At least it establishes some priority between the elements it joins, and imposes a fixed sequence. But what we notice about its use in *A Looking Glass* is that it turns into a compulsive mannerism, pressed into service no matter what the occasion; it comes to sound like a speech defect. Certainly the formulaic harping on one or two primitive modes of connection is common enough among illiterate or semi-literate people, but before a writer can make such speech interesting, to say nothing of comic or attractive, he must first have assimilated it into a fuller syntactic matrix, so that he can *suggest* monotony rather than merely succumbing to it himself. Again, then, we are faced with the fact that neither raw transcription of live language — if such was Lodge's purpose — nor automatic writing out of the author's own private speech habits — if this was Lodge's procedure — suffices to create a sound theatrical prose. A literary basis of some kind is indispensable, and in the sixteenth century, when a style could not be absorbed by osmosis from an already widely diffused and established style, it had to be invented, sometimes painfully. Whatever the defects of Lyly's somewhat eccentric rhetoric, it not only meets all of the elementary demands of dramaturgy, but it begins to take on a positive dramatic quality of its own: it permits effects of mood — lyric, satiric, ceremonious, and so on — achieved by largely verbal means, and it forms part of an aesthetic surface pleasant to contemplate in itself. Though style in drama is not all, as the example of Eugene O'Neill, among others, may serve to testify, a full command of the resources of language opens doors to the playwright that are closed to his less verbal colleagues. The Elizabethan theater was fortunate in having audiences with a taste for style; as a result it ended by producing, in Shakespeare, the greatest stylist, as well as the greatest playwright, in the history of the theater.

4

Shakespeare starts with the highly specialized set of expressive devices worked out by Lyly, inflects them variously, fills them with nuance, widens their range, and so finally transcends them, but without departing from the structural principles on which they are based. One tends not to notice the logicality of Shakespeare's prose because it is managed with such virtuosity as to seem as natural as breathing. But by his constant invention of fresh logical formulas, his endless improvising of new patterns, Shakespeare, if anything, carries logical syntax even further than Lyly.

The term logicality, here, refers not merely to the use of syllogisms and other formal schemes, though these are numerous enough,[17] but to a stylistic habit that includes these and goes deeper: the habit, first, of treating a piece of discourse as argument, of tracking effects back to causes, discovering consequences from antecedents, elucidating premises, proposing hypotheses, and the like; and second, more important, the habit of proceeding disjunctively, of splitting every idea into its component elements and then symmetrizing the elements so as to sharpen the sense of division between them.

Shakespeare's early plays tinker inventively, but perhaps also a bit facilely, with the kind of formal Euphuism in which pages pick apart each other's language and match wits with their masters. It is in the great middle comedies, as Bond has shown (I, 150–154), that Euphuism has been assimilated into the marrow of the language and reigns as the undisputed expressive principle. Somewhat less absolutely, it dominates the prose of the Lancastrian histories, and it continues to supply the chief structural basis for the prose of the tragedies and late romances, while gradually being absorbed and transformed into a style greater than itself.

A general discussion of Shakespeare's prose being clearly out of the question here,[18] the following pages will try to sketch out a glossary of some of his logical tactics in order to indicate their radical importance in his language. Examples from the tragedies and late romances will be included to support the contention that the logicality, though it evolves, remains an essential stylistic principle even in the final phase.

Like Lodge, Shakespeare makes a heavy-duty particle of the conjunction "for" — the "cause-renderer," as Jonson calls it in his *English Grammar* (Herford and Simpson, VIII, 550). Examples are legion, and citation would be useless. One point, however, seems worth noting: despite the frequency of the word in Shakespeare — he probably uses it oftener than any other playwright of the period, Lodge included — it never comes to sound like a nervous tic, because Shakespeare, unlike Lodge, is not enslaved to it. It forms only one of a variety of logical hinges that by their constant interchange maintain the syntactic sequence. A few specimens of the logical linchpin "therefore" may be given; the following are all from *Much Ado about Nothing*.

There is no measure in the occasion that breeds, therefore the sadnesse is without limit.[19]   (L.121; I.iii.3–4)

I am trusted with a mussell, and enfranchisde with a clog, therefore I haue decreed, not to sing in my cage.   (L.122; I.iii.34–36)

. . . marry once before he wonne it of mee, with false dice, therefore your Grace may well say I haue lost it.   (L.124; II.i.289–291)

I cannot be a man with wishing, therfore I will die a woman with grieuing.   (L.134; IV.i.324–326)

Foule words is but foule wind, and foule wind is but foule breath, and foule breath is noisome, therefore I will depart vnkist.
                                                                    (L.138; V.ii.52–54)

Instances of the numerous substitutes for "therefore" — "hence," "ergo," "thus," "so," and the like — may be omitted, as may the occasional "because" or "the reason is" that doubles for "for." [20]

It is well to remember, when discussing such humdrum phenomena as the use of "for," "therefore," and conjunctions and correlatives, that they are not mere inert forms just because they are common.

The greatest obstacle to recognizing the expressive value of rhetorical devices is the fact that they recur. One notices that Cicero uses a *litotes* or a *praeteritio* several times in a few pages, or so many hundreds of balances are counted in the *Ramblers* of Johnson. . . . The so-called "devices," really no more devices than a sentence is a device, express more special forms of meaning, not so common to thinking that they cannot be avoided, like the sentence, but common enough to reappear frequently in certain types of thinking and hence to characterize the thinking, or the style.[21]

What applies to "the so-called 'devices' " applies to sentence types and syntactic formulas. They are significant, indeed, in proportion to their frequency; if the following pages tax the patience of the reader, it is because one must demonstrate, if only in a limited fashion, that certain kinds of construction appear *often* in Shakespeare, often enough "to characterize the thinking, or the style."

The cause-and-effect relation that Shakespeare indicates rather formally with such conjunctions as "for" and "therefore" he may suggest more unobtrusively by such formulas as "so . . . that," where "so" indicates the way a thing is done and "that" describes its effect.

O she did so course o're my exteriors with such a greedy intention, that the appetite of her eye, did seeme to scorch me vp like a burning-glasse. (L.160; *MW* I.iii.72–75)

Hee must fight singly to morrow with *Hector*, and is so prophetically proud of an heroicall cudgelling, that he raues in saying nothing. (L.604; *Troil.* III.iii.248–249)

For the Nobles receyue so to heart, the Banishment of that worthy *Coriolanus*, that they are in a ripe aptnesse, to take al power from the people, and to plucke from them their Tribunes for euer. (L.637; *Cor.* IV.iii.20–26)

A related strategy, suppressing the "so," foretells the effect one hopes will follow a given cause. The "that" here is roughly equivalent to "in order that":

Let vs sit and mocke the good houswife *Fortune* from her wheele, that her gifts may henceforth bee bestowed equally. (L.204; *AYL* I.ii.34–36)

. . . therefore I shall craue of you your leaue, that I may beare my euils alone. (L.278; *TN* II.i.5–7)

Why I haue often wisht my selfe poorer, that I might come neerer to you. (L.697; *Tim.* I.ii.103–105)

Wee will giue you sleepie Drinkes, that your Sences (vn-intelligent of our insufficience) may, though they cannot prayse vs, as little accuse vs. (L.295; *WT* I.i.14–17)

One may also reach a conclusion by way of a qualification, first stating some real or imagined difficulty in a "though" clause, then overriding it in the main clause.

. . . though honestie be no Puritan, yet it will doe no hurt . . . (L.251; *Alls W* I.iii.97–98)

. . . though you change your place, you neede not change your
Trade.   (L.80; *MM* I.ii.110–111)

. . . though patience be a tyred [mare], yet shee will plodde . . .
                                    (L.427; *HV* I.ii.25–26)

Though this be madnesse, / Yet there is Method in't.
                                    (L.769; *Ham.* II.ii.208–209)

. . . though the wisedome of Nature can reason it thus, and thus,
yet Nature finds it selfe scourg'd by the sequent effects.
                                    (L.794; *Lear* I.ii.113–115)

Though I am not bookish, yet I can reade Waiting-Gentlewoman
in the scape.   (L.306–307; *WT* III.iii.73–75)

Though thou canst swim like a Ducke, thou art made like a Goose.
                                    (L.28; *Temp.* II.ii.134–135)

There is no reason why the "though" clause must precede the
main clause in such cases, but Shakespeare, with his penchant
for strongly marked disjunctions, usually makes it do so, and
by adding the antithetic particle "yet" at the head of the main
clause, he fences the two halves of the statement even more
rigidly off from each other.

One of the hallmarks, indeed, of a logical style is its taste
for disjunction. Needless to say, all language depends on disjunction, on separating strips of words into intelligible units,
and — to speak not very paradoxically — every conjunction
occurs at a point of disjunction. "Sir Cranberry stalked his
prey waited" does not become coherent discourse until some
division is made between the two halves, either with a vocal
pattern that we may represent by a semicolon ("Sir Cranberry
stalked; his prey waited") or a comma ("Sir Cranberry stalked
his prey, waited . . ."), or else with some word like "while,"
"but," or "and," which cuts apart the two elements at the
same time that it establishes some kind of relation between
them. What we find in Shakespeare and in writers like him is
a tendency to insist on the points of disjunction, to hold up

the two pieces of the sentence side by side, in full view, to symmetrize them and brandish them in their matched antagonism. "The dragon bellows if attacked" contains an unobtrusive disjunction marked by the "if." "If attacked, the dragon bellows" walls the two elements more firmly off from each other by making a heavier vocal suspension. A writer like Shakespeare will tend to prefer the second pattern, and in fact Shakespeare's prose is honeycombed with sentences of this type.

. . . if a Trassel sing, he fals straight a capring, he will fence with his own shadow. If I should marry him, I should marry twentie husbands: if hee would despise me, I would forgiue him, for if he loue me to madnesse, I should neuer requite him.

(L.183; Merch. I.iii.65–70)

If you head, and hang all that offend that way but for ten yeare together; you'll be glad to giue out a Commission for more heads: if this law hold in Vienna ten yeare, ile rent the fairest house in it after three pence a Bay: if you liue to see this come to passe, say Pompey told you so.   (L.84; MM II.i.251–257)

By placing the dependent clause before the major clause, Shakespeare achieves the maximum effect of climax, balance, and strong demarcation between the two halves. When the simple "if" formation is expanded by being doubled with its own antithesis ("If attacked, the dragon bellows; if ignored, he preens his scales"), we move into the domain of the highly disjunctive style, which pits each element rigidly against its opposite and matches it fiercely with its partner, dividing and binding in the same moment. "If thou beest a man, shew thy selfe in thy likenes: If thou beest a diuell, take't as thou list" (L. 30; Temp. III.ii.137–139); or, more elaborately:

. . . if you pricke vs doe we not bleede? if you tickle vs, doe we not laugh? if you poison vs doe we not die? and if you wrong vs shall we not reuenge? if we are like you in the rest, we will

resemble you in that. If a *Iew* wrong a *Christian*, what is his hu-
mility, reuenge? If a *Christian* wrong a *Iew*, what should his suf-
ferance be by Christian example, why reuenge?
(L.191; *Merch*. III.i.67–74)

A related discoupling mechanism, highly characteristic of
Shakespeare, is the "if . . . if not" formula. This stakes out
logical alternatives and specifies the possible consequences of
each.

Ile go sleepe if I can: if I cannot, Ile raile against all the first borne
of Egypt. (L.210; *AYL* II.v.62–63)

If it bee worth stooping for, there it lies, in your eye: if not, bee it
his that findes it. (L.278; *TN* II.ii.15–17)

. . . if your Father will do me any Honor, so: if not, let him kill
the next *Percie* himselfe. (L.392; *IHIV* V.iv.143–145)

When thou has[t] leysure, say thy praiers: when thou hast none,
remember thy Friends. (L.249; *Alls W* I.i.227–229)

If it be now, 'tis not to come: if it bee not to come, it will bee
now: if it be not now; yet it will come . . .
(L.788; *Ham*. V.ii.231–233)

If she will returne me my Iewels, I will giue ouer my Suit, and
repent my vnlawfull solicitation. If not, assure your selfe, I will
seeke satisfaction of you. (L.841; *Oth*. IV.ii.200–202)

. . . if you will take it on you to assist him, it shall redeeme you
from your Gyues: if not, you shall haue your full time of imprisonment . . . (L.93; *MM* IV.ii.10–13)

It is worth noticing here, as with most of Shakespeare's logical
schemes, that though the pattern itself is highly formulaic, the
completion of it is anything but predictable. "Ile go sleepe if
I can" may prompt us to suspect an antithesis; "if I cannot"
confirms the suspicion. But who could have foreseen the
bizarre outcome, "Ile raile against all the first borne of Egypt"?
Unlike Lyly, Shakespeare is never rigid. He achieves the
maximum amount of syntactic lucidity without sacrificing his

privilege of surprising us; he lures us into unexpected marshes
or drops us into brambles with a comical thud, or else conforms to expectation so generously and graciously that even
this comes as a surprise.

Another way of splitting things into antithetic alternatives
is to group them under opposed headings like "the one . . .
the other." This frequently produces even more strict patterning than the "if . . . if not" scheme.

. . . the one is too like an image and saies nothing, and the other
too like my Ladies eldest sonne, euermore tatling.
(L.122; *Much Ado* II.i.9–11)

— Who ambles Time withal?
— With a Priest that lacks Latine, and a rich man that hath not
the Gowt: for the one sleepes easily because he cannot study, and
the other liues merrily, because he feeles no paine: the one lacking the burthen of leane and wasteful Learning; the other knowing no burthen of heauie tedious penurie.
(L.215; *AYL* III.ii.337–343)

Out vpon thee knaue, doest thou put vpon mee at once both the
office of God and the diuel: one brings thee in grace, and the
other brings thee out. (L.269; *Alls W* V.ii.51–54)

Prethee peace: pay her the debt you owe her, and vnpay the
villany you haue done her: the one you may do with sterling
mony, & the other with currant repentance.
(L.399; *IIHIV* II.i.129–132)

You are mistaken: the one may be solde or giuen, or if there were
wealth enough for the purchases, or merite for the guift. The
other is not a thing for sale, and onely the guift of the Gods.
(L.880; *Cymb.* I.iv.89–93)

Shee had one Eye declin'd for the losse of her Husband, another
eleuated, that the Oracle was fulfill'd.
(L.319; *WT* V.ii.80–82)

Again one may notice the richness and variety that Shakespeare packs into his logical schemes, the colloquial sting of

Beatrice's "euermore tatling" in contrast to the more matter-of-fact "like an image"; the complex crisscross between the ignorant priest and the gouty rich man in Rosalind's lecture, which ends by making them sound like twins; the concise pun on "sterling mony" and "currant repentance" with which the Lord Chief Justice concludes his judgment on Falstaff; the surprising and affecting Latinisms — "declin'd" and "eleuated" — that portray the mingle of feelings in Paulina. Far from lending itself to stiffness, as it does in Lyly's romances, logical syntax in Shakespeare produces the utmost freedom and flexibility, like a ground bass on which an infinite number of variations may be played.

Schematic pointers such as "the one . . . the other" may of course be replaced by the nouns or pronouns to which they refer:

Yet it had not beene amisse the rod had beene made, and the garland too, for the garland he might haue worne himselfe, and the rod hee might haue bestowed on you, who (as I take it) haue stolne his birds nest. (L.124; *Much Ado* II.ii.235–238)

For the boxe of th'eare that the Prince gaue you, he gaue it like a rude Prince, and you tooke it like a sensible Lord.
(L.397; *IIHIV* I.ii.217–219)

Now blesse thy selfe: thou met'st with things dying, I with things new borne. (L.307; *WT* III.iii.115–116)

Nor is there any reason why the two alternatives cannot be expanded to include a third:

I maruell what kin thou and thy daughters are, they'l haue me whipt for speaking true: thou'lt haue me whipt for lying, and sometimes I am whipt for holding my peace.
(L.796; *Lear* I.iv.200–203)

Less fully developed alternatives may be expressed by the formula "either X or Y":

. . . in the managing of quarrels you may see hee is wise, for either hee auoydes them with great discretion, or vndertakes them with a Christian-like feare.   (L.127; *Much Ado* II.iii.197–200)

If this vncouth Forrest yeeld any thing sauage, I wil either be food for it, or bring it for foode to thee.

(L.210; *AYL* II.vi.6–8)

. . . there is eyther liquor in his pate, or mony in his purse, when hee lookes so merrily.   (L.62; *MW* II.i.197–198)

. . . thou hauing made me Businesses, (which none (without thee) can sufficiently manage) must either stay to execute them thy selfe, or take away with thee the very seruices thou hast done.   (L.307; *WT* IV.ii.15–19)

For he does neither affect companie, / Nor is he fit for't indeed.

(L.697; *Tim.* I.ii.30–31)

And if one of the alternatives is asserted over the other, the pattern may run, "not X but Y":

. . . the commendation is not in his witte, but in his villanie . . .

(L.123; *Much Ado* II.i.146)

. . . the yong Lion repents: Marry not in ashes and sacke-cloath, but in new Silke, and old Sacke.   (L.397; *IIHIV* I.ii.220–222)

For the Gods know, I speake this in hunger for Bread, not in thirst for Reuenge.   (L.617; *Cor.* I.i.24–25)

Expressions of choice, where the speaker asserts a preference for one thing over another, lend themselves naturally to anti-thetic formulation. The commonest disjunctive strategy here is the arrangement "rather X than Y."

I had rather (forsooth) go before you like a man, then follow him like a dwarfe.   (L.67; *MW* III.ii.5–6)

I had rather my brother die by the Law, then my sonne should be vnlawfullie borne.   (L.90; *MM* III.i.194–195)

I had rather be a Ticke in a Sheepe, then such a valiant ignorance.

(L.604; *Troil.* III.iii.313–315)

. . . I had rather had eleuen dye Nobly for their Countrey, then one voluptuously surfet out of Action.　　(L.620; *Cor.* I.iii.26–28)

You had rather be at a breakefast of Enemies, then a dinner of Friends.　　　　　　　　　　　　　(L.697; *Tim.* I.ii.78–79)

The antithetic halves, obviously, follow a variety of patterns. They may observe strict parison ("breakefast of Enemies," "dinner of Friends"), or exact antithesis without parison ("by the Law," "vnlawfullie"), or they may have no relation whatever outside the pattern in which they are set ("a Ticke in a Sheepe," "such a valiant ignorance"). And the same is true of such expressions of preference, or comparative judgments, cast in the form "more X than Y":

You haue Witch-craft in your Lippes, *Kate*: there is more eloquence in a Sugar touch of them, then in the Tongues of the French Councell; and they should sooner perswade *Harry* of England, then a generall Petition of Monarchs.

　　　　　　　　　　　　(L.448; *HV* V.ii.302–305)

I will no more trust him when hee leeres, then I will a Serpent when he hisses.　　　　　　　　(L.610; *Troil.* V.i.95–97)

The Swallow followes not Summer more willing, then we your Lordship.　　　　　　　　　　(L.705; *Tim.* III.vi.33–34)

If my Sonne were my Husband, I should freelier reioyce in that absence wherein he wonne Honor, then in the embracements of his Bed, where he would shew most loue.　(L.620; *Cor.* I.iii.2–6)

Kings are no lesse vnhappy, their issue, not being gracious, then they are in loosing them, when they haue approued their Vertues.
　　　　　　　　　　　　(L.308; *WT* IV.ii.30–32)

Preference may be expressed more modestly, or with a tinge of irony, by disposing the antithetic choices under the formula "as . . . as."

I had as liefe they would put Rats-bane in my mouth, as offer to stoppe it with Security.　　　　(L.396; *IIHIV* I.ii.47–49)

I had as lief haue the foppery of freedome, as the mortality of imprisonment.　　　　　　　　　(L.81; *MM* I.ii.136–138)

I had as liue haue a Reede that will doe me no seruice, as a Partizan I could not heaue.　　　　　　　(L.858; *Ant.* II.vii.13–15)

But the "as . . . as" disjunction may serve to affirm any kind of equivalence, literal or metaphoric:

It is as easie to count Atomies as to resolue the propositions of a Louer.　　　　　　　　　　　(L.214; *AYL* III.ii.245–246)

. . . they are as sicke that surfet with too much, as they that starue with nothing.　　　　　　　　(L.182; *Merch.* I.ii.6–7)

. . . thou art as ful of enuy at his greatnes, as *Cerberus* is at *Proserpina's* beauty.　　　　　　　(L.594; *Troil.* II.i.36–37)

. . . it is as dangerous to be aged in any kinde of course, as it is vertuous to be constant in any vndertaking.

(L.92; *MM* III.ii.237–239)

A more emphatic equation results from the pattern "as X, so Y," where "so" not merely insists on the identity between the two elements, but insinuates a causal relation between them.

. . . as *Alexander* kild his friend *Clytus*, being in his Ales and his Cuppes; so also *Harry Monmouth* being in his right wittes, and his good iudgements, turn'd away the fat Knight with the great belly doublet.　　　　　　　　(L.443; *HV* IV.vii.47–51)

. . . but as all is mortall in nature, so is all nature in loue, mortall in folly.　　　　　　　　　　(L.209; *AYL* II.iv.55–56)

. . . but as she spit in his face, so she defide him.

(L.83; *MM* II.i.86)

For, as it is a heart-breaking to see a handsome man loose-Wiu'd, so it is a deadly sorrow, to beholde a foule Knaue vncuckolded.

(L.849; *Ant.* I.ii.74–77)

One may observe that in the first example here, Captain Fluellen's Welsh dialect does not obscure the logicality of his syntax, just as, in the last example, Egyptian disorder and promiscuous living are suggested in the highly logical analogy of Iras. And so with virtually all the extracts so far cited. They are, at the same time, precise logical mechanisms, and completely appropriate to their speakers. The logical mechanism itself is an instrument that can be used in limitless ways. And there is hence no special moment or purpose for which Shakespeare employs it; rather, there are special moments and special purposes for which he deliberately discards it.[22]

When the two matching elements are to be semantically compounded rather than disjoined, Shakespeare still often contrives to emphasize the juncture, and hence the opposition between them, by some such device as the scheme "not only . . . but also."

. . . I shall not onely receiue this villanous wrong, but stand vnder the adoption of abhominable termes, and by him that does mee this wrong. (L.65; *MW* II.ii.307–310)

. . . and the cure of it not onely saues your brother, but keepes you from dishonor in doing it. (L.90; *MM* III.i.244–246)

. . . then must we looke from his age, to receiue not alone the imperfections of long ingraffed condition, but therewithall the vnruly way-wardnesse, that infirme and cholericke yeares bring with them. (L.793; *Lear* I.i.299–303)

There is not onely disgrace and dishonor in that Monster, but an infinite losse. (L.33; *Temp.* IV.i.209–210)

But Shakespeare's fertility in the invention and use of disjunctive devices is almost limitless, and it would be as pointless as it would be vain to try to classify them all. If the reader's patience is not quite exhausted, we may cite a few instances that do not conform exactly to any of the categories so far discussed, merely to illustrate the freedom with which he improvises.

O powerfull Loue, that in some respects makes a Beast a Man: in som other, a Man a beast. (L.76; *MW* V.v.4–6)

. . . where they feared the death, they haue borne life away; and where they would bee safe, they perish.
(L.438; *HV* IV.i.181–183)

What a merit were it in death to take this poore maid from the world? what corruption in this life, that it will let this man liue?
(L.90; *MM* III.i.240–242)

The Food that to him now is as lushious as Locusts, shalbe to him shortly, as bitter as Coloquintida. (L.823; *Oth.* I.iii.354–356)

Not so young Sir to loue a woman for singing, nor so old to dote on her for any thing. (L.795; *Lear* I.iv.40–41)

— He's a Lambe indeed, that baes like a Beare.
— Hee's a Beare indeede, that liues like a Lambe.
(L.624; *Cor.* II.i.12–14)

The foregoing tabulation makes no claim to completeness; it is intended only to be suggestive. (No mention has been made, for example, of the parisonic series, a logical formation on which Shakespeare relies throughout his career.) The cited extracts have been chosen partly for their brevity, so as to isolate the figures in question. But it goes without saying that Shakespeare is as versatile in combining them as he is resourceful in unearthing them in the first place. As we proceed from the simple schemes described above, we encounter more complex sentence structures, much less easy to classify, but often clearly reducible to composites of the simple figures, and hence stamped with the same logical clarity.

2. *Off.* 'Faith, there hath beene many great men that haue flatter'd the people, who ne're loued them; and there be many that they haue loued, they know not wherefore: so that if they loue they know not why, they hate vpon no better a ground. Therefore, for *Coriolanus* neyther to care whether they loue, or hate him, manifests the true knowledge he ha's in their disposition, and out of his Noble carelesnesse lets them plainely see't.

1. Off. If he did not care whether he had their loue, or no, hee
waued indifferently, 'twixt doing them neyther good, nor harme:
but he seekes their hate with greater deuotion, then they can
render it him; and leaues nothing vndone, that may fully discouer
him their opposite. Now to seeme to affect the mallice and displeasure of the People, is as bad, as that which he dislikes, to
flatter them for their loue.   (L.626; *Cor.* II.ii.7–26)

It needs no tedious explication to demonstrate that such a
passage consists of an intricate interlocking of many of the
rudimentary analytic schemes, and that despite its greater
intricacy, it displays the same clean edges and precision grinding that characterize its inner parts. Nothing floats ambiguously or tangentially from its reference; every element is
locked firmly in place by the logic of the syntax.

Shakespeare's prose, of course, encompasses enormous range
and variety, and one neither hopes nor wishes to classify it
under a single rubric. With his prodigious mimetic powers, he
could virtually erase his own voice and become his own
linguistic antiself. Nevertheless, he does have a voice, and that
voice emerges in the kind of passage we have been discussing.
When Shakespeare mimics the polysyndetic gabble of Pompey
or Shallow, or the gasping phrases of Mistress Quickly, or the
slovenly jawing of the carriers at Gadshill, his control of
decorum is so absolute that incoherence itself never falters.
But no tragic hero talks like Pompey; no romantic heroine
sounds like Mistress Quickly; no villain reminds us of Shallow.
Whereas the language of heroes, fools, and villains alike — of
Hamlet and the gravedigger, Falstaff and the Lord Chief
Justice, Rosalind and Touchstone, Don John and Dogberry,
Edmund and Lear's Fool, Autolycus and Polixenes — if we
track it back to its syntactic skeleton, shares the same basic
analytic structure, the logicality that in turn is traceable to
Euphuism. The logical style, in Shakespeare, represents a

37

norm from which the special idioms of Pompey or Shallow are purposeful departures. In Jonson, to anticipate, and to speak even more roughly, it is the other way around.

To the question of how these stylistic habits correspond to other aspects of Shakespearean drama, one can offer only hesitant answers. The argumentative character of the prose, its tendency to stick close to its syllogistic basis and to acknowledge this openly through the abundance of logical links — these one might relate to the network of causality that composes the intrigue plot. The intrigue plot depends on a multitude of chain reactions in which events spring out of other events and in their turn precipitate others. Lyly, who carries his own kind of logicality to extremes, tends to lay parallel or antithetic elements side by side without stressing the nexus between them. To speak more simply, he uses fewer connectives, and his plots display an analogous tendency to juxtapose scenes without binding them to each other in causal sequence. Shakespeare, in this respect, resembles more closely the popular playwrights with their "for's" and "therefore's," with the difference that he works with a fuller magazine of logical links; what in the plays of his contemporaries often reduces itself to a linear arrangement of "A leads to B leads to C," becomes in Shakespeare a dense tissue of inner relations, complexly interdependent on one another.

The symmetry and exact balance in Shakespeare's prose, on the other hand, form one aspect of the ceremoniousness of Shakespearean theater. In the prose as in the verse, we feel that we are never far from incantation or ritual. Even when the characters speak with the astounding lifelikeness that Shakespeare seems to command so effortlessly, we rarely lose the sense that they are talking a language superior to ours, more incisively rhythmical, more spacious, and more ordered. With the balanced, analytic syntax constantly feeding this sense even in moments of low tension, it requires only a slight tightening of the screws to bring us into the great formal harmonies of Falstaff's praise of sack, or Henry V's meditation on kingship, or Edmund's rejection of astrology. At such moments, even when the speaker himself is a spokesman for disorder, the resonant symmetries in the language seem to be reflecting a larger concord on which the plays repose as on a quiet.

Shakespeare's logicality, in any case, contributes to a prose style that — far from being "ungrammatical, perplexed and obscure," as Dr. Johnson complained [23] — is close to a model of clarity. And its clarity probably accounts in part for the unique hold its author's plays have maintained in the theater. Jonson's dramatic prose, winding and knotty, probably did not disturb an Elizabethan audience, but is likely to baffle a contemporary ear, which cannot predict where a sentence will go until it has already reached its destination. But Shakespeare maintains a balance between suspense and resolution just sufficient to satisfy the ear without taxing it. When we hear that "A good Sherris-Sack hath a two-fold operation in it" (L.412; IIHIV IV.iii.103–104), we have an advance blueprint of the discourse to be unfolded, and if Falstaff lingers over the description of Operation Number One, we wait expectantly but without irritation for Operation Number Two. When we hear that of two things, "the one" does such and such, we expect shortly to learn that "the other" does thus and so. When we hear "either," we know we shall soon confront the antithetic "or"; when we discover that someone would "rather" do something, we await the inevitable "than." And so with the dozens of other ways in which Shakespeare carves out divisions of thought. They not only foster clarity of exposition, they affect gesture and delivery, dictating antithetic or contrasting motion, and suggesting the proper weight for pauses and accents, enabling a speech to be heard slowly without fatigue or swiftly without bewilderment.[24] They form the building blocks of a speech that even today compensates for changes in the language, and carries an audience securely through any involutions of thought or plot. If these stylistic virtues play only a secondary role in the continuous presence of Shakespeare in the theater, their opposite (which is not a vice), a more irregular and captious syntax, may be held partly responsible for the unjust neglect of Jonson's great comedies.

❧ II ❧

Prose as Prose

In developing a series of assumptions about style, one might start with the hypotheses of Benjamin Lee Whorf in his essays on "metalinguistics." Whorf, inspecting such languages as Hopi, discovers that the radical differences in structure and pattern between them and such languages as English — "behavioral compulsions," as he calls them — amount to radical differences in ways of interpreting reality, that grammatical patterns are "interpretations of experience" reflecting deep-seated habits of response to the world. Indo-European languages, for Whorf, tend to "spatialize" experience, even those aspects of experience that on reflection have little to do with space. These languages carve up the world into collections of discrete "things" and "events," whereas in Hopi "events are considered the expression of invisible intensity factors, on which depend their stability and persistence, or their fugitiveness and proclivities"; [1] physical processes involving motion — waves, wind, lightning — are never compartmentalized into units, but regarded, in the very grammar of the language, as continuing processes. Grammar, then, is not a set of mere inert categories through which speakers "express" "their" "thoughts" about an "objective" reality, but is itself shot through with a highly partisan vision of reality from which no speaker can escape. Grammatical processes have a meaning beyond any consciously intended by their users, a meaning roughly translatable into a set of shared postulates about the world, and such meanings vary strikingly between languages like Hopi and English.

Within the range of a language group like the Indo-European, the differences will be smaller and more elusive. But that they exist one can assert by appealing to the experience of learning a foreign language, which always involves, to some extent, learning to think in a new way. The lexical habits and syntactic strategies of a new tongue imply, and impose, new habits of perception. Erwin Panofsky has described the salutary effect of having to learn to write in English after a lifetime of writing in German — salutary because the shift forced him for the first time to understand some of his own terms: "The German language unfortunately permits a fairly trivial thought to declaim from behind a woolen curtain of apparent profundity and conversely, a multitude of meanings to lurk behind one term"; German catchall terms like *taktisch* and *malerisch* now had to be reunderstood as composites of up to seven or eight distinct ideas, and broken down accordingly.[2] The French tongue is preferred for drawing up international treaties in Europe, because French, it is felt, by the nature of its grammar, binds the speaker (or writer) to a more logical form of expression than any other language; it discourages ambiguities and insists on clarity of reference. And without pretending to perceive all the terms of the comparison, one can see in the "multiplicity" of German and the "Cartesian" qualities of French, described by writers like Charles Bally,[3] a corollary to other significant cultural differences.

But languages may also differ within themselves, notably from one epoch to another, and here too the differences involve — whether as cause or effect — differences in modes of perception. The change that occurred when the language of the English Renaissance crystallized into that of the Restoration is bound up with a change in the whole form and texture of English thinking, a change symbolized by the names of John Locke and Isaac Newton. Behind all the observable stylistic details of the shift — the effort to make words express real "things" on the one hand, and embody the exactness of mathematical symbolism on the other, the narrowing range of meaning of words, the desire to write in clear and distinct ideas, to articulate sentences logically — "behind all the particular techniques," according to Andrews Wanning, "is a driving urge to reduce all the factors of discourse to tangible worldly things or to explicable abstractions from them." [4] The new view of the world embodied in the altered language expresses itself, needless to say, in virtually every phase of English culture.

But even at a given moment, within a single language, there may be a plurality of stylistic conventions, each a reduction of one or another aspect of current speech. The studies of Morris W. Croll [5] and others [6] attempt to educe from the literature of the Renaissance a set of characteristics that permits some writers to be termed "baroque" or "libertine" or "Stoic," others "Ciceronian" or "Euphuistic" — largely by virtue of the grammatical tactics these writers prefer. Complicating the situation is the fact that Croll's findings cut across linguistic boundaries to some extent. But indeed they would, in any epoch of European history: Europe shares a common past, and its languages evolve together as well as separately.

The narrowing circles of convention bring us closer and closer to the individual writer, and to conscious linguistic artistry. The gulf between Hopi and English exists on a deep, unconscious level, as does that between one Indo-European language and another until bridged (if at all) by study. Conscious purpose plays some part in the historical transformations of a single language, but here too no doubt the determining factor is still the imponderable calculus of thousands of instances of unreflecting usage. When we reach literary categories such as Croll's "baroque," we are dealing with a convention that is at the same time a collective style, since its practitioners have chosen more or less deliberately to adhere to one set of conventional practices rather than another.[7] When we move from the collective style to the individual artist, we reach the province of style *tout court*, where the writer stamps the shared style with the imprint of his own temperament. Often, however, within the limits of a collective style, individual accents may be difficult to distinguish; there are writers who simply adopt current clichés without ever conferring on them a distinctive stamp. And a powerful style may breed a race of imitations that — in fragments at least — can hardly be told apart from their parent. "Stylistic devices," one must remind oneself, "can be imitated very successfully," and "their possible original expressive function can disappear. They can become . . . mere empty husks, decorative tricks, craftsman's *clichés*. The whole relationship between soul and word is looser and more oblique than it is frequently assumed." [8]

Stylistic studies would seem to need an approach located somewhere between two pillars of unwisdom, between extreme statistic-hunting on the one hand and rank impressionism on the other, one that accepts the subjective basis for judgments of style but places this under conditions of maximum control. The method of Leo Spitzer, who urges first the scrutiny of an author's linguistic habits to discover what details of style are peculiar to him, and then — with the aid of provisional hypotheses — the use of these elements as keys to the artist's larger outlook, [9] seems to offer an approach at once definite enough and flexible. Spitzer's own admirable essays of this kind,[10] together with those of Vernon Lee,[11] Erich Auerbach,[12] Jean-Paul Sartre,[13] Harry Levin,[14] and R. A. Sayce [15] —to name a diversified group of brilliant performers working along similar lines — may be mentioned, not as models, but as indications of the general direction this study intends to pursue.

I

Since Jonson's stylistic habits differ so radically from Shakespeare's, a rapid comparison of representative passages may serve here as a convenient point of departure. First, the opening prose speech from the first part of *Henry IV*:

> *Falstaff*. Now *Hal*, what time of day is it Lad?
> *Prince Hal*. Thou art so fat-witted with drinking of olde Sacke, and vnbuttoning thee after Supper, and sleeping vpon Benches in the afternoone, that thou hast forgotten to demand that truely, which thou wouldest truly know. What a diuell hast thou to do with the time of the day? vnlesse houres were cups of Sacke, and minutes Capons, and clockes the tongues of Bawdes, and dialls the signes of Leaping-houses, and the blessed Sunne himselfe a faire hot Wench in Flame-coloured Taffata; I see no reason, why thou shouldest bee so superfluous, to demaund the time of the day. (L.369; *IHIV* I.ii.1–13)

Then, two opening speeches from *Every Man out of his Humour* and *Poetaster*:

> Come, come, leaue these fustian protestations: away, come, I cannot abide these gray-headed ceremonies. Boy, fetch me a glasse, quickly, I may bid these gentlemen welcome; giue 'hem a health here: I mar'le whose wit 'twas to put a prologue in yond' sackbuts mouth: they might well thinke hee'd be out of tune, and yet you'ld play vpon him too. (*EMO* Ind. 319–325)

> Young master, master OVID, doe you heare? gods a mee! away with your *songs*, and *sonnets*; and on with your gowne and cappe,

45

quickly: here, here, your father will be a man of this roome presently. Come, nay, nay, nay, nay, be briefe. These verses too, a poyson on 'hem, I cannot abide 'hem, they make mee readie to cast, by the bankes of *helicon*. Nay looke, what a rascally vntoward thing this *poetrie* is; I could teare 'hem now.

(Poet. I.i.4–11)

The first thing we notice is that the rhythm of the Shakespearean passage is slower, fuller, more oratorical, that of the Jonsonian passages more abrupt, staccato, and sharp. And these differences can be quickly traced to the fact that Shakespeare is using not only longer phrases, but a more oratorical, more symmetrical syntax than Jonson. In

> Thou are so fat-witted
> with drinking of olde Sacke,
> and vnbuttoning thee after Supper,
> and sleeping vpon Benches in the afternoone,

we find not only the parisonic exactness of "drinking," "vnbuttoning," and "sleeping," but the fact that the three phrases are arranged in climactic order: each succeeding one represents a more advanced stage in Falstaff's surrender to sloth, and each is longer than its predecessor; with "sleeping vpon Benches in the afternoone" we reach the fullest phrase and Falstaff's final collapse into indolence. But this sequence itself forms only a suspension, the first, or causal, half of the "so . . . that" pattern discussed in the previous chapter, and leads into a resolution, the assertion of an effect, which itself turns a somewhat intricate little antithesis on the object of "demand." The question that follows serves as a pause, and also to re-engage the logical machinery of the argument. After which the Prince embarks on another periodic sentence, more elaborate than the first, with a much more strongly marked climax —

vnlesse
houres were cups of Sacke,
and minutes Capons,
and clockes the tongues of Bawdes,
and dialls the signes of Leaping-houses,
and the blessed Sunne himselfe a faire hot Wench in
Flame-coloured Taffata

— and consequently a more incisive resolution, which forms
a cadence not only to the sentence itself but to the whole
speech, and crowns the argument of it at the same time. The
speech has thus a beginning, a middle, and an end — an introductory flourish, a development, and a full close — and its internal parts are constructed with similar solidity.

By contrast, the speeches of Carlo Buffone and Luscus
simulate live language much more closely, or seem to, and
the reason is that they reject the figures of balance, parallel,
and climax used by Shakespeare. They are heavily punctuated
with monosyllabic expletives like "Come, come," "gods a
mee," "Nay looke," which introduce a nervous stutter into
the rhythm and prevent it from achieving any full curve.
Occasional symmetrical details, such as the "fustian protestations" and "gray-headed ceremonies" of Carlo, jab at each other
instead of acting as rhythmic pairs, or else, as in "away with your
songs, and *sonnets*; and on with your gowne and cappe," they
suggest self-conscious cuteness on the part of the speaker.
Logical connectives are scarce. In "fetch me a glasse, quickly,
I may bid these gentlemen welcome; giue 'hem a health here,"
the expected "that" or its equivalent between the first two
clauses and the "and" that might have linked the second two
have both been suppressed, so that Carlo seems to be pouncing
convulsively from one idea to another. "Giue 'hem a health
here," stitched on in apposition, has the air of a sudden afterthought. Then the malicious remarks about the boy, who has

gone off-stage to fetch a glass, consist of three clauses glaringly unlike. Like Prince Hal in his final sentence, Carlo pursues a single metaphor through his, but the inequality among the members sets them tensely at odds with each other instead of engaging them in a cooperative enterprise, and the rhythm, as a result, is jagged and discontinuous instead of round and sonorous.

At such moments, Jonson reproduces the accent of living speech so convincingly that he seems to have abandoned rhetorical artifice. We are indebted to Morris Croll for showing that this kind of language, which moves in streaks and flashes rather than with a steady pulsation, springs itself from a highly articulate rhetorical theory, that of anti-Ciceronianism, that it has its roots in certain philosophical attitudes, chiefly Stoic and libertine, and that it has its own preferred masters of style in Seneca and Tacitus.

The writers whom Croll calls "baroque" — a term that will be adopted here for its convenience without any insistence on its exactness [16] — shared a distrust of the Ciceronian mode of sentence formation. This is not to say that they despised Cicero, the Vitruvius of Renaissance prose, or were uninfluenced by him, but only that they reacted against his oratorical manner. Jonson's admiration of Cicero is writ large (too large) in *Catiline*, and elsewhere, but Jonson was one of the least Ciceronian of writers. Ciceronian style was marked above all by the periodic sentence, as in the passage from *Henry IV* above,[17] where the syntax remains incomplete up to some well-defined turning point, with phrases and clauses tending to mass themselves in parallel formation on both sides of the turning point. The characteristic effects of this style were achieved by advance planning: one knew from the outset of a period where it was going and how it was going to get there. When it reached its destination, it afforded the gratification of a design finally complete, every piece falling into its place in the whole. Baroque style, on the other hand, aimed to give the impression, at least, of spontaneity, and hence its first concern was to break the stranglehold of the suspended sentence, to keep its syntax unencumbered and uncommitted, so as to be free to improvise in any way at any moment.

Now it may be objected with perfect justice at this point that Hal's speech *does* give the impression of spontaneity, that far from seeming artfully composed, it sounds as casually offhand as the speeches of Carlo or Luscus. Improvisation needs ground rules, and Hal's construction of a certain syntactic frame gives him freedom: he does not have to worry about what to do with his clauses, or where to put them. Having erected a rapid scaffolding that presupposes some degree of balance and likeness, he can proceed to forget it and concentrate on the details; he can extemporize, as he does, with lordly abandon. The suspended sentence, for him, is no stranglehold, but a set of strong struts. Shakespeare may be planning his effects with the utmost care, but Hal, at least, seems to be talking with perfect naturalness. One wonders, then, whether baroque writers were not misled, partly by abuses of Ciceronian style, partly by its origin in formal oratory, into thinking that it contained some intrinsic barrier to uninhibited thought; whether, tilting against the reader's expectations, they did not find themselves conducting campaigns of sabotage that involved more premeditation than the premeditated style they were warring against; whether, as a result, their own rhetoric is not parasitic in a peculiar way, unthinkable without the background of "normal" Renaissance practice.

In any event, baroque writers regarded Ciceronianism as an invitation to glibness and insincerity, and their first aim was to replace its logical schemes with various nonlogical maneuvers of their own, which Croll has grouped into the two categories of the "curt style" and the "loose style."

The curt style, illustrated above in the passage from *Every Man out of his Humour*, owes its name, and its other names of *stile coupé* and *stile serré*, to its abruptness and choppiness in contrast to Ciceronian "roundness"; its characteristic device is the so-called "exploded" period, formed of independent members not linked by conjunctions but set apart by a vocal pattern of stress, pitch, and juncture rendered typographically by a colon or a semicolon, sometimes a comma. The members of the exploded period tend to brevity, also to inequality of length, variation in form, and unpredictability of order; hence they are likely to suggest the effect of live thinking rather than of logical premeditation. The "mere fact" or main idea of the period is apt to be exhausted in the first member; subsequent members explore the same idea imaginatively, through metaphor or aphorism or example, but not through ordered analysis.

> *Natures* that are hardned to *evill*, you shall sooner breake, then make straight; they are like poles that are crooked, and dry: there is no attempting them.[18]   (*Disc.* 36–38)

> They are, what they are on the sudden; they shew presently, like *Graine*, that, scatter'd on the top of the ground, shoots up, but takes no root; has a yellow blade, but the eare empty.
>   (*Disc.* 685–688)

> *The great* theeves of a State are lightly the officers of the Crowne; they hang the lesse still; play the Pikes in the Pond; eate whom they list.   (*Disc.* 1306–08)

In each of these instances, the initial member encompasses the central idea at a single stroke; the members that follow illuminate or particularize with metaphor. In the last example, Jonson exchanges one metaphor for another: the officers of the crown start as thieves of the state and end as great pikes in a pond. And if one were to quote the period that follows, one would discover the same officers turning into fowlers who spread nets for harmless birds but allow the hawks and buzzards to escape. The progress of such a period, then, is typically not a logical sequence but "a series of imaginative moments occurring in a logical pause or suspension," [19] in which ideas develop out of each other associatively rather than according to any predetermined scheme. That the curt style cannot dispense with logic altogether is perhaps too obvious to need saying. What it can do is to excise logical ligatures, to play haphazardly and capriciously with its elements so as to minimize the sense of logical straitness.

Because of the freedom of its internal elements, the curt period lends itself to the expression of quick shifts in feeling, afterthoughts, self-corrections, unexpected interpolations or dislocations of attention, and since in so doing it simulates so convincingly the processes of live thought, it becomes an ideal instrument for certain kinds of theatrical prose. [20] Jonson uses it in a variety of ways. One characteristic way is to turn it into a vehicle for wit, allowing each successive clause, as it springs from its predecessor, to exploit the latent potentialities of a metaphor:

Ne're trust me, CVPID, but you are turn'd a most acute gallant of late, the edge of my wit is cleere taken off with the fine and subtile stroke of your thin-ground tongue, you fight with too poinant a phrase, for me to deale with.   (*CR* I.i.77–81)

Here the epithet "acute" used by Mercury in the first clause prompts its own figurative extension into the "thin-ground tongue" of the second, after which the pointed tongue becomes the sword with which Cupid "fights" his combats of wit. A related instance of the curt style used for purposes of wit proves to be an "exploded" period in more senses than one. Each clause ignites a verbal fuse that goes off as a pun in the next clause, after the manner of a chain of firecrackers.

> He walkes most commonly with a cloue, or pick-tooth in his mouth, hee is the very mint of complement, all his behauiours are printed, his face is another volume of *essayes*; and his beard an *Aristarchus*.   (*CR* II.iii.87–91)

The puns kindle each other by association. "Cloue" suggests a pun on "mint," which leads to an equivocation on "printed," which generates a quibbling metaphor on "volume" and *"essayes."*

In such cases, the language focuses sharply on its satiric object. The tone may be biting or not, but its primary purpose is to demolish its object, not to define its speaker. Used more complexly, the curt period does both at once: it sheds light on the creature being described, and it reveals the creature who is speaking.

> . . . a leane mungrell, he lookes as if he were chap-falne, with barking at other mens good fortunes: 'ware how you offend him, he carries oile and fire in his pen, will scald where it drops: his spirit's like powder, quick, violent: hee'le blow a man vp with a jest: I feare him worse then a rotten wall do's the cannon, shake an houre after, at the report.   (*EMO* I.ii.212–218)

Carlo Buffone, whose spiteful disposition is revealed chiefly in his penchant for coining scurrilous similitudes, leaps here from the figure of the starved dog to that of scalding oil and fire to that of gunpowder to describe Macilente, and then to a variation of the gunpowder figure in which he imagines himself as a rotten wall blasted by the cannon of Macilente's wit: a good illustration of the spiraling or rotating movement of the curt period, and of how its sputtering rhythms may be made to define an excitable temperament like Carlo's. The unstable tension of the curt period serves similarly to characterize another high-strung individual, Pantilius Tucca, whose invectives against Horace flicker back and forth between metaphoric and literal abuse, and whose speech rhythms tend even more than Carlo's to stumble and trip in nervous jabs of clauses.

Hang him fustie *satyre*, he smells all goate; hee carries a ram, vnder his arme-holes, the slaue: I am the worse when I see him.
(*Poet.* III.iv.367–369)

A sharpe thornie-tooth'd *satyricall* rascall, flie him; hee carries hey in his horne: he wil sooner lose his best friend, then his least iest. (*Poet.* IV.iii.109–111)

As these extracts suggest, the curt period serves especially well to characterize angry or indignant, impatient or volatile, or merely distracted or simple-minded people. Quarlous can dismiss Edgeworth in two irate clauses, and follow these with two more of stinging censure on his way of life.

But goe your wayes, talke not to me, the hangman is onely fit to discourse with you; the hand of Beadle is too mercifull a punishment for your Trade of life. (*BF* IV.vi.26–28)

Or the curt period can portray the spluttering, almost incoherent indignation of a Wasp, who states a proposition ("I am no Clearke") and particularizes it in a series of nonlogical convulsions.

That's well, nay, neuer open, or read it to me, it's labour in vaine, you know. I am no Clearke, I scorne to be sau'd by my booke, i'faith I'll hang first; fold it vp o' your word and gi' it mee; what must you ha' for't? (*BF* I.iv.6–9)

Or it can reproduce the idiotic flapping about of a half-witted mind, swayed aimlessly in opposite directions by the gusts of childish appetite.

53

I ha' paid for my peares, a rot on 'hem, I'le keepe 'hem no longer;
you were choake-peares to mee; I had bin better ha' gone to mum
chance for you, I wusse.   (*BF* IV.ii.73–75)

S'lid, this is an Asse, I ha' found him, poxe vpon mee, what doe I
talking to such a dull foole; farewell, you are a very Coxcomb,
doe you heare?   (*BF* IV.ii.105–107)

It may implement the language of abuse, as we have already
seen, or it may serve to convey the disordered prattle of
semisenility, as in the speeches of Venus in *Christmas his
Masque*.

Yes forsooth, I can sit any where, so I may see [my] *Cupid* act;
hee is a pretty Child, though I say it that perhaps should not, you
will say: I had him by my first Husband, he was a Smith forsooth,
we dwelt in Doe-little lane then, he came a moneth before his
time, and that may make him somewhat imperfect: But I was a
Fishmongers daughter.   (123–129)

The scatterbrained effect is secured by the multiplicity of
brief clauses, most of them syntactically unconnected; each
starts off afresh with its own new subject, so that the result
is a pepper pot of random remarks, loosely governed by
chronology but otherwise innocent of logic. The "But" that
introduces the final statement not only lacks logical force: it
is disruptive of logic, and so crowns the effect of incoherence.

It should perhaps be emphasized that the speeches of such
characters as Wasp, Tucca, and Carlo Buffone do not represent a mere tic of punctuation on the one hand or a mere
slavish transcription of heard language on the other, but a
distinct style; their barking phrases translate into stage idiom
the staccato effects of *stile coupé*. It is true enough that people
often speak so, and it is also true that one may find patches
of similar language in the popular comedy of the 1590's. But
what in earlier writers is a mere incidental twitch Jonson
transmutes into a structural principle. He takes the sprawling,

ramshackle popular language and disengages from it the strain congenial to his own rhetorical bent, thus effecting a kind of merger between colloquial speech and his own Stoic models. The result is a stage prose that combines the vitality of live language with the authority and expressive potency of a formed rhetoric.

The highly impressionable Shakespeare was not likely to be immune to influence from this rhetorical current, and it may be suggested that along with the primary voice discussed in the first chapter, Shakespeare has a subsidiary voice that sounds much like a modified version of the curt style. One might, however, prefer to call the Shakespearean variant something like "plain statement," since it tends to consist of a procession of simple declarative or imperative clauses with little of the "explosiveness" peculiar to curt style:

I haue dogg'd him like his murtherer. He does obey euery point of the Letter that I dropt, to betray him: He does smile his face into more lynes, then is in the new Mappe, with the augmentation of the Indies: you haue not seene such a thing as tis: I can hardly forbeare hurling things at him, I know my Ladie will strike him: if shee doe, hee'l smile, and take't for a great fauour.
(L.284; *TN* III.ii.81–89)

I would the Duke we talke of were return'd againe: this vngenitur'd Agent will vn-people the Prouince with Continencie. Sparrowes must not build in his house-eeues, because they are lecherous: The Duke yet would haue darke deeds darkelie answered, hee would neuer bring them to light: would hee were return'd.
(L.92; *MM* III.ii.183–190)

Looke, th'vnfolding Starre calles vp the Shepheard; put not your selfe into amazement, how these things should be; all difficulties are but easie vvhen they are knowne. Call your executioner, and off with *Barnardines* head: I will giue him a present shrift, and aduise him for a better place.   (L.95; *MM* IV.ii.219–227)

When I bestryde him, I soare, I am a Hawke: he trots the ayre:

the Earth sings, when he touches it: the basest horne of his hoofe, is more Musicall then the Pipe of *Hermes*.

(L.435; HV III.vii.16–19)

Leaue him to my displeasure. *Edmond*, keepe you our Sister company: the reuenges wee are bound to take vppon your Traitorous Father, are not fit for your beholding. Aduice the Duke where you are going, to a most festi[n]ate preparation: we are bound to the like. Our Postes shall be swift, and intelligent betwixt vs.

(L.807; Lear III.vii.6–13)

Alas, the storme is come againe: my best way is to creepe vnder his Gaberdine: there is no other shelter hereabout: Misery acquaints a man with strange bedfellowes: I will here shrowd till the dregges of the storme be past.

(L.27; Temp. I.ii.37–43)

Such speeches show certain traits of the *stile coupé*: its discontinuousness, its avoidance of logical particles, its shifts in grammatical form, perhaps above all its apparent innocence of rhetorical cunning. They differ from their Jonsonian counterparts in that the members tend to be more equal in length, and also longer, so that the rhythm is slower and gentler. Characteristically Shakespeare will insert into the middle of an otherwise highly wrought discourse one or two such clauses, which have the effect of tranquilizing the rhythm, of affording a moment's breathing-space for the actor and a pause in the forward march of the argument.

What the Shakespearean passages do not have is the bristling asymmetry of the Jonsonian speeches. George Williamson has objected to Croll's emphasis on this trait, and suggested that Croll, having committed himself to the analogy with baroque, was led to discover asymmetry in places where, in fact, symmetry predominates.[21] Williamson, by way of rejoinder, illustrates from Bacon, and with this correction, insofar as it applies to Bacon, one can only gladly agree: asymmetry, where it occurs in Bacon, remains tangential. But Jonson is another matter. "Asymmetrical" seems to define the shape of Jonson's prose so exactly that one is tempted to use it to describe the topography of his mind. Jonson delights in bending the logical axis of syntax a few degrees one way or another in order to interrupt a symmetrical pattern, to sprawl suddenly or compress unexpectedly in a way that pulls the reader up short. One may get at the difference between Bacon's style and Jonson's by comparing a passage from *The Advancement of Learning* with Jonson's adaptation of it in the *Discoveries*.

This grew speedily to an excess; for men began to hunt more after words than matter; more after the choiceness of the phrase, and the round and clean composition of the sentence, and the sweet falling of the clauses, and the varying and illustration of their works with tropes and figures, than after the weight of matter, worth of subject, soundness of argument, life of invention or depth of judgment.[22]

The thing that impresses itself on one immediately here is the careful regularity of the sentence. The exact antithesis "more after words than matter" undergoes artful expansion in the member that follows, first into four aspects of the hunt after words:

> the choiceness of the phrase,
> the round and clean composition of the sentence,
> the sweet falling of the clauses,
> the varying and illustration of their works with tropes and
>   figures.

The four phrases fall neatly into two sets of two each. In each set the second phrase is longer than the first, and each of the phrases of the second set is longer than its counterpart in the first. One result of this strict geometrical plotting is to produce an effect of climax, to bring us to a rhythmic plateau on the phrase "with tropes and figures," after which the second half of the antithesis elaborates itself serenely into a series of five component phrases that observe exact correspondence of parts. If one were to continue quoting at this point, one would discover Bacon launching into a new sequence of parallel statements extending through five sentences: "Then grew the flowing and watery vein of Osorius the Portuguese bishop, to be in price. Then did Sturmius . . . Then did Car of Cambridge . . . Then did Erasmus . . . Then grew . . . In sum . . ." As for the sentence preceding the quoted extract, it leads up to the antithesis between words and matter by enumerating four reasons why "eloquence and variety of discourse" came to be preferred to solidity of thought. The extract from Bacon, then, not only displays a high degree of formal clarity in itself: it forms part of a sequence that is highly articulated logically, that unfolds in parallel and antithetic statements, and that preserves parisonic correspondence in many of its inner parts in order to emphasize its logical divisions.

When we turn to Jonson's paraphrase, the first thing we notice is that the period in question is no longer a complete grammatical unit. It is fused to what precedes it, by virtue of the fact that its first verb, "make," simply forms the last in a series of subordinate verbs dependent on "Wee must" in the prior sentence. The prior sentence itself issues a plea for patience in the study of style that flickers restlessly back and forth between positive and negative counsel. The plea concludes, then, with the paraphrase from Bacon:

Then make exact animadversion where style hath degenerated, where flourish'd, and thriv'd in choisenesse of Phrase, round and cleane composition of sentence, sweet falling of the clause, varying an illustration by tropes and figures, weight of Matter, worth of Subject, soundnesse of Argument, life of Invention, and depth of Judgement. This is *Monte potiri*, to get the hill. For no perfect

Discovery can bee made upon a flat or a levell.   (*Disc.* 2116–24)

Jonson has eliminated Bacon's dichotomy between rhetorical curiosity and solidity of thought, and lumped together the phrases from both sides of Bacon's antithesis in a single top-heavy series. Further, he has cut away most of the articles and all the connectives, so that the period now produces an unexpected effect of abruptness. Finally, he has embedded the passage in what is itself, so to speak, an asymmetrical context, commencing with the freely zigzagging period that precedes the quoted excerpt, and ending with the two brusque periods that close the section like two hammer blows. He ends, hence, with a gnarled and knotted texture only remotely akin to the clearspun weave of the Baconian original.

One does find occasional stretches of exact or nearly exact symmetry in Jonson, but these tend to have a sledge-hammer brevity that transmits first of all a sense of power, and only secondarily the feeling of balance: "Some wits are swelling, and high; others low and still: Some hot and fiery; others cold and dull: One must have a bridle, the other a spurre" (*Disc.* 678–680). And when Jonson uses exact symmetry in his plays, he is almost always ridiculing it as an affectation on the part of the speaker. But in fact symmetrical repetition in Jonson infrequently extends — as it does here — beyond the bounds of a single clause. For the most part it is phrasal rather than clausal symmetry, which means that it appears in unpredictable clumps; and so instead of shaping the outlines of the syntax as a whole, and providing clear signposts from one unit of utterance to the next, it merely intensifies the prevailing irregularity.

There shall the Spectator see some, insulting with Joy; others, fretting with Melancholy; raging with Anger; mad with Love; boiling with Avarice; undone with Riot; tortur'd with expectation; consum'd with feare: no perturbation in common life, but

the Orator findes an example of it in the Scene. (*Disc.* 2537–43)
The violent verbal adjectives, the absence of linking terms, the
heavy pointing, place a greater and greater weight on each
member of the series, especially since nothing signals to us
when the series will end. The series erupts, flings itself at us
with steadily increasing pressure, and then gathers and collapses into the summary that follows the colon. The sentence
travels through fields of force rather than through preordained
paths of logic.

The fact is that although Bacon pioneered in anti-Ciceronianism, his own style remains conservative in another way.
As George Williamson has shown, Baconian prose has close
affinities with Euphuism,[23] and Euphuism imposes constraints
of its own. If the suspensions of a Ciceronian period demand
grammatical resolution, the symmetrical configurations of
Euphuistic prose demand psychological resolution — the more
so the more the logicality of the design becomes evident, the
more the reader comes to expect for each turn a counterturn.
In a context of precise antitheses, the first half of an antithesis,
no matter how self-contained grammatically, cries out for its
matching other half. "The unicorn is white; the hippogriff is
black. The unicorn is graceful; the hippogriff is clumsy. The
unicorn is caught by maidens; . . ." One might speak of such
a suspension as paratactic, occurring after a grammatically
closed unit, in the manner of a coordinate clause, in contrast
to the hypotactic suspension of Ciceronian style, where the
grammar remains "open" until the suspension is resolved. But
whatever term one applies to it, one must recognize that such
a technique sets up expectations as exigent as those of the
more familiar Ciceronian variety. Bacon's style, on the whole,
commits itself to satisfying such expectations. The baroque
writers properly speaking are those who eschew both sorts
of suspension, the hypotactic and the paratactic, or — even

more important — who initiate periodic or symmetrical motions only to frustrate them.

This is precisely Jonson's procedure. Where he arouses expectations of symmetry, it is usually for the purpose of violating it. When an implicitly symmetrical pattern is perpetually being disturbed and thwarted by small changes in form, we have the phenomenon of symmetry clashing with asymmetry that is at the heart of baroque stylistic practice.[24] The following passage, encompassing several periods, adheres as closely as Jonson ordinarily ever does to a strict oratorical pattern:

And an intelligent woman, if shee know by her selfe the least defect, will bee most curious, to hide it: and it becomes her. If shee be short, let her sit much, lest when shee stands, shee be thought to sit. If shee haue an ill foot, let her weare her gowne the longer, and her shoo the thinner. If a fat hand, and scald nailes, let her carue the lesse, and act in gloues. If a sowre breath, let her neuer discourse fasting: and alwaies talke at her distance. If shee haue black and rugged teeth, let her offer the lesse at laughter, especially if shee laugh wide, and open.   (*SW* IV.i.37–46)

The anaphoral "If shee" and "let her" establish a repeated figure on which Jonson plays constant and surprising variations. The short first member of each period undergoes its own vicissitudes: "If shee *be* short," "If shee *haue* an *ill foot*," "If a fat hand, and scald nailes" (the verb vanishes, and its object unexpectedly doubles), "If a sowre breath" (the object becomes single again), "If shee haue black and rugged teeth" (the verb re-enters with a new configuration of one noun and two modifiers as object). The parallel apodoses shift form even more fluidly, maintaining an air of exact symmetry and yet escaping from it at every moment. The result is not symmetry but asymmetry, perpetual displacements and dislocations of detail within a rhythmically symmetrical framework. This, moreover, from the play of Jonson's which more than any other simulates effects of balance in its dialogue.

61

2

The loose style, Croll's other subcategory of the baroque, differs from the curt style in that it prefers to multiply connectives rather than to suppress them. It tends also to longer members and longer periods, but its character is determined by its habit of heaping up conjunctions and by the kind of conjunctions it chooses: simple coordinates such as "and" and "or," which involve the least possible syntactic commitment to what has gone before, and, even more typically, the stricter relative and subordinating conjunctions used as though they were mere coordinates. And all this, as Croll urges, in order to free the period from formal restraints, to enable it to move with the utmost license from point to point, to follow nothing but the involutions of the thinking mind. For the enchaining suspensions of the Ciceronian period the loose style substitutes its own devices, the parenthesis and the absolute construction. The usefulness of the latter especially to a writer working in a resolved style is, as Croll has explained, that of all constructions it is "the one that commits itself least and lends itself best to the solution of difficulties that arise in the course of a spontaneous and unpremeditated progress." [25] It gives a writer carte blanche, enabling him to interrupt himself at will so as to travel in any cross-direction he pleases without dictating any alteration of the original syntax. It may be thrust in almost anywhere, and by its very nature — absolute, independent — forces most of the burden of logical connection upon the reader. Both the parenthesis and the absolute construction are favorites with Jonson, and sometimes he uses the two together in the same sentence:

. . . and presently goe, and redeeme him; for, being her brother, and his credit so amply engag'd as now it is, when she shal heare (as hee cannot him selfe, but hee must out of extremitie report it) that you came, and offered your selfe so kindly, and with that

respect of his reputation, why, the benefit cannot but make her
dote, and grow madde of your affections.   (*EMO* V.viii.14–20)

Jonson has here made the absolute construction elliptical, by
withholding the subject, "he," while the parenthesis intrudes
with the utmost casualness and tenuousness of reference into
the middle of a subordinate clause.

The most massive instance of Jonson's use of the absolute
construction may be quoted as a curiosity of the loose style:

Mary, your friends doe wonder, sir, the *Thames* being so neere,
wherein you may drowne so handsomely; or *London*-bridge, at a
low fall, with a fine leape, to hurry you downe the streame; or,
such a delicate steeple, i' the towne, as *Bow*, to vault from; or, a
brauer height, as *Pauls;* or, if you affected to doe it neerer home,
and a shorter way, an excellent garret windore, into the street;
or, a beame, in the said garret, with this halter; which they haue
sent, and desire, that you would sooner commit your graue head
to this knot, then to the wed-lock nooze; or, take a little sublimate,
and goe out of the world, like a rat; or a flie (as one said) with a
straw i' your arse: any way, rather, then to follow this goblin
matrimony.   (*SW* II.ii.20–32)

In this quintessentially Jonsonian loose period, we are confronted immediately either with a drastic ellipsis, which must
be filled in with some phrase ("Mary, your friends doe
wonder, sir, *why you do not make away with yourself at
once*") in order to complete the sense, or else with a huge
series of absolute constructions that seems to behave as a suspension and yet never leads to a resolution. Seems to behave
so, at least, to a reader. A reader is likely to demand the completion of syntactic patterns much more stringently than a
listener, who is accustomed, in talk, to hearing such patterns
form, dissolve, and drift off into others without ever fulfilling
themselves. The reader awaits with a certain tension the decisive return that will close the orbit; a listener may be perfectly

content to let the syntax turn into a wandering fire. And since Jonson was in this case writing for the stage, he may simply have pushed to an extreme the tendency of the baroque period to deal brusquely with its own syntactic commitments.

The absolute constructions here, it may be noticed, are in themselves, after the first, somewhat elliptical, requiring the reinstatement of the verbal phrase "being so neere" in each case. Then the extreme irregularity of the parallel members should be observed; each has its own unique configuration of subordinate clauses or modifying phrases or epithets, so that gradually the sense of parallel form all but evaporates, and we are left with a series of defiantly dissimilar constructions hooked together with "or's" and "and's," spinning freely in grammatical space and almost uncontrolled by any center of gravity. The effect of climax proceeds partly from the simple agglomeration of details and partly from the rhythmic speed-up toward the end that leads into the recapitulary formula, "any way, rather, then to follow this goblin *matrimony*."

A further trait of loose style illustrated in this passage is what Croll has called the "linked" or "trailing" period, occurring "when a member depends, not upon the general idea, or the main word, of the preceding member, but upon its final word or phrase alone." [26] The effect of such tactics is, as usual, to reduce to its minimum the interdependence of the successive members, to give the period, at any moment, a thrust forward into new areas. Truewit enumerates several of the high places from which Morose may fling himself before leading up to the mention and then to the proffering of a noose. At this point a shift to the relative "which," dependent as it is solely on the word "halter," deflects the absolute constructions from their course and leaves them stranded, at the same time catapulting the period into new grammatical territory. The period now follows a trajectory determined by the verb "desire," and lands finally a great distance from its starting point. This technique of pushing a period forward into fresh syntactic domain with scarcely a backward glance at the ground already traveled is one way in which anti-Ciceronian writers avoided the oratorical or "circular" Ciceronian period with its necessary return to some initial syntactic postulate. And it was this disregard of what he considered self-evident principles of grammatical law and order that led Coleridge to describe Senecan style as a series of thoughts "strung together like beads, without any causation or progression," [27] and caused Saintsbury to complain of the abuse of conjunctions among seventeenth-century writers, who tended "apparently out of mere wantonness, to prefer a single sentence jointed and rejointed, parenthesised and postscripted, till it does the duty of a paragraph, to a succession of orderly sentences each containing the expression of a simple or moderately complex thought" [28] — a stricture from which he unaccountably exempted Jonson.

But the writers in question intended to be wanton as the mind is wanton, to transcribe the process of thought onto the page instead of stifling it, as they thought, within prescribed logical schemes. "Je ne peints pas l'estre. Je peints le passage: non un passage d'aage en autre, ou, comme dict le peuple, de sept en sept ans, mais de jour en jour, de minute en minute." [29] Whether in fact a process of thought has any verifiable reality apart from the words that incarnate it, and whether, if so, the irregular modes of syntax preferred by most of the anti-Ciceronians are necessarily any truer to thought, any more "natural," than the suspensions of the Ciceronians or the perfected antitheses of Euphuism, are questions that Renaissance authors did not raise. They assumed that regularity was artful, irregularity natural and spontaneous, and they wrote accordingly. In the case of Jonson, a mild paradox emerges: despite his fervent belief in the hard labor of composition, for which he was both admired and ridiculed by his contemporaries, he adopted a rhetorical mode associated with improvisation. Probably — despite his own protestations to the contrary (*Disc.* 695–700) — he worked as hard to roughen and ir-regularize his prose as others did to polish and regularize. As George Williamson has demonstrated, imitation of Seneca could lead to something very close to Euphuism.[30] In Jonson's case it did not. He copied in Seneca only the vein of curtness and asymmetry for which he had a temperamental affinity, and in so doing produced a style more Senecan than Seneca's, insofar as Senecanism implied rebellion against rhetorical constraint.

The spontaneity implied in the loose style triumphs most decisively, as Croll points out, just when it seems most in danger of succumbing to orthodox periodicity. It falls into complex syntactic movements and then extricates itself in hair-breadth fashion by improvising fresh members or absolute constructions. Jonson finds himself entangled characteristically in his own habit of multiplying relative pronouns; he escapes from his own snares not by unraveling the constructions he has initiated, but by effectively cutting the Gordian knot of the constructions and then proceeding undisturbed. He will, for example, substitute a new subject that shunts the old one onto a siding and allows the thought to advance unimpeded on a new track. In the following excerpt Crites has been exclaiming against the use of perfume by men:

Yet, I doe like better the prodigalitie of jewels, and clothes, where-of one passeth to a mans heires; the other, at least weares out time: This presently expires, and without continuall riot in rep-aration is lost: which who so striues to keep, it is one speciall ar-gument to me, that (affecting to smell better then other men) he doth indeed smell farre worse. (*CR* V.iv.334–340)

(marginalia: more asymmetry in Jonson than Bacon)

Parenthetically one may notice here a signal feature of the loose style in the fact that the member that elaborates the second half of the antithesis grows and grows until it outweighs everything that has preceded it, almost engulfing the period, and inhibiting all possibility of exact balance. More germane to our present purpose is the way it grows: the linking relative *which*, referring back to *this* (which in turn refers back to the perfume previously mentioned), becomes the object of a complex syntactic motion vice-governed by "who," but this motion is instantly sidetracked by the introduction of a new indefinite-pronoun subject, "it." The member commencing with "it" is elliptical, since we do not know except by implication what "it" is a special argument *of*, and it starts syntactically from scratch, so that the clause "which who so striues to keep," perilously close to the "nonchalant" anacoluthon of which Croll speaks,[31] dangles in mid-air even after the fresh start has come to its rescue and completed the period.

One may add that it is probably as much as anything else Jonson's practice with relative conjunctions that has led his editors and critics to speak of his style as "packed" and "weighty." On the one hand he will employ relative connectives that cross-refer and intertwine densely with one another, and that may, while still incomplete, sprout further subsidiary relative clauses, as in the passage just cited. But he may, on the other hand, at any moment that it pleases him, throw them overboard for new constructions and leave them shipwrecked. Some fairly drastic instances of this kind of procedure appear in *The Entertainment at Highgate*.

. . . vouchsafe your eare, and forgiue his behauiour, which (euen to me, that am his parent) will no doubt be rude ynough, though otherwise full of salt, which, except my presence did temper, might turne to be gall, and bitternesse; but that shall charme him.   (199–203)

In this jungle of relatives and ellipses, the phrase "though otherwise full of salt" refers back to "which," itself dependent on "behauiour." A second "which," dependent solely on "salt" immediately preceding it, now makes its entry, introducing a trailing semiperiod half again as long as the member from which it springs, and subverting the initial construction entirely. The final demonstrative "that" refers back over a considerable distance to "my presence." The "packed" and "weighty" texture, then, seems to spring from the conflict of two opposing tendencies: the centrifugal force of the loose style struggling against the centripetal impulse of the Latinate conjunctions. A tightly integrated syntax is implied by the connectives and then carefully left unrealized.

If the curt style is peculiarly suited to expressions of quick wit, excitement, distraction, and the like, the loose style, by virtue of its greater floridity, lends itself well to purposes of formal declamation. It can be and is used by Jonson in a variety of ways: straightforwardly, as in Crites' censure of perfume, or with self-conscious exaggeration and heightening, as in Truewit's tirade against matrimony — or it may become the vehicle for the affected eloquence of fops like Amorphus and Fastidious Brisk eager to show off their aureate vocabularies. But whereas the dramatic versions of the curt style derive in part at least from prose as it was used in the popular drama of the 1590's, Jonson's theatrical adaptations of the loose style are his own original creation. Nothing in the comic prose of the preceding decade, whether in plays, novels, or pamphlets, really prepares us for such a baroque virtuoso piece as Fastidious Brisk's rhapsody on the court:

A man liues there, in that diuine rapture, that hee will think himselfe i' the ninth heauen for the time, and lose all sense of mortalitie whatsoeuer; when he shall behold such glorious (and almost immortall) beauties, heare such angelicall and harmonious voyces, discourse with such flowing and *ambrosian* spirits, whose wits are as suddaine as lightning, and humorous as *nectar*; Oh: it makes a man al *quintessence*, and *flame*, & lifts him vp (in a moment) to the verie christall crowne of the skie, where (houering in the strength of his imagination) he shall behold all the delights of the HESPERIDES, the *Insulae Fortunatae*, ADONIS gardens, *Tempe* or what else (confin'd within the amplest verge of *poesie*) to bee meere *vmbrae*, and imperfect figures, conferr'd with the most essentiall felicitie of your court.   (*EMO* IV.viii.18–32)

3

Having glanced at the major landmarks on Croll's baroque landscape, and having tried to show their relevance to Jonson's practice, we may carry the discussion into more particularly Jonsonian country by mentioning a few traits of style that, though not always exclusive with Jonson, are habitual enough with him to be regarded as idiosyncratic. These will in every case exemplify further the baroque syntax already outlined.

One of Jonson's customary techniques is to disturb, by one means or another, what we would ordinarily regard as logical word order. The frequent result of such tactics is to promote oddness of emphasis, to undermine expectations of "normal" arrangement; words will fail to appear in looked-for places and then emerge bizarrely where we least expect them. Jonson's simplest transposition of this sort is to add some element — subject, object, or modifier — postgrammatically, and thus to isolate it. In the statement "Men are decay'd, and *studies*" (*Disc.* 127), "Men are decay'd" forms a self-contained grammatical unit onto which Jonson has tacked an extra subject. The delayed subject comes as a kind of afterthought, and lends an improvisatory flourish to the remark. At the same time, paradoxically, it completes a rhythmic curve. If we put it back into its "normal" place in the sentence ("Men and studies are decay'd"), we make a more orderly period, and a flatter one. The same detail that roughens the syntax in one way, by separating elements that grammatically go together, smooths it out in another way by producing a cadence. And so with most instances of this device. One might, then, tentatively add to Croll's types of baroque effect the kind of tension that arises when the syntax is doing one thing grammatically and another rhythmically. And this could be classified as a further species of asymmetry, since the grammatical logic and the rhythm are out of phase with each other, instead of synchronized as in Euphuistic or Ciceronian prose. The effect of irregularity in such cases depends on the distance between the postscripted element and its natural grammatical mate.

A Trumpet should fright him terribly, or the Hau'-boyes?
(*SW* I.i.160–161)

. . . when some groome of his has got him an heire, or this barber . . .
(*SW* I.ii.54–55)

Some Diuine must resolue you in that, sir, or canon-Lawyer.
(*SW* IV.iv.148–149)

I'll tell you, Morose, you must talke diuinitie to him altogether, or morall philosophie.
(*SW* IV.iv.81–82)

If there bee neuer a *Seruant-monster* i'the *Fayre;* who can helpe it? he sayes; nor a nest of *Antiques?*
(*BF* Ind. 127–128)

The fact that this pattern occurs so much oftener in the plays than in the *Discoveries* suggests that Jonson was seeking to vitalize his language rhythmically for the stage in ways that would have been needless for the library.

Another way of driving a wedge between two words grammatically related is to separate a relative pronoun from its antecedent by interposing a word or phrase between them:

Come forward, you should be some dull tradesman by your pigheaded Sconce now, that thinke there's nothing good any where; but what's to be sold.
(*NNW* 12–14)

Nor is that worthy speech of *Zeno* the Philosopher to be past
over, without the note of ignorance: who being invited to a feast
in *Athens* . . .   (*Disc.* 370–372)

Jonson, one observes, does not assume that a relative or subordinate clause must tread like a porpoise on the tail of its
antecedent. He constantly, and sometimes perplexingly, delays
the pronoun while he interpolates other matter.[32] This habit
probably stems in part from Latin, a language in which, since
inflected endings carry the burden of grammatical connection,
the word order tends to be abstract — capable of manipulation
for purposes of emphasis and design. At the same time, the
cavalier distribution of elements recalls colloquial speech,
which rarely pauses to pickle over the logicality of its word
order. So that with this detail as with others, Jonson's "Ro-
manizing" tendency and his fascination with living speech
unexpectedly reinforce each other; the same device that on
the page can suggest pressure of thought and evoke memories
of classical prose, can in the theater serve to create a sense of
conversational *désinvolture*.

Sometimes Jonson deliberately suppresses some grammatical
element in order to avert an impending symmetry, to sabotage
in advance what threatens to evolve into too fussy a balance:
"But now be pleased to expect a more noble discovery worthie
of your eare, as the object will be [of] your eye" (*NNW* 301–
303). Here the ellipsis of an introductory *as* ("a more noble
discovery, *as* worthie of your eare, *as*") leaves the reader un-
prepared for the exact antithesis that follows and hence unable
to feel its full impact. Since symmetry depends to a large extent
on preparation, and unfolding according to plan, it may be
upset by a refusal to usher it in with recognizable anticipatory
formulas. Conversely, a severely antithetic scaffolding may be
erected in one clause only to be knocked to pieces in the next:
"A woman, the more curious she is about her face, is com-

71

monly the more carelesse about her house" (*Disc.* 192–193); "His modesty, like a riding Coat, the more it is worne, is the lesse car'd for" (*Disc.* 1328–29). No reader of Euphuistic prose could have failed to expect perfect matching between the two halves of the antithesis ("the more it is worne, the lesse it is car'd for"), but Jonson wrenches askew the second member so as to produce a lopsided rather than a balanced antithesis. Or, again, the effect of balance may be undone by the interpolation of a qualifying phrase between symmetrical elements: "If I doe not, let me play the mounte-bank for my meate while I liue, and the bawd for my drinke" (*SW* IV.i.151–152).

If we leaf through Jonson for the symmetrical formulas so abundant in Shakespeare, we find that where Jonson uses them he commonly manages to derange their stability in one way or another. The "as . . . so" parallelism, in Jonson, is likely to come out like this: "In short, as Vinegar is not accounted good, untill the wine be corrupted: so jests that are true and naturall, seldome raise laughter, with the beast, the multitude" (*Disc.* 2657–59), where the second half invents an entirely unforeseen syntactic combination for itself, abandoning in particular the notion of change from sweetness to corruption and embarking on explicit mention of those who are judging and condemning. The "though . . . yet" antithesis is liable to emerge in a form like this: "For though the *Prince* himselfe be of most prompt inclination to all vertue: Yet the best *Pilots* have need of *Mariners*, beside Sayles, Anchor, and other Tackle" (*Disc.* 1246–49), where the antithetic "yet" clause takes a sudden leap into metaphor, and elaborates that metaphor almost to the point of obscurity. In all of these instances, Jonson contrives to balk the kind of satisfaction that arises from a regular design fully articulated. Instead of a sense of fulfillment, he seeks effects of tension, instead of the feeling of repose as the pattern rounds itself out, a feeling of energy from the breaking of the pattern.

The asymmetry peculiar to baroque prose appears in Jonson in still another stylistic mannerism: the coupling in parallel relation of two elements that are either grammatically non-congruent or, if congruent on one level, so aggressively non-parisonic as to produce a feeling of incongruity, creating that slight sense of *offness* that baroque writers, their ears surfeited by Lylian parison or Ciceronian periodicity, evidently delighted in.

. . . they find nothing new, or to seeke.   (*Disc.* 1677)

But, beware of presuming, or how you offer comparison with persons so neere Deities.   (*Pan* 154–155)

. . . to doe this with diligence, and often.   (*Disc.* 1704–05)

. . . to taste all by degrees, and with change.   (*Disc.* 1654–55)

. . . has a yellow blade, but the eare empty.   (*Disc.* 687–688)

. . . with a Funnell, and by degrees, you shall fill many of them . . .   (*Disc.* 1794)

The parallel elements of a series may of course be set at odds with each other in the same way. In the following example, the third member rebelliously refuses to conform to the pattern of infinitives established by the first two: "*For* a man to write well, there are required three Necessaries. To read the best Authors, observe the best Speakers: and much exercise of his owne style" (*Disc.* 1697–99). In the next, Jonson charges headlong from a past participle, "*banish't*," to the nouns "want" and "disease": "As to wish a friend *banish't*, that they might accompany him in *exile:* or some great want, that they might relieve him: or a disease, that they might sit by him" (*Disc.* 440–443).

But irregularity need not restrict itself to a habit of interfering with symmetry, nor need it be confined within the compass of one period. Jonson's prose is marked by an almost dizzying variety of mutations of form. There are passages in which the subject changes from clause to clause, or from sentence to sentence:

His language, (where hee could spare, or passe by a jest) was nobly *censorious*. No man ever spake more neatly, more presly, more weightily, or suffer'd lesse emptinesse, less idlenesse, in what hee utter'd. No member of his speech, but consisted of the owne graces: His hearers could not cough, or looke aside from him, without losse. Hee commanded where hee spoke; and had his Judges angry, and pleased at his devotion. No man had their affections more in his power. The feare of every man that heard him, was, lest hee should make an end. (*Disc*. 888–898)

Despite a certain regularity here — from the steady march of subject, predicate, subject, predicate, subject, predicate — the effect of irregularity predominates because of the nervous mobility of the subject, in which respect Jonson outdoes the passage from Seneca that serves as his model. One result is to emphasize the independence and, so to speak, defiant integrity of each clause, to brace it sharply against its neighbors and force the reader to readjust his perspective at every pause. Jonson demands similar reaccommodations when he causes a subject to materialize out of thin air: "Then men were had in price for learning: now, letters onely make men vile. Hee is upbraydingly call'd a *Poet*, as if it were a most contemptible *Nick-name*" (*Disc*. 279–282).

He is no less in revolt against regularity in his handling of verbs. Sometimes he pitches abruptly from the declarative mood into the imperative:

In Picture, light is requir'd no lesse then shadow: so in stile, height, as well as humblenesse. But beware they be not too humble; as *Pliny* pronounc'd of *Regulus* writings: You would thinke them written, not on a child, but by a child. (*Disc*. 1541–45)

74

The change of pace here jolts the reader even more sharply because at the same time there erupts from nowhere the pronoun "they," for which the reader must scramble to invent an antecedent. At other times Jonson will suddenly shift gears into neutral, so to speak, by switching into the infinitive:

A strict and succinct style is that, where you can take away nothing without losse, and that losse to be manifest.[33] (*Disc.* 1970–72)

Have not I seen the pompe of a whole Kingdome, and what a forraigne King could bring hither. Also to make himselfe gaz'd, and wonder'd at, laid forth as it were to the shew, and vanish all away in a day? (*Disc.* 1404–07)

And sometimes he will without warning shift a plural verb (with its plural subject) into the singular: ". . . what Iustice or Religion is to be expected? Which are the only two Attributes make *Kings* a kinne to *Gods;* and is the *Delphick* sword, both to kill Sacrifices, and to chastise offenders" (*Disc.* 1288–91). Or he will coolly switch tenses within the space of a single period. "But the fees of the one, or the *salary* of the other, never answer the *value* of what we received; but serv'd to gratifie their labours"[34] (*Disc.* 476–478). This happens especially when he is recounting the scenic effects of a masque, as if he were aiming to convey a vivid sense of immediacy together with the precision of objective reporting:[35]

In his hand he bore a golden censor with perfume, and censing about the altar (hauing first kindled his fire on the toppe) is interrupted by the *Genius*. (*King's Ent.* 551–553)

When the Spectators had enough fed their eyes, with the delights of the *Scene*, in a part of the ayre, a bright cloud begins to breake forth. (*Chlor.* 28–30)

And finally there is the kind of irregularity that occurs when members of a sequence not only vary internally one from another, but from the start are launched in diverse directions by differing conjunctions:

> *Metaphors* farfet hinder to be understood, and affected, lose their grace. Or when the person fetcheth his translations from a wrong place. As if a Privie-Counsellor should at the Table take his *Metaphore* from a Dicing-House . . .   (*Disc.* 1905–09)

It scarcely matters, in short, what sort of regularity or continuity one presupposes in prose style: Jonson manages to avoid them all. Discontinuity, change of pace, interruption of design, are the materials with which he works. Despite a certain amount of incidental symmetry, Jonson's prose is irregular on principle, and the irregularity transmits itself from the largest phenomena of style down to the smallest, from the formation of the most massive block of loose periods down to the parallel coupling of discongruent adverbs. Saintsbury's dictum that Jonson "preserves — his kind cannot but preserve — the balance of Ascham and Lyly as his chief rhetorical instrument" [36] must then be severely emended, if indeed it is to stand at all. If Jonson preserves balance, he does so only to upset balance. If he deploys symmetrical patterns, he does so only to violate their symmetry. Everywhere he is restlessly interfering with the expected structure of a phrase or clause. The asymmetrical tactics that pervade his writing form a rhetoric distinct from, and as distinct as, any of the more orthodox rhetorics, an antirhetorical rhetoric that seeks to disguise itself almost as a nonrhetoric. The necessarily stricter attentiveness of the reader to such a style, since he cannot let his mind coast in the suspensions of a periodic sentence or in the exact correspondences of the aculeate style, perhaps suggests why the laborious Jonson adopts a manner apparently most congenial to effects of improvisation. In the hands of writers like Burton, baroque prose ambles or scampers with skittish whimsicality. Jonson, by his reluctance to fulfill expectation, his defiance of stock responses to syntax, creates an impression of granitic strength: the participation of the reader or listener becomes an exercise in rock-climbing over the jagged, twisted, craggy terrain of the syntax.

4

An inquiry into the relation between these stylistic habits and larger aspects of technique might suggest rather quickly that the structure of the *Discoveries*, at least, resembles that of the curt and loose periods. Like Donne's *Devotions*, Selden's *Table Talk*, and Traherne's *Centuries of Meditations*, the *Discoveries* belong to a genre — named after the most distinguished example of it — the *pensées*, a disconnected series of jottings that explores a few dominant themes in as many ways as the writer chooses. Each *pensée* constitutes a separate quantum, a bundle of words peculiar to itself, differing in size, shape, color, and texture from all the other bundles, just as the members of the curt period differ from each other. Truth is presented in fragments, in scattered glimpses, rather than steadily and whole. There may or may not be an ordered vision behind the fragments, but the technique, at least, implies groping, exploration, tentative forays; the vision is seen only intermittently and in pieces.[37]

With the plays, the problem is more complex. It may, however, be conjectured that just as a writer who repeatedly uses causal connectives is thinking in terms of cause and effect, so a writer who shuns them is thinking in other terms, perhaps of a world so static that nothing in it is subject to change, perhaps of a world so bewildering and disintegrated that nothing in it seems causally related to anything else, a world in which the atoms of impulse, act, and event collide haphazardly in a void. It may be excessively obvious to observe that Shake-

speare's plays constitute a dense network of cause and effect:
but set them beside Jonson's, and the fact becomes overpowering. Coleridge's description of Iago's soliloquies as "the mo-
tive-hunting of motiveless malignity," [38] the endless efforts to
account for Hamlet's madness, Lear's folly, and the rest,
suggest the extent to which we expect effects in Shakespeare
to be adequately motivated. Shakespeare, by repeatedly raising
the question himself, sanctions such expectations. One might
compile a repertory of occasions on which characters inter-
rogate the motives behind acts or feelings:

> Why haue these banish'd, and forbidden Legges,
> Dar'd once to touch a Dust of Englands Ground?
> <div align="right">(L.354; <i>RII</i> II.iii.90–91)</div>

> Why do'st thou say, King <i>Richard</i> is depos'd . . .
> <div align="right">(L.360; <i>RII</i> III.iv.77)</div>

> Wherefore doe you so ill translate your selfe,
> Out of the Speech of Peace, that beares such grace,
> Into the harsh and boystrous Tongue of Warre?
> <div align="right">(L.409; <i>IIHIV</i> IV.i.47–49)</div>

> But wherefore did hee take away the Crowne?
> <div align="right">(L.414; <i>IIHIV</i> IV.v.89)</div>

> Fellow, why do'st thou show me thus to th'world?
> <div align="right">(L.80; <i>MM</i> I.ii.120)</div>

> Where are the vile beginners of this Fray?
> <div align="right">(L.681; <i>Rom.</i> III.i.146)</div>

> Princes:
> What greefe hath set the Iaundies on your cheekes?
> <div align="right">(L.591; <i>Troil.</i> I.iii.1–2)</div>

> Good my Lord, what is your cause of distemper?
> <div align="right">(L.777; <i>Ham.</i> III.ii.350–351)</div>

> Why brand they vs / With Base?
> <div align="right">(L.793; <i>Lear</i> II.i.9–10)</div>

> Wherefore to Douer?   (L.808; <i>Lear</i> III.vii.52)

But wherefore could not I pronounce Amen?

(L.744; *Mac.* II.ii.31)

And this would be only the merest beginning, to be followed by an inquiry into occasions on which characters vouchsafe explanations of acts and feelings — and still one would have barely scratched the surface of Shakespeare's densely causal world and his dynamic conception of character.

Jonson's world, by contrast, is not causal, and character does not interact with character. A seeming cause produces no effect; an apparent effect springs from no discoverable cause. The archetypal Jonsonian situation is that in which an individual pursues his humor oblivious of everything else about him. Fungoso, his eyes fixed greedily on Fastidious Brisk's fine suit, makes half-answers to his uncle while privately calculating how much it will cost him to duplicate the suit. Sogliardo, in the same moment, is too engrossed by the prospect of vulgar pleasures in London to notice Fungoso's inattention. Sordido, scarcely aware of the others on the stage, gazes into the sky for signs of the rain that will raise the value of his wheat. The characters remain as isolated, as blocked off from each other, as immobilized in their humors, as the members of an exploded period. Instead of a chain of circumstances, dependent one on another, the plot presents a kaleidoscopic series of characteristic stances.

Jonson modifies this technique in his mature comedies. Certainly the hoaxes and conspiracies that form the mainsprings of action in *Volpone*, *Epicene*, and *The Alchemist* involve causal sequence. But the sequences tend to be simple rather than multiple, and even so they often run aground and require relaunching. The fifth act of *Volpone* provides a notorious example: the mainspring of the plot having run down, Jonson must forcibly rewind it in order to bring on the catastrophe. Similarly, the denouement of *The Alchemist* depends on Love-

79

wit's unexpected return to London, but where another playwright might have motivated the return, accounted for it
through some specific circumstances connected with other
facts of the plot, and where a playwright bent on suspense
would have provoked our curiosity about it beforehand, Jonson characteristically allows it to come as a total surprise and
then does not bother to explain it, because he cares only for
the series of brilliant confusions it will produce. Even in his
major comedies, that is, Jonson prefers to create his effects by
means other than causal linkage: the true center of interest
lies in the shifting configurations of character confronting
character. Few dramatists of his stature depend so little on suspense, on tying episode to episode and evolving one incident
out of another. In Shakespeare, each scene germinates out of
causes planted in previous scenes, and becomes in turn the
germ of future scenes. In Jonson, scene after scene has only
its own existence to contemplate. In Shakespeare, people have
missions, they go on errands, they seek each other out. In
Jonson, they meet by accident; they just happen to turn up.

Poetaster, for instance, opens with a lively debate on the
status of poetry between Ovid, his father, Tucca, Lupus, and
some servants. The scene projects concisely and forcefully a
whole range of attitudes toward art. But the narrative links
between it and the rest of the play are exceedingly tenuous.
Ovid Senior has come to visit his son — for a purpose, we
assume; but we never learn what the purpose is, since when he
finds his heir reciting verses, he loses his temper and forgets
his errand. Then, though he threatens to disinherit his son for
neglecting the law and persisting with poetry, and though
Ovid Junior defies the threat, nothing further is heard of the
matter. There are no repercussions for Ovid, nor does his
father ever reappear on the stage. Again, Tucca has attached
himself to Ovid Senior to wheedle a few drachmas out of him.

The scene gives us a picturesque sample of Tucca's methods of cadging, but it also sets up a relation between the two that is never pursued. Tucca, we know, will not repay the loan; Ovid Senior, we know, will be incensed; but none of this is ever referred to again. Finally, by including Lupus, the tribune, in the scene, Jonson adds to the philistine contemners of poetry the political enemies of it. But why Lupus should happen to be a friend of Ovid Senior's, why he should meet him on this particular morning and accompany him to his son's quarters, is left wholly to conjecture: the entente between them begins and ends in the scene in question. Jonson, in short, assembles a group of characters so as to exhibit them in significant postures, but does not, except in the most perfunctory manner, account for their simultaneous presence on the stage, and does not attempt to follow through with the narrative elements planted in the scene.

Something similar may be said — and will be said in due course — concerning *Epicene*. For the moment we may pause to notice that when Marcel Achard adapted the play for Charles Dullin in 1925,[39] the chief thing he did with it was to revise it as far in the direction of the intrigue plot as it would go. By suppressing minor characters, by hooking all subsidiary action directly into the main plot, by motivating Dauphine's scheme itself more substantially, he turned the whole play into the network of cause and effect that his generation prized in the theater. Family links are specified: Achard's hero, Dauphin, is not simply Morose's nephew, but "le fils bien-aimé de sa bien-aimée soeur" (p. 149). He intrigues for Morose's inheritance not as an end in itself but to enable him to compete successfully for the hand of a rich heiress, Lady Juliet, with whom he is in love. Sir John Daw and Sir Amorous La Fool are collapsed into a single character, Sir Sottenville des Amourettes, a doltish rival of Dauphin's, whose reading of the madrigal now has the effect of inflaming Dauphin's jealousy, and whose discomfiture in the last act has the specific purpose of exposing his unworthiness before Lady Juliet, so that she will appreciate Dauphin. Truewit, now Delesprit, delivers his recommendations on fashionable folly, seduction, and feminine adornment with the precise aim of assisting Dauphin in his courtship and of reconciling him to Juliet's worldliness. The play ends, needless to say, with a triumphant union between the hero and his lady.[40]

The language reflects this new state of affairs. It now swarms with exact symmetries and logical particles. In the opening scene, Jonson's idle conversation between Clerimont and Truewit concerning the *longueurs* and secrecies of the dressing-table becomes Dauphin's complaint over the behavior of his mistress:

Elle reçoit trop aimablement les beaux esprits, les fatuités du jour. Je ne puis pénétrer dans sa chambre qu'après une longue et terrible attente. Elle m'acceuille le dernier parce que je n'ai pas l'esprit chargé de madrigaux et que je ne la sais pas comparer habilement à la lune aux étoiles et au soleil. J'attends donc les deux heures encore qu'elle consacre à parer, baigner, peindre, parfumer et ajuster sa noble personne. Car elle donne dans le travers du temps, et se défigure par des poudres, des crèmes et des onguents.

(p. 143)

The sense of motive, intention, and causality that figures so strongly in the adaptation appears in the multiplication of causal conjunctions, in the "parce que," "donc," and "car." Lady Juliet's behavior is ascribed to a certain set of attitudes; its effects on Dauphin are equally specific. Or, for the more conventional symmetry of Achard's style, one might compare Truewit's boast, "If I doe not, let me play the mountebank for my meate while I liue, and the bawd for my drinke," with Delesprit's, "Je la rendrai amoureuse de toi, ou je veux gagner mon pain sur la place publique et mon vin dans un mauvais lieu" (p. 147), with its reiteration of purpose and its more pat antithesis. Finally, to see how Achard alters the Jonsonian loose period, one might compare the long passage quoted earlier (in section 2) with its equivalent from Delesprit:

Vos amis s'étonnent, Monsieur, que la Tamise étant si près, où vous pouvez vous noyer si agréablement, ou bien le pont de Londres, d'où une belle chute peut vous précipiter au fond de la rivière; qu'ayant à votre disposition nos jolis clochers de la ville, tel que celui de Bow, celui de Saint-Paul dont la hauteur vous offre encore un saut plus rapide; ou si vous préférez un endroit plus près de votre maison, les fenêtres de ce grenier qui donne sur la rue; qu'ayant dans ce même grenier une poutre, et cette corde que vos amis vous envoient, ils s'étonnent, dis-je, et préféreraient vous voir commettre votre tête vénérable à ce noeud coulant qu'à celui du mariage. Ils aimeraient certes vous voir prendre du sublimé et mourir comme un rat ou comme une mouche, — dit-on, — d'une paille au derrière, . . .   (p. 166)

The major change here is precisely the break-up of the long winding baroque movement into a series of rationally ordered members, periodically reintroduced by a "que," reconfirmed by a "dis-je," and then halted entirely and recommenced afresh when it begins to grow top-heavy.

   La femme silencieuse, in short, reintroduces logical *engrenage* into the language and causal continuity into the lives of the characters. In Jonson, the avoidance of logical particles and the preference for the exploded period reflect the discontinuous plot structure; society is conceived as a collection of disconnected atoms, in which each character speaks a private language of his own, pursues ends of his own, collides from time to time with other characters, and then rebounds into isolation.

It goes without saying, but it must be said nevertheless, that none of this is meant to imply inferior workmanship, second-rate dramaturgy, or a deficient sense of the "dramatic" on Jonson's part. Jonson's sentences, Jonson's plots, are not un-dramatic: they are dramatic in a special and somewhat uncommon, perhaps a Joycean, sense. They constitute a series of epiphanies. Their pictorial fullness and verbal density embody a vision: they show us that the things we see are those things that they are and no other things. Harry Levin has appropriately urged us to criticize Shakespeare in terms of "movement and warmth," Jonson in terms of "pattern and colour." [41] Disapproving the heavy plotting of most Elizabethan drama, Jonson replaces it with something akin to the kaleidoscope, where blocks of color are put in strange conjunction, then shaken to produce new conjunctions, or, as Levin has suggested, to the chess game, in which each character "has only his characteristic move, . . . and the object of the game is to see what new combinations have been brought about." [42] One might compare this emphasis on abstract design with that in Gabrieli's brass *canzone* for St. Mark's, or Stravinsky's *Agon*, where the manipulation of textures, contrasting sonorities, competing rhythms, resembles the clash of jargons, the shrill rivalry of character pitted against character, of the Jonsonian stage.

For an analogy that included more of the expressive and realistic content of Jonsonian theater, one might cite Eric Bentley in defense of Brecht. Speaking of the lack of suspense in Brecht's plays, Bentley likens them to paintings by Brueghel, where the dramatic whole is conceived as an aggregate of small dramas, as a picturesque assemblage of minor tensions rather than as a single dominant tension. Brueghel's "Battle between Carnival and Lent" offers a swarming villagescape in which the queer little figurines engage in dozens of diverse activities — watching a Lenten play, dancing in a ring, huddling around a bonfire — activities related for the most part only analogically to the weird combat taking place in the foreground. In Bosch's "Temptation of St. Anthony," the saint himself is only a spectator to the eerie scene, in which snouted creatures, astride mooncalves, strum harps, or wizened homunculi go fishing from dolphins rigged as boats. Similarly, in Brecht's patchwork of the Thirty Years' War, or Jonson's crazy quilt of Bartholomew Fair, "swift, strong sensation" is avoided. The eye is invited "to linger on this detail or that. The eye that accepts the invitation discovers one 'drama' after another in the picture and even a total drama of the whole." [43]

What is true of the design as a whole obtains for the smaller unit of the period or sentence: instead of the closely woven, climactic effect of the Ciceronian period, Jonson's prose affords the clash of clause against clause, the abrupt reversals and unexpected prolongations, that defeat the wish for suspense but gratify the craving for "pattern and color"; instead of the single, imperious tension, the diffracted tension that allows the ear "to linger on this detail or that."

5

To detect the "psychological etymon" [44] behind this stylistic behavior is not easy, far less easy, certainly, than for other baroque writers. One can, of course, point to Jonson's neo-Stoicism, his admiration for the anti-Ciceronian prose of Seneca and Tacitus. But Bacon revered Tacitus and writes a prose akin to Euphuism. Seneca himself is more Euphuistic, more word-catching, than Jonson. One can point also to Jonson's mimetic preoccupation, his fascination with the sounds of live language. But one has still not explained why he preferred the stutter of the curt style to the rotunder polysyndetic effects equally common — one supposes — in Elizabethan speech.

What follows, then, is to be regarded as speculative and exploratory.

If we assume that the restlessness of baroque style expresses some restlessness within the writer, some inner conflict or war with the world at large, we can see that it lends itself admirably to the needs of authors like Donne, Browne, Milton, Burton, Montaigne, and Pascal. Donne's tensions are not merely obvious: they form the subject matter of his art. In sermon and poem alike he dramatizes his own paradoxes of feeling, his struggles between carnal love and religious devotion, his craving to unite matter and spirit. There are the obvious doubts and the obvious suffering. *Mutatis mutandis*, much the same may be said of Pascal. In Sir Thomas Browne we have a milder personality, but one still caught between different kinds of belief: committed on the one hand to hieroglyphic mysteries like the quincunx, and on the other to the sober reappraisal of popular errors. *Religio medici* expounds the writer's theology with such minute particularity, such pondering of every nuance, that despite its orthodoxy as a whole it becomes an absolutely private vision. In Milton — verse and prose alike — we have the passionate assertions of a spirit whose Protestant self-sufficiency leads him steadily further from the center of orthodoxy into an area of belief uniquely his own, and recognized by him as such. In *The Anatomy of Melancholy*, individualism takes the form of eccentricity; Burton revels in his own crotchets, and makes out of the baroque rhetoric an appropriately crotchety style in which to do so, just as his philosophical master, Montaigne, reveled in the oddities of *his* temperament.

The common denominator among these writers seems to be an intense, sometimes rebellious subjectivity, for which the skittishness of baroque prose provides an ideal instrument. But when we approach Jonson with similar expectations, we seem to run into a blank wall. Jonson goes through no dark night of the soul like that of Donne or Pascal, nor does he feel impelled to record his own configuration of belief and discriminate it from those of others, as do Browne and Milton. Unlike Montaigne, Jonson would never have admitted to any pleasure in reading his own entrails. Far from courting eccentricity, like Burton, Jonson satirizes it scornfully, the whole theory and dramatic practice of "humors" comedy being an attempt to scourge deviations from the social norm. Instead of listening to the inner voice, the private idiosyncrasy, Jonson respects only the standards of the humanist tradition, the consent of the learned, the congress of the good, and he never expresses the slightest doubt that he speaks for the learned and the good of all ages. What distinguishes the *Discoveries* from the *Devotions*, the *Pensées*, the *Table Talk*, and the *Centuries of Meditations* is precisely the suppression of all doubt and personal revelation — the frequent paraphrases, marginally acknowledged, from other authors, giving the work more the air of a compilation than of a private meditation.

In short, where the other baroque writers explicitly dramatize their tensions, in Jonson the tensions remain buried. The other writers manage to relate their private disturbances to large cultural crises, theological, ecclesiastical, or political, but Jonson, by refusing to acknowledge his, can express them only in oblique and devious ways, which makes them less easy to isolate. But no one has ever doubted their existence. The presence of tension in Jonson reveals itself most obviously in his insistent claim to be without tension; the oftener he protests his imperturbability, the less we are inclined to believe it. Jonson cannot, like the stoic he longs to be, remain indifferent to the vicissitudes of fortune. He cannot despise the acclaim or the scorn of others; he exults in approval and smarts painfully under criticism. He cannot cleanse himself of the petty passions he would like to disown.

Nor can he find the post in society that he claims as his due, that of the teacher-poet standing at the elbow of the monarch, unfolding wise and sane counsel, instructing his peers in the good life and flicking off the insect malice of envious rivals. The casting of himself in just such a role in *Cynthia's Revels* and *Poetaster* is in both cases an act of extravagant wish-fulfillment, yet even in these fantasies of Crites and Horace, the serenity is only skin-deep: just below the surface lurks the marsh of insecurity, envy, and suspicion. If it would be rash to suggest that Jonson is exorcising his own eccentricity in the fops and fools of the comical satires, he is certainly doing something like it with Morose, Wasp, and other characters of the mature comedies. Jonson himself cannot believe in the ideal image of himself to which he would like the world to subscribe; he can only inch toward it by loading onto the gulls and victims of the comedies his own hampering tensions, and casting them out.

The result is that Jonson's most successful art is that in which unmasking and casting out have fullest scope. More and more often into the ceremoniousness of the masques intrude outbreaks of the critical spirit that cannot credit the reality of the vision being created. Satiric comedy affords the only lightning rod by which Jonson's high tension can release itself in ordered, concentrated form. The massive voltage streaks down in the great comedies, igniting everything in its path, creating by destroying and destroying by creating. The positive standard, the ethical humanism and solid sense to which he is always appealing, remains for the most part in the background, and every effort to incarnate it dramatically (Bonario, Surly, Grace Wellborn) is a failure.

In Jonson, in short, we have a subjectivity as intense as

Donne's masquerading as its opposite, a thin-skinned suspiciousness masking itself as a benign imperturbability, and an acute social insecurity clothing itself in the mantle of achieved status, in a fashion similar to that in which the social-climbing citizens of Jonson's own comedies clothe themselves in the jargon and gestures of a superior class in order to be accepted by it. And it is dissonances like these, no doubt, within Jonson himself, that lead him to adopt baroque style, with its broken rhythms and perilous balances, rather than the stabler rhetorics of Euphuism or Ciceronianism, with their implicit sense of integration into a harmonious, ordered cosmos.

❦ III ❦

Rhetoric's Tinkling Bell

T wo well-known passages in the *Discoveries* will indicate how Jonson uses prose in his plays. One, paraphrased
from Vives, concerns the relation of language to character:

Language most shewes a man: speake that I may see thee. It
springs out of the most retired, and inmost parts of us, and is the
Image of the Parent of it, the mind. No glasse renders a mans
forme, or likenesse, so true as his speech.   (*Disc.* 2031–35)

The other, adapted from Seneca, specifies the link between
language and morality:

Wheresoever, manners, and fashions are corrupted, Language is.
It imitates the publicke riot. The excesse of Feasts, and apparrell,
are the notes of a sick State; and the wantonnesse of language, of
a sick mind.   (*Disc.* 954–958)

A man's speech, in short, the faculty that distinguishes him
from the brutes, provides the truest index to his disposition
and his moral health. Corruption of speech implies corruption
of thought and feeling. If states reveal their rottenness in "excesse" of feasts and apparel, individuals disclose their sickness
in "wantonnesse" of language. But what constitutes "wantonnesse" in language? Dramatizing the answer to this question occupies Jonson throughout much of his career. One may

summarize his numerous answers by saying that it includes any kind of verbal showiness, such as the use of jargon or exotic terms or hard words, or the use of ornamental schemes like those of Euphuistic or Arcadian prose; any kind of convulsive linguistic tic recognizable as an addiction; and above all, mimicry, the imitation of any way of speaking not normally one's own, whether of another social class, a coterie, or a trade, or of books or the stage.

Mimicry, in fact, which tends to draw the other vices into itself, is the symptom of a universal disease:

> I *have* considered, our whole life is like a *Play:* wherein every man, forgetfull of himselfe, is in travaile with expression of another. Nay, wee so insist in imitating others, as wee cannot (when it is necessary) returne to our selves: like Children, that imitate the vices of *Stammerers* so long, till at last they become such; and make the habit to another nature, as it is never forgotten.
>
> (*Disc.* 1093–99)

The compulsion to parrot the "expression of another" thus leads to the loss of one's own authentic voice, and hence of oneself. Mimicry is in the narrowest sense a "behavioral compulsion": the mimic remains trapped in a vocabulary, a syntax, and a whole idiom confected by someone else, and in consequence he can never perceive his own feelings or desires, but must live a hand-me-down existence filched from another. By failing to make a language of his own, the mimic forfeits the making of himself; he remains a half-man, or moral cretin.

The playwright himself, to be sure, is a mimic, and so is the actor. Both practice that "singerie sublime" of which Diderot speaks,[1] the professional ventriloquism of the artist seeking to create personae for purposes of theatrical illusion. But the mimicry the playwright practices he projects, in varying degrees, onto his characters. Hence the capital importance of impersonation in most of the world's great drama, especially comedy. The playwright's craft provides him with a basic metaphor for problems of identity and existence, truth and hypocrisy, self-knowledge and self-ignorance; he mimics mimicry in order to deride or admire it. Jonson's later contemporary, Jean Rotrou, shows the actor Genest assuming in sober earnest the role of martyred Christian he has begun by merely "playing" before a pagan emperor. Our own contemporary, Jean Genêt (likewise "comédien et martyr") represents the clients of a brothel acting out various fantasy personae that momentarily become "real" during an insurrection. Pirandello's Henry IV preserves in sanity the bizarre guise he has unwittingly adopted in madness; Osborne's Archie Rice tries vainly to shed at home the role of vulgar jokester he has donned in the music hall. In all these cases, one line to be drawn is that between creative and slavish mimicry. Pirandello's Henry IV is largely creative, Osborne's entertainer largely slavish. In Jonson, the creativeness appears in figures like Mosca, Volpone, Subtle, and Truewit, who can within limits control their own personae, command their own metamorphoses. The butts in the plays are those who try to live within an alien persona, adopting the kind of mask that flatters their ambitions but exceeds their capacities, and so failing to realize either.

I

The identity of language with character, in Jonson, leads to an especially acute concern for decorum, the law which demands that a character speak like himself at all times. Mimicry, however, introduces a complication: a violation of decorum, so to speak, on the part of the character, who is straining *not* to speak like himself, *not* to play his proper role. The playwright then has the task of observing decorum while his character is offending against it. And this he may do either by insinuating, through the texture of the language, that all is false, or else by intermingling the "true" and "natural" in his character's speech with the unnaturally appropriated expressions, the forms of wantonness. The latter is Jonson's more usual procedure. Preoccupation with viciousness of language begins to emerge even within the old-fashioned "romantic" plot of his early comedy *The Case is Altered*.[2] At least one of the prose characters, the cobbler Juniper, has learned to inflate his speech with "wantonnesse." Juniper is fascinated by the mere sound of words, by the portentous, oracular clang of magniloquent polysyllabicisms, and refuses to interest himself in their meaning:

> *Iuniper.* Nay, slid I am no changling, I am *Iuniper* still, I keepe the pristinate ha, you mad *Hierogliphick*, when shal we swagger?
> *Valentine. Hieroglyphick*, what meanest thou by that?
> *Iuni.* Meane? Gods so, ist not a good word man? what? stand vpon meaning with your freinds? Puh, *Absconde*.
> *Valen.* Why, but stay, stay, how long has this sprightly humor haunted thee?
> *Iuni.* Foe humour, a foolish naturall gift we haue in the *Æquinoctiall*.   (I.iv.5–14)

His vocabulary includes not only dinosaur words but foreign phrases, Petrarchan conceits, and scraps of verse from popular plays, which he tumbles out with the eagerness of a child spilling the contents of a Christmas stocking. The sense of wonder is heightened by Juniper's habit of speaking in excitement, in rapid-fire barrages of short clauses, hooked together with commas and semicolons in the manner of the exploded period.

What are you mad, are you detestable, would you make an Anatomy of me, thinke you I am not true Ortographie?   (IV.viii.24–26)

For Gods sake be not so inuiolable, I am no ambuscado, what predicament call you this, why do you intimate so much?

(IV.viii.28–30)

Ha Bully? vext? what intoxicate? is thy braine in a quintescence? an Idea? a metamorphosis? an Apology? ha rogue? Come this loue feeds vpon thee, I see by thy cheekes, and drinkes healthes of vermilion teares, I see by thine eyes.   (IV.v.8–12)

Juniper's flamboyant style proves seductive enough to provoke emulation from his fellow-servant Onion, who copies it fitfully when he can remember to do so.[3] But it is not at all clear who or what Juniper is trying to imitate; the only demand he makes on a word is that it be novel and arresting. One can discover certain links between what Juniper and Onion say and what they do. One might find in their irresponsibility with language a counterpart to the moral irresponsibility that leads them to steal Jaques' treasure. One might also see in the dueling lesson an awkward effort to be gentlemanly, just as their language is stuffed with words too "gentlemanly" for their station. And one might see in the scene of their drunkenness, where they dress like peacocks on their stolen gold, a love of visible finery corresponding to their love of verbal finery. So much would doubtless be true, and to this extent Jonson's moral and linguistic judgments coincide. The trouble is that one can find no clear motivating center for the acts and words of these two, apart from simple high spirits. Although they practice the noble science of fencing, and talk of buying coats of arms with their loot, it is plain that they have no serious pretensions — no pretensions whatever, in fact — to gentility, but are merely playing at it like children. No one, in fact, is more earnestly anxious than Onion to discharge his duties as a serving-man properly. And Juniper's gentlemanly terms enter only by accident into a vocabulary chosen mostly for its glitter. Like the older clowns on whom they are modeled, they enjoy revelry and bright colors, and their talk betrays a childlike pleasure in the bright colors and fine sounds of words, an attachment to shine and surface. Attachment to surfaces, in Jonson, ordinarily implies moral superficiality, but this is usually clinched by being associated with some palpable folly or even criminality. In the case of Juniper and Onion, there is no necessary or probable relation between their language and the rest of their behavior. Their verbal capers are freakish in too many different ways at once, and refer too haphazardly to the situations in which they occur. Like the colored lozenges of the harlequin's costume, their festive words are a kind of free-floating decoration patched onto their dialogue to give it gaiety and movement, but little else.

Nevertheless, this same language paves the way for Jonson's future successes in the representation of folly. While he could doubtless have approximated the same effects in verse if he had wanted to, prose gave him more elbowroom. Through its freedom from metrical recurrence, it lent itself to the imitation of irregularity — of extreme irregularity — and hence of incoherence. Marlowe had resorted to prose to convey Zabina's tragic distraction at the sight of her husband's body (*I Tamburlaine* V.ii). Jonson too wishes to suggest distraction, of a more continuing kind, that of rattle-headed folly, and by adopting the nonregular rhythm of prose, and insisting, both rhythmically and semantically, on its nonregularity, he achieves the effect of mental clutter he is after. Juniper and Onion thus become stylistic prototypes for the legions of gulls and fops that prance through later Jonsonian theater.

In the prose of Maximilian, on the other hand, we have an experiment that Jonson was never to repeat. Maximilian, Milanese general and friend to the irascible old count, forms the exception to the rule in this play that noble personages speak verse while their social inferiors speak prose. One may account for this by observing that Maximilian is intended as a spokesman for reason and judgment. Where the other characters indulge in various kinds of emotional outpourings, he maintains a dignified and judicial reserve, and Jonson may have felt that the cooler element of prose would be a fitting medium for his cooler temperament. Unfortunately it cannot be said that he has succeeded in making of him more than a cardboard cutout of noble sentiments. Maximilian's speeches strike one limp pose of politeness after another, with a perfunctory propriety that chills. A further difficulty appears in speeches like this:

Mounsieur *Gasper* (I take it so is your name) misprise me not, I wil trample on the hart, on the soule of him that shall say, I will wrong you: what I purpose, you cannot now know; but you shall know, and doubt not to your contentment. Lord *Chamount*, I will leaue you, whilest I go in and present my selfe to the honourable *Count*; till my regression so please you, your noble feete may measure this priuate, pleasant and most princely walke.

(IV.i.37–44)

Aside from mere insipidity, one notices here in the closing lines, in the flowery "regression," in the pseudo elegance of "your noble feete may measure," and above all in the inane alliteration of "priuate, pleasant and most princely walke," precisely the kind of verbal dandyism that within a year would have aroused only the most stinging contempt from Jonson — that he would have called into being only to blast into oblivion. Maximilian's language regularly verges on preciosity: now he is quoting morsels of Latin wisdom; now he is frigidly punning; now he is striking an attitude with a line from rodomontade tragedy, rather in the manner of Juniper. Yet there is nothing else to indicate that he is less than the perfectly rational, noble, chivalrous soul he appears. Whether Jonson thought he was here approximating aristocratic speech it is impossible to know, but he succeeded in making his aristocrat absurd, without himself apparently recognizing the absurdity. His artistic tact, however, kept him from perpetrating the same absurdity twice. With a single exception, Jonson never again tried to use prose, as Shakespeare so often uses it, as a purely "neutral" medium. For Jonson, than whom few authors have been less neutral, few so passionately committed to framing an indictment, to use language was to criticize, to rebuke, to condemn; to ridicule or admire; to distort, exaggerate, or belittle. In the last analysis, he could mimic successfully only a language stamped with oddness or derangement, or in which mimicry itself played a part, and his inability to portray the speech of healthy normalcy marks one limit to his immense gift as a mimetic artist.

The most finished prose in *The Case is Altered* occurs in Balladino's scene, usually regarded as a later addition,[4] and in Valentine's diatribe against theater audiences:

And they haue taken such a habit of dislike in all things, that they will approue nothing, be it neuer so conceited or elaborate, but sit disperst, making faces, and spitting, wagging their vpright eares, and cry filthy, filthy. Simply vttering their owne condition, and vsing their wryed countenances in stead of a vice, to turne the good aspects of all that shall sit neere them, from what they behold.   (II.vii.76–82)

The authority and solidity here, the vividness of detail, are achieved, however, only at the expense of relevance. Valentine exists only for these moments of incidental satire; otherwise he has virtually no dramatic meaning. And the satiric episodes themselves have nothing to do with the business of the play. At best, they remain pleasant digressions. They suggest, further, that while Jonson was already — or shortly — writing excellent critical prose, he had not yet learned to bind it tightly into a dramatic structure, nor to harness it to the needs of character. And they illustrate the kind of didactic digression that Jonson, throughout his career, remained prone to, and had to fight to subordinate to larger artistic concerns.

2

With *Every Man in his Humour*,[5] Jonson takes a huge step forward. The uncertainty stamped on nearly every page of *The Case is Altered* has almost vanished; only an occasional clumsiness, an infrequent breach of decorum, betray the hand of the apprentice. Each character now possesses his own idiom, and is revealed by it: Jonson bids his creatures speak, and they tell us what they are. When he came to revise the play for inclusion in the Folio of 1616, he found much to add, but little to change.

Prose predominates over verse in *Every Man in his Humour* (Quarto version of 1601) in a ratio of three or four to one, and thus becomes the staple language from which verse is a deviation. Only two major characters, Thorello the *jaloux* and Lorenzo Senior the Terentian elder, normally speak verse, the one standing somewhat outside the events of the plot, the other possessed by a passion so fierce that Jonson may have felt unequal, at this time, to rendering it without the assistance of meter. Even so, he has not troubled to maintain anything like exact consistency, and one must confess, once and for all, that though one can often discern rough criteria governing the alternations between prose and verse, these can never be regarded as absolute. Jonson changes them or departs from them at his pleasure, for reasons of momentary convenience that often can better be guessed at than explained.

The prose of *Every Man in his Humour* is both more incisive and more dynamic than that of *The Case is Altered*. Jonson has learned to write dialogue that can annihilate its object and transfix its speaker at one and the same time, as in Cob's description of Matheo:

He vseth euery day to a Marchants house (where I serue water) one M. *Thorellos*; and here's the iest, he is in loue with my masters sister, and cals her mistres: and there he sits a whole afternoone sometimes, reading of these same abhominable, vile, (a poxe on them, I cannot abide them) rascally verses, *Poetrie, poetrie*, and speaking of *Enterludes*, 't will make a man burst to heare him: and the wenches, they doe so geere and tihe at him; well, should they do as much to me, Ild forsweare them all, by the life of Pharaoh, there's an oath: how many waterbearers shall you heare sweare such an oath? oh I haue a guest (he teacheth me) he doth sweare the best of any man christned . . .   (I.iii.63–75)

This excerpt from Cob's opening monologue illustrates the associational movement, as one may term it, of much of Jonson's dramatic prose. Cob's unflattering account of Matheo courting his "mistres" turns unpredictably into a loud bray of scorn against poetry and "*Enterludes*." The recollection of Matheo surrounded by his giggling wenches provokes a silly and pointless brag as to how he, Cob, would behave in such circumstances; the idea of "forswearing" reminds him of a fine oath he has just learned, "by the life of Pharaoh," and the oath in turn reminds him of its inventor, his guest Bobadilla, who now becomes the object of an admiring eulogy. Cob's unstable train of thought starts and stops and jolts crookedly from one detail to another without the least attention to logical exposition: neither he nor the audience knows that he will interrupt his reminiscences of Matheo in order to vent his abhorrence of poetry, or that his fantasied rejection of the wenches will spill over into a panegyric on Bobadilla. The process reveals a mind myopically in pursuit of the object nearest it, unable to hold more than one thing at a time, streaked by the kind of coarse skepticism that can perceive the quackery in Matheo without being able to tell this apart from the real thing, and by the credulousness that falls victim to Bobadilla's suaver pose. The speech, in short, combines self-revelation with formal exposition in a masterly way.

The characteristic winding involutions of the loose period make their first appearance in this play, but they have an occasionally unfortunate tendency to wind around their subject so long that they strangle it with detail. Lorenzo Junior confides to Prospero that Musco's disguise as a soldier has completely fooled him:

Fore God . . . I might haue been ioind patten with one of the nine worthies for knowing him. S'blood man, he had so writhen himselfe into the habit of one of your poore *Disparuiew's* here, your decaied, ruinous, worme-eaten gentlemen of the round: such as haue vowed to sit on the skirts of the city, let your Prouost & his half dozen of halberders do what they can; and haue translated begging out of the olde hackney pace, to a fine easy amble, and made it runne as smooth of the toung, as a shoue-groat shilling.

(III.ii.7–16)

Here the typically fused manner of the loose style, which does not stop to survey or articulate its parts — the offhand way, for example, in which, after the digression on the Provost and his halberders, the "and" introduces two unexpected long clauses concerning the gentlemen of the round — seems to lead Jonson astray. The description of the Disparviews, which commences merely as an account of Musco's disguise, turns into such a minutely engraved satiric vignette that we all but forget about Musco. Much of it, then, remains undigested observation, picturesque but encumbering. And it illustrates what was to remain a cardinal temptation for Jonson: his fascination with the picturesque, over and above the strict demands of plot and character.

In the language of the butts of this play Jonson scores his

first solid triumph. The styles of the country gull Stephano, the town gull Matheo, and the *miles gloriosus* Bobadilla are rendered with an exquisite attention to minute degrees of folly. The crudest of the three, Stephano, betrays a grasp of sequence as weak as Cob's, whether he is advertising his own gentility or indulging in fits of childish sulkiness. Encountering Matheo and Bobadilla, he is spurred to instant emulation by the sound of their rich, fruity diction and bizarre oaths. Matheo, who has moved for some time in Bobadilla's orbit, has already been working hard to deform his own speech by imitating Bobadilla's. Bobadilla himself, the fountainhead of eccentricity of this group, has evolved his own style, partly through an eclectic use of cant terms from dueling and "polite" locutions, partly through his coinage of strange oaths. "Wantonnesse of language," it may be noticed, is here linked firmly to social aspiration and moral slackness. Stephano and Matheo, the mimics, have almost literally no minds of their own, but automatically soak up the attitudes of their associates, preferably such companions as Bobadilla, whose manner offers a suitably flamboyant object of imitation. The moment they are confronted with moral choices, they collapse into meanness, as in Stephano's theft of the dropped cloak, or Matheo's plagiarisms. Bobadilla, who has worked up the language of the duello from books and learned to cause a stir by swearing picturesquely, uses the first as a cloak for cowardice and the second as a badge of singularity. A far more accomplished fool than his pathetic satellites, he becomes contemptible in direct proportion to the skill and effort he expends on his impostures.

Less obviously than by his affected singularity, Bobadilla proclaims his insatiable self-absorption at every moment by his fixation on the first-person pronoun, as in his verdict on *The Spanish Tragedy*: "I would faine see all the Poets of our time pen such another play" (I.iii.129–130); his rebuff to

Matheo for his clumsy fencing technique: "I haue no spirit to play with you, your dearth of iudgement makes you seeme tedious" (I.iii.214–216); his appraisal of Stephano's new sword: "A Fleming by *Phoebus*, ile buy them for a guilder a peece and ile haue a thousand of them" (II.iii.147–148); his judgment on Giuliano: "I hold him the most peremptorie absurd clowne (one a them) in Christendome: I protest to you (as I am a gentleman and a soldier) I ne're talk't with the like of him" (I.iii.165–168). Bobadilla's mode of expression manages to imply that his every sentiment is a matter of the keenest interest to others: "I professe my selfe no quack-saluer" (III.ii.84), "I delight not in murder: I am loth to beare any other but a bastinado" (IV.ii.48–50), "I loue few wordes" (II.iii.75). Insistent disclaimer thus becomes a covert form of self-eulogy.

Bobadilla's language at one point shows another kind of wantonness; Jonson is beginning to grope toward the effects implicit in traditional rhetorical schemes. After the beating administered to him by Giuliano, Bobadilla replies to a question from Matheo by losing himself in a forest of asyndetic clauses, stiffened by anaphora, that suggest the extent to which he can "bewitch" himself with his own rhetoric:[6]

Matheo. I but would any man haue offered it in *Venice?*
Bobadilla. Tut I assure you no: you shall haue there your *Nobilis*, your *Gentelezza*, come in brauely vpon your reuerse, stand you close, stand you ferme, stand you fayre, saue your retricato with his left legge, come to the assaulto with the right, thrust with braue steele, defie your base wood. But wherefore do I awake this remembrance? I was bewitcht by Iesu: but I will be reuengd. (IV.iv.10–17)

The parisonic members, hardened by alliteration, set up a kind of incantation which permits Bobadilla to forget his recent humiliation and triumph once more in fantasy. His repeated use of the impersonal "your" heightens the effect of complacency. The fantasy, no doubt, becomes choreographic as well as verbal: with each phrase, Bobadilla thrusts, lunges, parries, retreats, miming with his whole body the gratifying victory that his cowardice has in fact denied him. Years of poring over books on the duello have ended in his being able to mesmerize not only Matheo and Stephano but himself into a belief in his own valor.

A similar use of balanced language creeps into the begging pleas of the disguised Musco:

. . . you seeme to be gentlemen well affected to martiall men, els I should rather die with silence, then liue with shame: how e're, vouchsafe to remember it is my want speakes, not my selfe: this condition agrees not with my spirit. (II.i.50–53)

Where Bobadilla's chanting represented a species of self-delusion, Musco, in his role as mendicant soldier, adopts the antithetic turn and the sophistical distinction in order to deceive others, and with a certain malicious pleasure in the smoothness of his own tongue. But in each case the elaborately logical structure implies fraud, falsity of language directed toward the falsification of truth. And we shall find other occasions on which Jonson uses this pat logicality to signal moral deficiency.

So much, perhaps, will serve to demonstrate the remarkable gain in stylistic control of *Every Man in his Humour* over *The Case is Altered*. The rather slapdash linguistic portraits of Juniper and Onion have been refocused into a series of precisely discriminated fools, each with his particular syndrome of folly, each with his linguistic deformities to match. Every effect that Jonson can command is now lashed firmly to the dramatic context. Nevertheless, as the revision will serve to indicate, Bobadilla is probably the only character

whose language already fully and consistently fills in the outlines predicated for it by the action. The final realization of
the other creatures, fools and wise men alike, awaits the hand
of the reviser a dozen years later.

3

With *Every Man out of his Humour* [7] all traces of appren-
ticeship have vanished. In full command now of his prose
style, Jonson commences to experiment with new uses for it.
Instead of turning to Plautine commonplaces for his plot, he
sets out to invent one wholly his own, discarding conventional
intrigue formulas with a boldness that may well be termed
revolutionary. But one result of this fresh start was to pro-
long the period of experimentation. It was perhaps inevitable
that one who refused to adopt ordinary ways of making a
play should have to struggle to perfect a method of his own.
In Jonson's case the struggle was intensified because, for the
moment, he rejected even the minimal suspense needed to hold
an audience in the theater, which normally even the most
tendentious playwrights — like Shaw — are delighted to supply, since it guarantees them the attention of the spectators.
In a sense, Jonson's dramatic development from this point on
is the history of his gradual coming to terms with his audience.
Even the "understanding" spectator, to whom Jonson addressed himself, is likely to balk at spending an evening in the
theater while characters parade their eccentricities in isolation across the stage, only to be stage-managed out of them
at the eleventh hour. But if *Every Man out of his Humour* is
a failure, it is at least a heroic failure, a brilliant and original
failure; in all respects other than that of simple stageworthiness
it leaves its predecessor far behind.

The proportion of prose to verse in this play is very high,
nearly six to one, enough in itself, perhaps, to notify us that

Jonson now feels equal to all occasions in the unfamiliar medium. The criteria governing the alternations from prose to verse have altered somewhat from those of *Every Man In*, but they are scarcely more rigorously applied. Only one character, Macilente, speaks verse with any regularity. Macilente, it will be recalled, performs two functions. As a character with his own dominant humor, envy, he is subject to ridicule and conversion along with the rest. But his manner of self-exposure — to rail at other men's good fortune — enables Jonson to make him also a vehicle for satiric comment. One would like to be able to see in this dual function an explanation of his shifts from verse to prose, to find that when Macilente soliloquizes on folly or breaks out into his bitter asides he speaks verse, and turns to prose only in conversation with others. But this would only be partly true. Exceptions occur often enough to warn us that if Jonson did indeed intend any such division, he was willing to settle for far less than perfect consistency. And the even more striking departures into verse in the two Sordido scenes and in the first scene between Fallace and Deliro resist rational explanation even more stubbornly.

The prose now displays everywhere great energy, versatility, and characterizing power. Carlo Buffone's running fire of insult combines with the harsh metrical asides of Macilente to form a constant rain of savage comment amidst which the other creatures perform their various antics. Carlo, a personified Detraction, speaks a restless asyndetic language based chiefly on the simple device of apposition, which allows him to improvise as many abusive afterthoughts as possible on any theme:

. . . his spirit's like powder, quick, violent . . .   (I.ii.215–216)

. . . they are impudent creatures, turbulent spirits, they care not what violent tragedies they stirre . . .   (I.ii.122–124)

O, we must not regard what hee saies man, a trout, a shallow
foole, he ha's no more braine then a butter-flie, a meere stuft
suit . . .   (I.ii.198–200)

. . . it's a proiect, a designement of his owne, a thing studied, and
rehearst . . .   (II.ii.35–36)

Sometimes Carlo will uncork his venomous similes before he
has tagged them with a subject:

. . . a lanke raw-bon'd anatomie, he walkes vp and downe like
a charg'd musket, no man dares encounter him.   (IV.iv.25–26)

A good bloud-hound, a close-mouth'd dogge, he followes the sent
well, mary he's at a fault now, me thinkes.   (IV.iv.10–11)

If *Every Man out of his Humour* is a "pictorial" play, as has
been suggested,[8] wherein one character after another drapes
himself in the posture of his humor in the manner of a *tableau
vivant*, nothing in the language conveys the pictorial element
better than Carlo's visual caricatures. Appearances, here, even
rancorously described, tell the truth. Though Carlo distorts
for satiric effect, his malignant eye sees in each of the other
personages exactly what Jonson wishes the audience to see,
and time after time his similes take on the frozen, arrested
quality of an allegorical tableau or a sculptured title page.

He lookes like a colonell of the *Pigmies* horse, or one of these
motions, in a great antique clock: he would shew well vpon a
habberdashers stall, at a corner shop, rarely.   (II.i.5–8)

Looke, looke; as if he went in a frame, or had a sute of wanescot
on: and the dogge watching him, lest he should leape out on't.
                                                        (II.ii.89–91)

I, this is hee; a good tough gentleman: hee lookes like a shield of
brawne, at *Shrouetide*, out of date, and readie to take his leaue: or
a drie poule of ling vpon *Easter-eue* . . .   (IV.iv.109–112)

S'lud, hee lookes like an image carued out of boxe, full of knots:
his face is (for all the world) like a *dutch* purse, with the mouth

downeward; his beard the tassels: and hee walkes (let mee see) as melancholy as one o' the Masters side in the *Counter*.

(V.vi.33–37)

. . . when he is mounted, he lookes like the signe of the *George*, that's all I know; saue, that in stead of a dragon, he will brandish against a tree, and breake his sword as confidently vpon the knottie barke, as the other did vpon the skales of the beast.

(II.i.131–135)

With similes like these, Carlo freezes his colleagues in heraldic attitudes that express iconographically their proper selves, but more direct ethical comment is left to Macilente. Carlo's malevolent eye finds the absurdity in appearances. Macilente finds the emptiness underneath. He rarely speaks of externals, and when he does, it is to distinguish the splendid exterior from the rotten interior: Sogliardo is "a transparent gull / That may be seene through" (I.ii.33–34); Fungoso a "painted jay, with such a deale of out-side," and barren of "inward merit" (II.v.42, 47); Fastidious and his fellow fops are richly clothed but "naked in desert," with "wretched soules" (IV. vi.137, 139). To the extent that the verse-prose alternations of Macilente remain consistent, we may say that the verse signifies his power to penetrate surfaces. But surfaces reflect the truth in this play. Many of the characters have no reality at all apart from their appearances; the elaborateness of their wardrobes is matched by their inner aridity. Carlo's inventory of their physical and sartorial oddities hence becomes the central means of exposure.

Jonson begins, in this play, to experiment with a wider range of traditional rhetorical figures. These tend to group themselves most heavily, or at least to become most evident, at certain key moments, notably at the point in the stage life of each character when he abandons himself without restraint to his ruling passion. Sordido, for example, reaches a kind of fever of frustrated usury in the scene of attempted suicide, and his language grows as stiff as painted waves. He enters lamenting the perversity of the good weather.

Nay, gods-precious, if the weather and season bee so respectlesse, that beggars shall liue as well as their betters; and that my hunger, and thirst for riches, shall not make them hunger and thirst with pouertie; that my sleepes shall be broken, and their hearts not broken; that my coffers shall bee full, and yet care; theirs emptie, and yet merry! Tis time, that a crosse should beare flesh and bloud, since flesh and bloud cannot beare this crosse.

(III.vii.1–8)

The arrangement here is unusually symmetrical for Jonson, each antithesis being supported by exact parison. Also unusual is the old-fashioned, quasi-Ciceronian period, starting with a suspended "if" clause, to which are subordinated four sets of antithetical "that" clauses, which gather momentum until resolved in the final outburst. Most unusual of all, for Jonson, is the Euphuistic word play: the clinking of "beggars" and "betters"; the repetition of "hunger" and "thirst," as nouns, then verbs, first in a metaphoric, then in a literal sense; the fussy iteration of "broken," likewise in two different senses; and the chiastic pattern of the conclusion. These echoes of Lyly become here a weapon of great satiro-comic potency. The mechanical rigidity of the antitheses accentuates to the point of fantasy the contrast between Sordido's love of his money and his hatred of others. It is not enough that his hunger and thirst for riches be satisfied: the satisfaction of them must provoke physical hunger and thirst in others. It is not enough for his sleep to be unbroken; the hearts of others must be broken. The juxtaposition of "broken" sleeps and "broken" hearts, by its very extravagance, produces the effect of comic viciousness that Jonson is aiming at.

The extent to which Sordido's language has jumped the rails

of realism here may be judged by confronting it with a soliloquy by a similar character, old Lucre in *A Trick to Catch the Old One:*

My adversary evermore twits me with my nephew, forsooth, my nephew: why may not a virtuous uncle have a dissolute nephew? What though he be a brotheller, a wastethrift, a common sur-feiter, and, to conclude, a beggar, must sin in him call up shame in me? Since we have no part in their follies, why should we have part in their infamies? For my strict hand toward his mort-gage, that I deny not: I confess I had an uncle's pen'worth; let me see, half in half, true: I saw neither hope of his reclaiming, nor comfort in his being; and was it not then better bestowed upon his uncle than upon one of his aunts? — I need not say bawd, for every one knows what aunt stands for in the last translation.[9]   (II.i.1–13)

This speech too is a tissue of antitheses and pat balances, but the sense of parody is absent. Lucre is a hypocrite rationalizing his hypocrisy, an extortioner trying to persuade himself that he has acted rightly. His thoughts turn on concrete persons and events: a rival usurer, a penniless nephew, an ill-gotten mortgage. The tone, for all its exaggeration, remains a humanly possible one. Sordido's speech, in contrast, has broken the bounds of plausibility entirely, and Sordido has become a kind of goblin or malevolent troll, divorced from all human pre-occupations except greed. His fantastic litany of sorrows turns into a kind of Black Mass, a travesty of the Passion — instead of suffering for others he would have others suffer for him — whereupon the preposterous conclusion follows almost naturally: since others are *not* suffering, he will proceed to self-crucifixion.

Similar rhetorical heightening occurs after the terrible-tempered Fallace has been reduced to groveling admiration by the sight of the courtier Fastidious Brisk. Her first glimpse of him leads to some rapturous soliloquizing, the second to a kind of apotheosis:

Oh, sweete Fastidivs Briske! ô fine courtier! thou art hee mak'st me sigh, and say, how blessed is that woman that hath a courtier to her husband! and how miserable a dame shee is, that hath ney-ther husband, nor friend i' the court! O, sweet Fastidivs! ô, fine courtier! How comely he bowes him in his court'sie! how full hee hits a woman betweene the lips when he kisses! how vpright hee sits at the table! how daintily he carues! how sweetly he talkes, and tels newes of this lord, and of that lady! how cleanely he wipes his spoone, at euery spoon-full of any whit-meat he eates, and what a neat case of pick-tooths he carries about him, still! O, sweet Fastidivs! ô fine courtier!   (IV.i.29–41)

Here the direct apostrophe to Fastidious, the "intimate" use of the second person singular pronoun, the passionate exclama-tions introduced by the anaphora of "how," the thrice intoned refrain of "sweet Fastidivs!" "fine courtier!" all contribute to an effect of tumultuous passion that jars ludicrously with the triviality of the details — the excellent table manners, the clean wiping of the spoon, the neat case of picktooths.[10] Jon-son is making comic capital out of the misapplication of devices sacred to classical oratory, and it might be added that the absurdity of the little bourgeoise apostrophizing the peacock gallant in this vein of lofty sublimity is far more comic than most of the harshly realistic husband-and-wife wrangles that he loved to dramatize.

The fine courtier, sweet Fastidious Brisk, has his own patches of purple prose, notably his celebrated dueling narra-tive and his highly charged encomium on the court:

A man liues there, in that diuine rapture, that hee will thinke him-selfe i' the ninth heauen for the time, and lose all sense of mor-talitie whatsoeuer; when he shall behold such glorious (and al-most immortall) beauties, heare such angelicall and harmonious voyces, discourse with such flowing and *ambrosian* spirits, whose

wits are as suddaine as lightning, and humorous as *nectar*; Oh:
it makes a man al *quintessence*, and *flame*, & lifts him vp (in a
moment) to the verie christall crowne of the skie, where (houering in the strength of his imagination) he shall behold all the
delights of the HESPERIDES, the *Insulae Fortunatae*, ADONIS gardens, *Tempe* or what else (confin'd within the amplest verge of
poesie) to bee meere *vmbrae*, and imperfect figures, conferr'd
with the most essentiall felicitie of your court.   (IV.viii.16–32)

This rhapsody, absurd enough in itself, acquires added ironic
force from our having already witnessed (III.ix) a meeting
between Fastidious and his mistress, Saviolina, "the wonder
of nations," in all its pathetic emptiness. Fastidious' prime
technique is "copy," abundance. He doubles his adjectives:
"glorious (and almost immortall)," "angelicall and harmonious," "flowing and *ambrosian*"; his nouns as well: "*quintessence*, and *flame*," "*vmbrae*, and imperfect figures"; and sometimes both at once: "as suddaine as lightning, and humorous
as *nectar*." The sense of surfeit produced by a language so
choked with exaggeration is almost overpowering. If Fallace
succeeds in remaking Fastidious into a prince of gallantry,
Fastidious succeeds in turning the court into a dizzying confusion of celestial and terrestrial paradises. The Latinate diction is not there by accident: it exaggerates the discrepancy
between the court itself and what is claimed for it, as well as
between the speaker's image of himself as a silver-tongued
phrasemaker and the image of vain posturing he presents to
others.[11] The characteristically loose syntax, always exfoliating
in fresh directions, keeps the speaker gasping for breath until
he brings the period home with its absurd Latinism, causing
the acid Macilente to observe, "Well, this *Encomion* was not
extemporall, it came too perfectly off" (IV.viii.33–34) —
further evidence, if any were needed, of Jonson's deep distrust of premeditated speech in normal social circumstances.

But an even better comment on Fastidious' speech, as on Fallace's praise of its speaker, is to be found in the *Discoveries*, where Jonson remarks that "that which is high and lofty, declaring excellent matter, becomes vast and tumorous, speaking of petty and inferiour things" (2052–54). With Fallace and Fastidious, as with many of Jonson's self-bewitched babblers, we enter the domain of what can be slightingly called "rhetoric," and the patently hysterical note in their voices sounds a warning as clear as that issued to the young scholars in *The Pilgrimage to Parnassus:* "Take good aduise from him that lous youe well, / Plaine dealing needes not Retoricks tinklinge bell" (26–27).

"Wantonnesse" of language thus takes more elaborate form in this play than hitherto. It now includes a much wider variety of types of linguistic exhibitionism, and those types are more incisively etched. In the case of Sogliardo, we have a country clown whose rag bag of jingles, proverbs, and silly puns turns him into a creature of stupefying blockishness. In the case of Puntarvolo, we hear a weird, stilted, bookish prose falling from the lips of a knight whose whole existence centers about the re-enactment of scenes from chivalric romance. In Fallace, Sordido, and Fastidious Brisk, we have purple passions and maniac rages, carried to a point of comic extravagance made possible only by the parody of traditional rhetoric. If we compare any of these figures with Juniper in *The Case is Altered*, we can see how decisively Jonson now welds a specific linguistic vice to its moral equivalent. And if we compare them with the gulls of *Every Man In*, we notice that the newer group is more specialized and more extravagantly caricatured. Types like Sordido and Puntarvolo burst the bonds of realism altogether and carry the whole play into the realm of the semifabulous. Despite its avoidance of the Terentian plot, and despite much energetic realism of detail, *Every*

Man out of his Humour seems far less realistic than its predecessor: Jonson's rhetorical innovations produce marvels of the grotesque, not of the plausible. As we shall see, many of these observations apply to the play that follows, *Cynthia's Revels*.

4

In *Cynthia's Revels*,[12] Jonson seeks, and finds, ways of avoiding the somewhat rigid structure of *Every Man Out*. *Cynthia's Revels* is less a vaudeville than its predecessor, more a well-knit construction that starts with Echo's curse on the fountain, proceeds through the mounting follies of the parasite courtlings, and concludes with their discomfiture at the masque of Cynthia. The fact that the "humors" characters constitute a homogeneous group of fools, nesting on the fringes of the court that is destined to reject them, also increases the structural coherence. But Jonson pays a terrible price for this greater cohesiveness; his increasing preoccupation with fine shades of affectation — for which the quartet of he-fools and she-fools makes a brilliant exhibition piece — ends in excess. Despite the vigor of the writing, and a promising first three acts, *Cynthia's Revels* begins to suffocate the reader with boredom just when it should most strongly claim his interest. The final act — a mere 1600 lines in the Folio version — is stupefyingly dull, and bears painful witness to the extent to which Jonson's passion for detail and surface has stifled his feeling for movement in the theater.

If in *Every Man out of his Humour* Jonson shows increasing reluctance to mix verse and prose in the same scene, this tendency reaches its logical conclusion in *Cynthia's Revels*, where the verse, though there is much more of it, is crystallized out into full scenes or lengthy monologues. Strictly speaking, no scenes of mixed prose and verse occur in this play. Crites, the satiric commentator, speaks prose along with the fools.

Only when the stage has been cleared does he break out into his scornful verse tirades. A new criterion, then, for distinction between prose and verse has evolved. In the world of the court, presided over by a divine Cynthia, where truth and virtue reign unchallenged, only verse is spoken. In the world of folly that hovers illicitly about the edges of the true court, only prose is heard. Crites, who inhabits both worlds and acts as intermediary between them, alters his verbal mode to suit the company he is in. The same is true of Arete and, in a different way, of Mercury.

Elaboration of rhetoric and baroque syntax reach their height in this play. The slight dramatic situation has a heavy load of set pieces to digest, including eight full-length satirical *caractères*, a lengthy discourse from Amorphus on the classification of faces, the minutely elaborated fantasies of the court ladies, the duello and the masque in Act V, and those engines of refined Jonsonian torment, the games of Substantives and Adjectives and A Thing Done and Who Did It, not to mention the formal verse satire in III.iv delivered by Crites, and Cynthia's speeches in the final scenes. The undramatic nature of Jonson's procedure may be judged from the fact that on two successive occasions scenes of sound comic potentiality are passed up and simply alluded to in static scenes of talk. In III.i, Amorphus enters commiserating with Asotus on a recent misadventure, "Sir, let not this dis-countenance, or dis-gallant you a whit: you must not sinke vnder the first disaster," and proceeds to give his pupil a lesson in courtship; but we never learn what "this" was or how it was disastrous, and though the scene of Asotus' first discomfiture would have made an admirable comic episode, Jonson prefers to ignore it, using it merely as an excuse for the first lesson in etiquette. III.ii opens with an even more cryptic and tantalizing complaint from Hedon: "Hart, was there euer so prosperous an inuention thus vnluckily peruerted, and spoyl'd by a whore-sonne booke-worme, a candle-waster?" The whoreson bookworm, as we learn a moment later, is Crites, but the other details arouse a curiosity Jonson has no intention of satisfying. He never informs us what Hedon's "inuention" was or how Crites has "spoyl'd" it; clearly the whole allusion serves only as an excuse for Hedon and Anaides to begin their railing against Crites and for Crites to retort with his counterblast, though a staging of the imaginary episode would have shown us more about all three characters than the pages of invective. Jonson, in short, seems deliberately to side-step the theatrical possibilities of the plot in favor of formal satiric comment.

Again, if we compare Cob's account of Matheo and Boba-dilla, already quoted, with Cupid's or Mercury's sketches of the fools in the present play, the untheatrical nature of the latter becomes painfully clear. Cob's monologue tells us as much about Cob as it does about the two gulls. In the process of describing, he is also reacting; a continuous kinetic interplay takes place between him and his environment. But Cupid and Mercury serve as little more than colorless megaphones for the voice of the omniscient satirist. If we are surprised, in the final scene, when Cupid is chased from court and Mercury urged to stay, it is because Jonson is belatedly, at the last moment, restoring to them the familiar mythic personalities that he has suppressed during most of the action.

Moreover, the character-sketches delivered by these two observers relate only tenuously to the plot, since they omit information relevant to it, and in consequence, being overloaded with extraneous detail, they end by teaching us little even of the persons they are supposed to describe. It is useful, in *Every Man in his Humour*, to have a foretaste of Matheo's pretensions to poetry, since we see him later in the exact posture described by Cob, and so with the other details in

Cob's monologue. But it is worse than useless, it is positively mischievous, to be burdened with information about Hedon's wardrobe, his allergy to baths, or his relations with his tailor, about Anaides' stinginess or his cheating at cards, since none of these matters proves of the slightest consequence in the unfolding of the plot; most, in fact, are never alluded to again. Significantly, the Folio revision transfers a phrase concerning Anaides ("Like a squeez'd *Orenge*, sower") almost without change to Asotus ("His face is like a squeez'd orange" — IV.i.117), suggesting how imperfectly the four gallants are differentiated even in the satiric sketches of them. It is the lack of correspondence with the observed facts of the narrative, the discrepancy between what we see of a character with our own eyes and what we are told about him, that makes these *caractères* — well-written though they unquestionably are — hard to swallow. The least unsuccessful one, that of Crites, succeeds precisely insofar as it avoids inundating the reader in detail. Being laudatory, it deals mostly in ethical generalities. It fails insofar as the sweetly reasonable Crites it portrays differs from the thin-skinned Crites who actually appears on the stage. Jonson is not only using techniques of formal satire; he is using them to thrust upon the audience interpretations of the plot that the plot itself scarcely sustains.

Last, one may object that the prose in *Cynthia's Revels* does not sufficiently distinguish the dramatis personae. Anaides' swearwords, Phantaste's similes, and other tiny mannerisms hardly produce a ripple on the surface of sameness. Jonson's preoccupation with the microtones of courtly parlance ends in differences inaudible to the naked ear. The fact that the sameness is a consequence of the restricted milieu does not alter one's longing for the babel of *Every Man out of his Humour*, where every speaker seems to possess his own unique vocal apparatus.

There is, however, one exception to the sameness, the language of Amorphus, in which most of the stylistic interest of the play is concentrated. Amorphus is the supreme exponent among Jonsonian creatures of the style of "complement," the affected, magniloquent, periphrastic discourse of those who imitate, or think they are imitating, the court. If Bobadilla and Fastidious Brisk cull an occasional flower of rhetoric to stick into their otherwise sandy style, Amorphus has plucked them all and made his speech into a tropical garden. He carries the floridity of baroque syntax to its extremest point:

What should I inferre? If my behauiours had beene of a cheape or customarie garbe; my accent, or phrase vulgar; my garments trite; my countenance illiterate; or vnpractiz'd in the encounter of a beautifull and braue-attir'd peece; then I might (with some change of colour) haue suspected my faculties: but (knowing my selfe an essence so sublimated, and refin'd by trauell; of so studied, and well exercis'd a gesture; so alone in fashion; able to tender the face of any states-man liuing; and to speake the mere extraction of language; one that hath now made the sixth returne vpon venter; and was your first that euer enricht his countrey with the true lawes of the *duello*; whose *optiques* haue drunke the spirit of beautie, in some eight score and eighteen Princes courts, where I haue resided, and beene there fortunate in the *amours* of three hundred fortie and fiue ladies (all nobly, if not princely descended) whose names I haue in catalogue; to conclude, in all so happy, as euen admiration her selfe doth seeme to fasten her kisses vpon me:) Certes, I doe neither see, nor feele, nor taste, nor sauour the least steame, or fume of a reason, that should inuite this foolish fastidious *Nymph*, so peeuishly to abandon me.   (I.iii.24–45)

Here, as in the set pieces of Fastidious Brisk, the large-scale asymmetry of the loose period affords a perfect vehicle for the speaker's self-congratulatory copiousness. The doubled terms — "cheape or customary," "accent, or phrase," "sublimated, and refin'd," "studied, and well exercis'd," "steame, or fume" — spill out from every corner like water from a baroque fountain. The affected verbal phrases, "drunke the spirit of beautie," "fasten her kisses vpon me," the syntactic shifts, with their parentheses within parentheses, writhe and gurgle in an uninterrupted stream and then fall over the brink with a splash in the quadrupled verb and the lengthy cadence of the final phrases. Where Fastidious Brisk musters his eloquence only for special occasions, when a proper audience is assembled, Amorphus speaks this way all the time, even, as here, when there is no one else about and nothing more important than vexation to be expressed. The passage, incidentally, though perhaps overloaded, characterizes its speaker far more effectively than the later formal portrait drawn by Mercury, where we hear of his picktooth, his cowardice, his shifts of shirt, his intervention in quarrels, and other matters none of which has much bearing on the action.

Another fragment of self-revelation from Amorphus may be quoted for what it shows of Jonson's use of detail as a structural element. Crites has appeared near the fountain, with Asotus at his heels, and Amorphus is racking his brains for a way to introduce himself to Asotus.

Since I trode on this side the *Alpes*, I was not so frozen in my inuention. Let mee see: to accost him with some choice remnant of *spanish*, or *italian?* that would indifferently expresse my languages now: mary then, if he should fall out to be ignorant, it were both hard, and harsh. How else? step into some *ragioni del stato*, and so make my induction? that were aboue him too; and out of his element, I feare. Faine to haue seene him in *Venice*, or *Padua?* or some face neere his in similitude? 'tis too pointed, and open. No, it must be a more queint, and collaterall deuice. As — stay: to frame some *encomiastick* speech vpon this our *Metropolis*, or the wise magistrates thereof, in which politique number, 'tis ods, but his father fill'd vp a roome? descend into a particular admiration of their iustice; for the due measuring of coales, burning of cannes, and such like? As also their religion, in pulling downe a superstitious crosse, and aduancing a VENVS, or PRIAPVS, in place of it? ha? 'twill doe well. Or to talke of some hospitall, whose walls record his father a *Benefactor?* or of so many buckets bestow'd on his parish church, in his life time, with his name at length (for want of armes) trickt vpon them? Any of these? Or to praise the cleannesse of the street, wherein hee dwelt? or the prouident painting of his posts against hee should haue beene *Praetor?* or (leauing his parent) come to some speciall ornament about himselfe, as his rapier, or some other of his accoutrements? I haue it: Thanks, gracious MINERVA. (I.iv.79–105)

With this little debate between self and soul we may usefully compare Falstaff's soliloquy on honor:

Well, 'tis no matter, Honor prickes me on. But how if Honour pricke me off when I come on? How then? Can Honour set too a legge? No: or an arme? No: Or take away the greefe of a wound? No. Honour hath no skill in Surgerie, then? No. What is Honour? A word. What is that word Honour? Ayre: A trim reckoning. Who hath it? He that dy'de a Wednesday. Doth he feele it? No. Doth hee heare it? No. Is it insensible then? yea, to the dead. But wil it not liue with the liuing? No. Why? Detraction wil not suffer it, therfore Ile none of it. Honour is a meere Scutcheon, and so ends my Catechisme. (L. 390; *IHIV* V.i.130–144)

The point about this passage, for present purposes, is its logicality, or its mock logicality. Falstaff, after a punning antithesis between "prick off" and "prick on," inquires whether honor can remedy (a) a wounded leg, (b) a wounded arm, or, indeed, (c) any wound at all? Negative replies in each case lead to a summary conclusion: honor has no skill in surgery. Its presumptive virtues thus disposed of, Falstaff proceeds to define it — correctly enough — as "a word"; a word in turn is definable as "air." But to whom, he asks, with Elizabethan textbook logic, to whom does honor belong? Of what subject is it an adjunct? And this question satisfactorily answered — it belongs to the dead — the next question investigates the possessor's consciousness of his possession, which proves to be nonexistent. An objection is now forestalled: does it not belong to the living? The answer: it does not; calumny filches it away. Therefore, concludes the catechist, such an unreal, chimerical commodity he will have none of.

One may say of this kind of language that it is all nerve and sinew, all process of thought. Details are few, and those few of a highly generalized nature, so that they might easily be replaced by others — "arm" and "leg" by "hand" and "foot," or "died a Wednesday" by "died a Thursday" — without impairing the logical sequence or substantially violating the meaning. The comic effect stems from the agility with which Falstaff twists logic to his own purposes in order to arrive at conclusions contributory to his own safety and subversive of traditional idealism. As we watch Falstaff's mind at work, we discover unexpected weaknesses in the petrified concept he is anatomizing.

Amorphus' monologue proceeds along entirely different lines. There is logic of a rough sort, enough to keep the details in place, but the essence of the passage lies in the tissue of details themselves. These fall into two groups. In the first group, Amorphus is concerned primarily about himself and the effect he would like to make on a stranger. Each of his proposed maneuvers illustrates the boastfulness of the ignorant traveler anxious to make social capital out of his travels, eager to discuss affairs of state, drop foreign phrases, and the like. These progress only to the extent that they imply increasing doubt of Asotus' capacity to respond properly. The second group involves no particular progression at all, but moves in the associative manner typical of Jonson's eccentrics. Each proposal here involves flattery of Asotus through praise of the city magistrates, and the comic effect springs entirely from the patronizing foolishness or the outlandishness of the details themselves.[13] The idea that a social-climbing son of the middle class would be enchanted to hear his father praised for promoting clean streets or regulating the measurement of coal is captivating in its absurdity. Throughout it is the choice of details that amuses us. Once the main theme has been stated, it can be varied ad libitum; there is no sequence of thought from one point to another, but rather the fixing on a point and gyrating about it to uncover all of its ludicrous possibilities. The danger of such a method is that the accumulation of detail will overwhelm all logical movement whatever, and this, as we have intimated above, is nearly what happens in *Cynthia's Revels*.

Had Jonson been wholly indifferent to movement, its absence would probably not matter. The trouble is, he *wants* the play to move; he wants to show us the evolution of folly into self-love and thence to purgation. At the same time, and even more, he wants to present a minutely engraved, fully realized, immobile image of folly, an emblem from an emblem book with every curlicue in place. The second purpose, finally, submerges the first. Jonson fails to correlate details tightly enough with his own evident dramatic purpose, and the result is a great fossilized dinosaur of a play, "like the mammoth and megatherion, fitted and destined to live only during a given period, and then to exist a skeleton, hard, dry, uncouth perhaps, yet massive and not to be contemplated without [a] mixture of wonder and admiration," [14] to borrow words applied by Coleridge to all of Jonson.

5

Poetaster,[15] even more than Jonson's other plays, seems to gaze with Januslike doubleness in two directions at once, back toward the plays that preceded it, ahead toward those still in embryo. In its heightened moral intensity, its more complex ethical situation, the Roman setting, and the somber power of the Apologetical Dialogue, it inaugurates a new phase of Jonson's dramatic development that continues in *Sejanus* and culminates in *Volpone*. The Augustan tribunal that jolts the offending poetasters out of their humors, on the other hand, recalls the appearance of the queen at the end of the first version of *Every Man Out* and the masque in *Cynthia's Revels*, and marks the literal, medicinal climax of the whole notion of purgation of humors common to the "comicall satyres." In still another way, in the matters of prose style and prose usage, *Poetaster* seems to revert to the techniques of *Every Man in his Humour*.

The action of *Poetaster*, like that of *Cynthia's Revels*, moves between two worlds: one virtuous, the imperial court, and one vicious, the household of the jeweler Albius and his social-climbing wife Chloe. In a rough way this polarity governs the choice of style. Caesar and Virgil, at one extreme, only speak verse; Albius, Chloe, Tucca, and Crispinus at the other gabble entirely in prose. But in the middle area, where these two spheres intersect, all is uncertainty and vacillation. Both Ovid and Horace tend to use verse under one kind of circumstance — the solemn, the serious, the ceremonial — and prose under another — the frivolous. But in neither case is the distinction consistently maintained, and in view of the otherwise unbroken development that leads from the tentative mixtures of *The Case is Altered* and *Every Man In* to the all-verse plays *Sejanus* and *Volpone* on the one hand and the all-prose plays *Epicene* and *Bartholomew Fair* on the other, one is forced to assume that Jonson simply did not have time to finish *Poetaster* as he might have liked. We know that he hurried the completion of the play in order to forestall the expected counterblast from Dekker and Marston. But why, if this is so, he failed to revise accordingly for the Folio of 1616, must remain a mystery.

Stylistically, the prose of *Poetaster* marks a return to the relative colloquial simplicity of *Every Man in his Humour*. There is nothing in it to compare with the bursts of rhetorical artifice that punctuate *Every Man Out* or the densely woven periods of *Cynthia's Revels*. The syntax tends toward extreme plainness, avoiding the involutions of the loose period in favor of the spatter of the *stile coupé*. In fact, if one might speak of *Cynthia's Revels* as an experiment with the dramatic potentialities of loose style, one might think of *Poetaster* as an essay in the possibilities of curt style.

Language defines character with uniform incisiveness and vividness throughout, but achieves its major triumph in the figure of Captain Pantilius Tucca, who probably speaks a more bizarre lingo than any other character in Jonson. Arthur H. King, in his exhaustive study, *The Language of Satirized Characters in Poëtaster*, has catalogued many of Tucca's linguistic peculiarities, his lexical addictions, his vocative style, his devices of repetition, and shown that Tucca's vocabulary is drawn from those of all social classes at once, from the pseudocourtly lexicon of "complement" down to the cant of the underworld.[16] A further word may be added concerning the syntax of this style. Like Carlo Buffone, Tucca possesses an edgy, asyndetic verbal manner that gives the effect of crackling high tension. The energy, blocked and released, blocked and released, never discharges fully enough to produce a corresponding wave of relaxation, but sputters uninterruptedly throughout the play, perhaps emblematic of Tucca's inability to commit himself fully to anyone or anything but his own mean appetites while he is constantly pretending to commit himself to everyone. A consistently asyndetic style, as we have seen, is likely to crystallize into the curt style, and, in fact, insofar as an abstraction like "curt style" may be said ever to achieve absolute embodiment, it does so in Tucca's speeches, the short members hovering restlessly about a single idea, sometimes exploring it from different points of vantage, sometimes merely rephrasing it for the sake of emphasis.

A sharpe thornie-tooth'd *satyricall* rascall, flie him; hee carries hey in his horne: he wil sooner lose his best friend, then his least iest. What he once drops vpon paper, against a man, liues eternally to vpbraid him in the mouth of euery slaue tankerd-bearer, or water-man; not a bawd, or a boy that comes from the bake-house, but shall point at him: 'tis all dogge, and scorpion; he carries poison in his teeth, and a sting in his taile.   (IV.iii.109–116)

Sometimes the range of metaphoric suggestion is much nar-rower. Instead of extending the idea or discovering fresh pos-sibilities in it, Tucca simply worries it with small fidgets of vocabulary. In extreme cases, the shifting members of the curt period may amount to simple tautology.

You did not? where was your sight, OEDIPVS? you walke with hares eies, doe you? I'le ha' 'hem glas'd, rogue; and you say the word, they shall be glaz'd for you: come, we must haue you turne fiddler againe, slaue, get a base violin at your backe, and march in a tawnie coate, with one sleeue, to Goose-faire, and then you'll know vs; you'll see vs then; you will, gulch, you will?
                                                    (III.iv.130–136)

Here in two instances a member of the period does nothing but rephrase the previous member: "I'le ha' 'hem glas'd, rogue; and you say the word, they shall be glaz'd for you," "then you'll know vs; you'll see vs then," demonstrating the tendency of the curt period, at one extreme, to stall all forward move-ment entirely, while the central idea shifts its syntactic gar-ments. And this device lends itself well to the characterization of one in a state of perpetual agitation, who must always be talking, but often with nothing new to say.

As we have seen earlier, one of the typical features of the curt style in Jonson is its use, especially with appellatives, of apposition. Apposition fits naturally into such a style, since it requires no linking conjunction and thus preserves the asyndetic jaggedness of the manner, and since, like the absolute construction, it may be located anywhere within a reasonable distance of its reference. It permits a half-articulate speaker like Tucca to be constantly shaping and reaffirming his statements as he delivers them, without lapsing into nonsense.

They are growne licentious, the rogues; libertines, flat libertines.
(I.ii.52–53)

Doe not denie thine owne MINERVA, thy PALLAS, the issue of thy braine.   (V.iii.267–268)

IVPITER saue thee, my good *poet*; my noble *prophet*; my little fat HORACE.   (IV.vii.23–24)

The syntax thus marks time while variations are played on one element.

Perhaps the most obsessive kind of repetition in Tucca's speech is the short phrase composed of a verb and its subject, often an auxiliary verb and its subject, reiterated at the end of a statement like an extra hammer blow after the nail has been driven home.

Men of worth haue their *chymaera's*, as well as other creatures: and they doe see monsters, sometimes: they doe, they doe, braue boy.   (I.ii.195–197)

. . . thou hadst ill fortune, THISBE; the fates were infatuate; they were, punke; they were.   (IV.iii.42–44)

Doe, you perpetuall stinkard, doe, goe . . .   (I.ii.32)

What, you are proud, you rascall, are you proud? ha? you grow rich, doe you?   (III.iv.124–125)

The brevity of the final element in each case accentuates the slashing abruptness of effect. Extreme brevity of phrase, in fact, together with a remarkable absence of connectives, is probably the most significant operative element of Tucca's discourse. His inability to pursue an idea without self-interruption is linked to his flair for the scurrilous epithet. Scarcely a clause goes by without its quota of interpolated insult:

He will eate a legge of mutton, while I am in my porridge, the leane POLVPHAGVS, his belly is like *Barathrum*, he lookes like a mid-wife in mans apparell, the slaue.   (III.iv.280–283)

Why, how now, my good brace of bloud-hounds? whither doe you dragge the gent'man? you mungrels, you curres, you bandogs, wee are Captaine TVCCA, that talke to you, you inhumane pilchers.   (III.iv.1–4)

So much is perhaps in itself enough to suggest the extreme and, if one may say so, substantial oddity of Tucca's language. When to these mannerisms we add his addiction to expletives like "what" and "I meane," thrust in at random and so often that they become mere stitches to replace genuine conjunctions, as well as his habit of coining allusive epithets, metaphoric and mythological, and his compound words and strings of opprobrious adjectives, we have a style that is an absolute marvel of strangeness. And this despite its evident realism and the fact that it was apparently copied from life, from a certain Captain Hannam.

Language so highly idiosyncratic ought to be easy to imitate, but an imitation would run the risk of straying from the exact boundaries staked out by the original; it might easily fall into an uncharacteristic gesture. When Dekker (and Marston?) [17] tried to put Tucca back onto the stage in *Satiromastix*, in order to beat Jonson with his own stick, they managed to catch a good many of the captain's incidental mannerisms, but frequently failed to produce convincing parody, because they had not grasped the underlying principle of his style.[18] King has spoken of the relative monotony of the *Satiromastix* Tucca, the smaller range of diction and verbal devices; one might notice further how often his speech is thrown out of focus by "mistakes" of syntax. Apart from petty errors, which are legion, one may observe that the chief thing that gives Jonson's Tucca his distinctive idiom, and which the authors of *Satiromastix* reproduce only fitfully, is its absence of connectives. Tucca suppresses most conjunctions most of the time; logical conjunctions like "for," "therefore," and "because" he suppresses entirely. Dekker and Marston catch this discontinuous manner from time to time and then unexpectedly abandon it, loading Tucca's speeches with complex sentences and subordinate clauses. The telltale logical particles drift back in quantities, to spoil the effect.

Go too, let not thy tongue play so hard at hot-cockles; for Gammer Gurton, I meane to bee thy needle, I loue thee, I loue thee, because thy teeth stand like the Arches vnder London Bridge, for thou't not turne Satyre and bite thy husband; No, come my little Cub, doe not scorne mee because I goe in Stag, in Buffe, heer's veluet too; thou seest I am worth thus much in bare veluet. (III.i.199–204)

Saue thee, my most gracious King a Harts saue thee, all hats and caps are thine, and therefore I vaile: for but to thee great *Sultane Soliman*, I scorne to be thus put off or to deliuer vp this sconce I wud.[19] (V.ii.163–166)

At moments like these (and there are many in *Satiromastix*), the illogical stumble of the *Poetaster* Tucca settles into an explanatory trot, and the linguistic resemblance between Tucca the First and Tucca the Second all but breaks down. Except for the silly alloquialisms (Gammer Gurton, Sultan Suleiman), not much here distinguishes their speaker from the other dramatis personae; still less reminds us of the original.

The faltering ventriloquism of Dekker and Marston serves to remind us, by contrast, how thoroughgoing and strongly rooted Jonson's sense of decorum is, how completely his characters are projected stylistically. Nothing in Jonson's dialogue stands idle. Every comma contributes its mite to the realization of the strident, wheedling, bullying roarer. The language of Tucca, to borrow T. S. Eliot's phrase, is "poetry of the surface," but of surfaces rendered so precisely and so substantially that the reader's demand for the kind of reality they present is fully satisfied, and craves no stimulation of the kind in which "swarms of inarticulate feelings are aroused." [20]

It is perhaps not irrelevant to mention another and much later echo of Captain Tucca, in Congreve. Congreve must have assimilated Jonson even more deeply than he himself realized, to have reproduced, apparently without intending to, the ring of Tucca in some speeches of Sir Sampson Legend.

Nor no more to be done, old Boy; that's plain — here 'tis, I have it in my Hand, old *Ptolomee*; I'll make the ungracious Prodigal know who begat him; I will, old *Nostrodamus*. . . . Where's my Daughter that is to be — hah! old *Merlin*! body o'me, I'm so glad I'm reveng'd on this undutiful Rogue.

(*Love for Love*, II.v.1–17)

Body o'me, I have gone too far; — I must not provoke honest *Albumazar*, — an *Egyptian* Mummy is an Illustrious Creature, my trusty Hieroglyphick; and may have Significations of Futurity about him. . . . What, thou art not angry for a Jest, my good *Haly* — I reverence the Sun, Moon and Stars with all my Heart.[21]

(II.v.82–90)

"Body o'me" comes from Bobadill, but most of Sir Sampson's locutions here — "old Boy," "old [anything]," "hah!," "Hieroglyphick," "good," "trusty" — are specialties of Tucca's, used much as Tucca would have used them. With

"What, thou art not angry for a Jest, my good *Haly*," one might compare Tucca's "Why, thou art not angrie, rascall? art thou?" (III.iv.36). However, the rapid absorption of these Tuccan mannerisms into a somewhat different style suggests that the borrowing on Congreve's part was unconscious.

Poetaster, a play in which causal connectives are rare, affords a good illustration of Jonson's "darkly deterministic" view of character,[22] and it may be suspected that the absence of connectives is related to the fixity of temperament. Tucca does not, cannot, change. He can be punished, symbolically, by having a "case of vizards" clapped on his head, to signify his two-facedness, but the punishment seems to confirm and corroborate, rather than correct, his disposition. The Rabelaisian purgation inflicted on Crispinus leaves him, as a character, nonexistent, and it leaves us, as auditors, doubtful of the possibility of any real conversion, in view of the fact that Caesar's tribunal exists only in Jonson's longing fantasy and not in the actual world. In the actual world, the aggrieved poet can strike back at his detractors only by writing a play against them. But within the play itself, as in *Every Man out of his Humour*, the molecules of character collide and rebound, leaving no sensible imprint on each other, unless it is the intensification of an original egoism. With the deflation of humor comes the collapse of character, after which, if the character is to renew its existence, it must do so from scratch, like the members of a curt period; a new entity must be born, discontinuous with the old. But Jonson never takes us this far into the afterlives of his dramatic personages.

Poetaster, in any case, though it marks a retreat from the rhetorical expansiveness of *Every Man Out* and *Cynthia's Revels*, produces within its narrower limits Jonson's greatest triumph of characterization to date, in Pantilius Tucca. Whatever may have prompted his reversion to the mixed prose-verse method of *Every Man In*, this was to be his last specimen of the kind. Before discussing the two great prose comedies of his maturity, however, we must glance at the Folio version of *Every Man in his Humour*, to see what Jonson had learned of his craft as a prose playwright since the premiere of that play in 1597.

6

It is unnecessary to settle here the exact date of the revision of *Every Man in his Humour*. Jonson may have rewritten the play for a revival at court in 1605, as Chambers suggests (III, 360), in which case the recent collaboration with Marston and Chapman on *Eastward Ho* would not have been without effect in determining the transfer of the scene to England; or, more plausibly, he may have done so in 1612, when he was preparing his plays for the 1616 Folio, and recasting *Poetaster*, *Cynthia's Revels*, and *Sejanus* for inclusion in the new volume.[23]

The distribution of prose and verse remains nearly the same in the new version. Four odd lines of verse of Lorenzo Junior's in I.ii.11–14 have been struck out, as well as his fervent metrical defense of poetry in Act V.[24] These excisions leave Lorenzo's counterpart, Young Knowell (we shall henceforth use chiefly Folio nomenclature), an exclusively prose-speaking character and very much more of a piece than before. Old Knowell's complaint of his son's poetical leanings is irrelevant even in the Quarto until the sudden interchange on the subject between his son and Justice Clement in Act V. In the Folio, the complaint is preserved, but it is now wholly irrelevant. Young Knowell is simply the witty young gallant about town, unafflicted, so far as we can see, with poetical symptoms. By removing most of the serious remarks on poetry and by dismissing Matthew's plagiarisms more casu-

ally, Jonson reduces to its strictly comic aspects the war between good and bad poets he had explored so strenuously in
the comical satires. The lighter sentences accorded Matthew
and Bobadill now resemble the indulgent treatment of Sir John
Daw in *Epicene*. The whole exhausting question of the
antagonism between Poetry and Humor is thus momentarily
shelved, or at least soft-pedaled, and this tends to set the revised *Every Man in his Humour* apart from the trio of plays
that precede it. On the other hand, as we shall see in a moment,
revisions of a different sort tend to emphasize the resemblances.

Setting aside the occasional clarifications of verse rhythm
or prose rhythm, and the orthographic changes that contribute to a more phonetic realism, one might classify the
Folio changes roughly into three groups: first, those that
heighten the vividness or precision of the dialogue without
actually affecting character; then, those that correct flaws in
decorum or fill in more exactly the outline of character as
premised in the Quarto; finally, those that transform character or add a fresh dimension to it.

The first group demonstrates most plainly Jonson's fascination with detail, since this kind of change does not spring from
any need to clarify motive or illuminate action, but simply
embroiders on what was already blocked out in the Quarto.
In some cases Jonson merely particularizes more fully a statement from the Quarto:

By this good ground, I was faine to pawne my rapier last night
for a poore supper, I am a Pagan els: sweet Signior.
(Q, II.ii.58–60)

. . . by this good ground, I was faine to pawne my rapier last
night for a poore supper, I had suck'd the hilts long before, I am
a pagan else: sweet honor.   (F, II.v.89–92)

Elsewhere, the substitution of a more concrete or specific
term for a general one infuses new vitality into the language:

. . . (as Gods my iudge, they should haue kild me first) . . .
(Q, IV.i.35)

. . . (as I protest, they must ha' dissected, and made an *Anatomie*
o' me, first, and so I told 'hem) . . .   (F, IV.vi.36–37)

Or Jonson may replace a simple literal statement with a
metaphoric one, or vitalize it by subjoining a simile to it:

. . . he is come to towne of purpose to seeke you.
(Q, II.iii.206–207)

. . . he has follow'd you ouer the field's, by the foot, as you
would doe a hare i' the snow.   (F, III.ii.46–48)

. . . oh that my bellie were hoopt now, for I am readie to burst
with laughing.   (Q, II.ii.101–103)

O that my belly were hoopt now, for I am readie to burst with
laughing! neuer was bottle, or bag-pipe fuller.   (F, II.v.133–135)

Changes such as these, to be sure, are not wholly without effect on character. If nothing else, they imply Brainworm's
increased slyness and self-confidence, his sharper powers of
observation. Still one feels that the impulse behind them is less
psychological than decorative: the desire to fill every nook
and cranny with its appropriate bits of design, over and above
the bare necessities of narrative.

A larger group of changes involves clear considerations of
character. In the first place, there is a crescendo of courtly
jargon in the speeches of Bobadill and Matthew. Where the
original Bobadilla summoned the hostess to "lend vs another
bedstaffe here quickly" (Q, I.iii.195–196), his later counterpart commands her to "accommodate vs with another bed-
staffe here, quickly: Lend vs another bed-staffe. The woman
do's not vnderstand the wordes of *Action*" (F, I.v.126–128),
thus replacing the simple "lend vs" with the high-flown verbal
phrase "accommodate vs," and retranslating it back into plain
English so as to be able to plume himself on his smart vo-

cabulary and rebuke the hostess for her ignorance at the same time. Similar touches heighten Bobadill's already evident egoism. His original impatience with Matthew was sufficiently self-preoccupied: "Why you do not manage your weapons with that facilitie and grace that you should doe, I haue no spirit to play with you" (Q, I.iii.213–215). The Folio makes the self-reference even more pronounced: "Why, you doe not manage your weapon with any facilitie, or grace to inuite mee: I haue no spirit to play with you" (F, I.v.146–148). On the other hand, Bobadill's manner toward Downright, at the moment of the beating, becomes more obsequious and cowardly. Instead of "Signior heare me! . . . Signior, I neuer thought [on] it till now" (Q, IV.ii.109–111), he tries to conciliate his antagonist with flattery: "Gentleman of valour, I doe beleeue in thee, heare mee . . . . Tall man, I neuer thought on it, till now" (F, IV.vii.122–125).

Bobadill's vocabulary of cant and his elegant periphrases, amplified in the Folio ("*chartel*" [F, I.v.111] for "challenge" [Q, I.iii.184]; "the fume of this simple" [F, III.v.81] for "Tabacco" [Q, III.ii.74]), infect his pupil Matthew, who strives more zealously after the lordly tone and the arcane manner in the Folio than in the Quarto. For "beautifull" (Q, I.iii.159), Matthew now says "peremptory-beautifull" (F, I.v.82–83); for "verie rare skill" (Q, I.iii.191) he coins the grotesque superlative "vn-in-one-breath-vtter-able skill" (F, I.v.121); for "O Gods mee" (Q, I.iii.138) he devises an oath of his own, "O, the *Muses*" (F, I.v.61). The edict against blasphemy in the Act of Assizes forced Jonson to suppress a good many oaths in the revision, or to find less offensive ones, but he turned the handicap into a triumph. The new oaths are more weirdly appropriate to their speakers than the old ones, and the gulls now show a tendency to grope more palpably after their oaths. Master Stephen, raging over a fancied insult, exclaims in the Quarto, "Well I will not put it vp, but by Gods foote, and ere I meete him — " (Q, II.iii.157–158). Jonson had to retrench the blasphemous allusion to God's foot, but he did so with a stroke of genius: "Well, I will put it vp, but by — (I ha' forgot the Captaynes oath, I thought to ha' sworne by it) an' ere I meet him — " (F, III.i.176–178), thus replacing a bit of straightforward mimicry with a piece of pathetic would-be mimicry, and so exchanging a single comic effect for a double one.

Stephen's fatuousness is heightened throughout by small mutations in the Folio. Greeting a messenger, he exclaims foolishly enough in the Quarto:

> Welcome good friend, we doe not stand much vpon our gentilitie; yet I can assure you mine vncle is a man of a thousand pounde land a yeare; hee hath but one sonne in the world; I am his next heire, as simple as I stand here, if my cosen die: I haue a faire liuing of mine owne too beside. (Q, I.i.81–85)

The Folio expands this slightly:

> Nay, we do' not stand much on our gentilitie, friend; yet, you are wel-come, and I assure you, mine vncle here is a man of a thousand a yeare, *Middlesex* land: hee has but one sonne in all the world, I am his next heire (at the common law) master STEPHEN, as simple as I stand here, if my cossen die (as there's hope he will) I haue a prettie liuing o' mine owne too, beside, hard-by here. (F, I.ii.2–8)

It should perhaps be explained that the phrase "we do' not stand much on our gentilitie" is an idiotic echo of the advice his uncle has just finished giving him concerning his social pretensions. The rest of the speech, in both versions, under-scores the extent to which the advice has been wasted. In the Folio, every new stroke heightens the pointlessness of his boasting. By placing "you are wel-come" after the disclaimer of pride in his gentility, Stephen contrives to suggest that there is some connection between them, that the messenger is welcome in spite of the fact that Stephen does not stand much on his gentility — a stunning piece of illogicality. Of the two added parentheses, the first is a vain display of parts, the second a stroke of monumental imbecility, considering that the uncle who stands beside him, and whose wealth he expects to inherit, is also the father of the "cossen" whose death he is complacently hoping for. The pleased self-identification "master STEPHEN" and the change from "faire" to the more simpering word "prettie" complete the effect of infantine self-congratulation. Similar alterations elsewhere in Stephen's dialogue produce similar results.

In a few cases Jonson rectifies lapses from decorum, usually by substituting a colloquial phrase for a pedantic one. Cob's too mincing stream of grateful epithets, "O diuine Doctor, thankes noble Doctor, most dainty Doctor, delicious Doctor" (Q, III.iii.119–120), at the end of his scene with Justice Clement, has been cut short and made more appropriate to Cob: "O, the Lord maintayne his worship, his worthy worship" (F, III.vii.79–80). Brainworm now says "remou'd" (F, III.ii.37) instead of "sublated" (Q, II.iii.198), "drum extraordinarie" (F, III.ii.35–36) instead of "God *Mars* extraordinarie" (Q, II. iii.196–197), and Young Knowell, "Ile be gelt" (F, I.iii.62) for "Then will I be made an *Eunuch*" (Q, I.ii.58). At the same time, Jonson does not hesitate to replace a common word with an elegant one if the situation prompts it. Brainworm as Brainworm speaks a saltier lingo than the original Musco, but Brainworm as skeldering soldier tends toward preciosity, and this is intensified rather than toned down in revision. Finally, one must observe that in two or three spots the attempt to expunge minor improprieties dulls the effect. Downright, vowing retaliation against the poetasters, declares in the Quarto, "Ile marre the knot of them ere I sleepe perhaps:

especially signior *Pithagoras*, he thats al manner of shapes"
(Q, III.iv.173–175). But the Folio, doubtless in order to remove a learned allusion from the aggressively philistine Downright, transmutes the cuttingly Jonsonian "signior *Pithagoras*,
he thats al manner of shapes" into the much weaker, tamer
"Bob, there: he that's all manner of shapes" (F, IV.iii.16–17).

The third group of changes, not always absolutely distinct
from those so far discussed, produces actual extension or en-
largement of character. At least three of the dramatis personae
— Downright, Brainworm, and Young Knowell — emerge
as more substantial and complex creations than their Quarto
prototypes.

Downright, the choleric humor, becomes more choleric,
but a fresh thread has been woven into the texture of his
language. This is signaled to us in advance in Bobadill's disdainful description, much enlarged in the Folio:

I protest to you (as I am a gentleman and a soldier) I ne're talk't
with the like of him: he ha's not so much as a good word in his
bellie, all iron, iron, a good commoditie for a smith to make
hobnailes on. (Q, I.iii.167–170)

I protest to you, as I am a gentleman, and a souldier, I ne're
chang'd wordes, with his like. By his discourse, he should eate
nothing but hay. He was borne for the manger, pannier, or pack-
saddle! He ha's not so much as a good phrase in his belly, but all
old iron, and rustie prouerbes! a good commoditie for some smith,
to make hob-nailes of. (F, I.v.92–98)

Aside from such inevitable nuances as the replacement of
"talk't" by the affected "chang'd wordes," the new details
add little to our knowledge of Bobadill, but they introduce
us more adequately to Downright, whose new attribute is
precisely his habit of larding his speech with "rustie prouerbes." "It will neuer out o' the flesh that's bred i' the bone"
(F, II.i.71–72), "counsell to him, is as good, as a shoulder of

mutton to a sicke horse" (F, II.i.73–74), "as he brewes, so he shall drinke" (F, II.ii.34), "he has the wrong sow by the eare, ifaith: and claps his dish at the wrong mans dore" (F, II.i. 78–79). In a sense Jonson has merely realized more concretely a pattern already clear in the Quarto. Downright is perhaps not so much changed as he is substantiated, but this in itself amounts to a change of some importance, since his substantiality is the very thing that sets him in contrast to the anemic Bobadill and the scarce-existent Matthew. On the one hand the pseudo soldier and would-be gentleman lisping exotic oaths; on the other the plain-spoken bourgeois, whose language smells of the stable and market place. On the one hand the chirping little plagiary; on the other hand the gruff philistine to whom verses are "worse then cheese, or a bag-pipe" (F, IV.ii.21–22). The vividness of these confrontations depends to a large extent on the greater solidity of Downright's language in the revision.

The metamorphosis of Musco into Brainworm and of Lorenzo Junior into Young Knowell, however, not only substantiates these characters, it reorients them: both come to resemble the satiric expositor of the comical satires. Exposure of humors, in the comical satires, required not merely that a fool exhibit his folly, but that he be held up to ridicule by a commentator provided for the purpose, an Asper, Crites, Macilente, Carlo Buffone, Mercury, or Cupid. The Folio text of *Every Man in his Humour* remodels Brainworm and Young Knowell so as to make them perform this function more clearly; they now flout the gulls more openly, and so deflate them more emphatically. The scene in Q, I.ii.28–52, as an instance, where Musco and Stephano confer over the latter's boot, undergoes a marked shift of tone in F, I.iii.14–55. Brainworm's formerly unfocused verbal high spirits now turn into an instrument of irony directed steadily at Stephen. His silly quibble on "boot" in the Quarto is transferred to Stephen, and now figures as one more item in Stephen's long inventory of folly. Brainworm's reiterated "master STEPHEN" this, "master STEPHEN" that, ends by itself becoming a form of sly ridicule. His deferential praise of Stephen's leg in the Quarto is banished in the revision; the Folio allows Stephen to introduce the commendation of his own leg, "How dost thou like my legge, BRAYNE-WORME," to which the reply, ostensibly judicious, is now sardonic, "A very good leg! master STEPHEN! but the woollen stocking do's not commend it so well." Finally, Musco's parting words in the Quarto, "You haue an excellent good legge, sir: I pray you pardon me, I haue a little haste in" (Q, I.ii.51–52), completely lack the suave mockery of Brainworm's speech at the same point: "You haue an excellent good legge, master STEPHEN, but I cannot stay, to praise it longer now, and I am very sorie for't." Brainworm's dry raillery not only draws the attention of the audience more sharply to Stephen's stupidity, it heightens that stupidity itself, since Stephen does not grasp the fact that he is being laughed at, and this affords a further contrast with those occasions on which, quite gratuitously, he takes it into his head to imagine that he *is* being laughed at.

In the case of Young Knowell, there is a sadistic rasp to many of his speeches in the Folio, where the prevailing tone in the Quarto was one of playful banter. His grandiloquent exhortation to Stephen, good-natured in the first version, is full of concealed barbs in the later one:

. . . why cousin, a gentleman of so faire sort as you are, of so true cariage, so speciall good parts; of so deare and choice estimation; one whose lowest condition beares the stampe of a great spirit; nay more, a man so grac'd, guilded, or rather (to vse a more fit *Metaphor*) tinfoyld by nature, (not that you haue a leaden constitution, couze, although perhaps a little inclining to that temper, & so the more apt to melt with pittie, when you fall into the fire of rage) but for your lustre onely, which reflects as bright to the world as an old Ale-wiues pewter againe a good time; and will you now (with nice modestie) hide such reall ornaments as these, and shadow their glorie as a Millaners wife doth her wrought stomacher, with a smoakie lawne or a blacke cipresse? Come, come, for shame doe not wrong the qualitie of your desert in so poore a kind: but let the *Idea* of what you are, be portraied in your aspect, that men may reade in your lookes; *Here within this place is to be seene, the most admirable rare & accomplisht worke of nature*; Cousin what think you of this?

(Q, I.ii.94–112)

A gentleman of your sort, parts, carriage, and estimation, to talke o' your turne i' this companie, and to me, alone, like a tank-ard-bearer, at a conduit! Fie. A wight, that (hetherto) his euery step hath left the stampe of a great foot behind him, as euery word the sauour of a strong spirit! and he! this man! so grac'd, guilded, or (to vse a more fit *metaphore*) so tin-foild by nature, as not ten house-wiues pewter (again' a good time) shew's more bright to the world then he! and he (as I said last, so I say againe, and still shall say it) this man! to conceale such reall ornaments as these, and shaddow their glorie, as a Millaners wife do's her wrought stom-acher, with a smokie lawne, or a black cypresse? O couss! It cannot be answer'd, goe not about it. DRAKES old ship, at *Detford*, may sooner circle the world againe. Come, wrong not the qualitie of your desert, with looking downeward, couz; but hold vp your head, so: and let the *Idea* of what you are, be pourtray'd i' your face, that men may reade i' your physnomie, (*Here, within this place, is to be seene the true, rare, and accomplish'd monster, or miracle of nature*, which is all one.) What thinke you of this, couss? (F, I.iii.108–128)

Among other things, the new version clarifies the sense a good deal by breaking up the long intricate period into a series, by reducing the jugglery with modifying phrases and trailing clauses, and by readdressing itself at regular intervals to the subject and object, Stephen. The exclamatory outbursts that punctuate the series, and afford further clarification, also heighten the bombast of the mock encomium. "One whose lowest condition beares the stampe of a great spirit" in the Quarto is ironic, to be sure, but "one whose euery step hath left the stampe of a great foot behind him, as euery word the sauour of a strong spirit" caps a ludicrous bathos with a still droller pun on brandy-tainted breath, the ambiguities producing an irony more complex and more cutting than that of the Quarto equivalent, which is ironic chiefly by courtesy of context. At length emerging from behind the cloud of grandiose comparisons under cover of which he has been mocking his cousin, Knowell ends by exchanging for the implied sarcasm of *"admirable rare & accomplisht worke of nature"* the open derision of *"true, rare, and accomplish'd monster, or miracle of nature."*

The Folio regularly transforms Knowell's colorless gestures of politeness into caustic rejoinders, often altering other speeches so as to make room for such rejoinders. Bobadill's revised speech of self-introduction now ends with the announcement, "I loue few wordes," so as to draw a sardonic answer from Young Knowell, "And I fewer, sir. I haue scarce inow, to thanke you" (F, III.i.84–86). Later, when Bobadill has dismissed Stephen's sword as a mere Fleming, Matthew, unexpectedly contradicted by his idol, is forced to reverse his own previous judgment and declare that on closer view it must be a poor Fleming after all: "Masse I thinke it be indeed" (Q, II.iii.154). The Folio amplifies at this point — "Masse, I thinke it be, indeed! now I looke on't, better" — so as to draw another wicked gibe from Knowell: "Nay, the longer you looke on't, the worse" (F, III.i.172–174).

Where the Quarto text already contains mockery of the gulls, the Folio frequently adds to it. In the former, Wellbred compares Stephen "to nothing more happely, then a Barbers virginals; for euery one may play vpon him" (Q, II.iii.184–185). In the latter, he likens him, more devastatingly, "to nothing more happily, then a drumme; for euery one may play vpon him." To which Young Knowell makes a further correction: "No, no, a childes whistle were farre the fitter" (F, III.ii.23–25). A barbershop virginal can be played by many, but not by all; it requires a certain minimum of training and skill. But absolutely anyone can bang on a drum, and the drum is hence a more degrading comparison. But a drum produces loud booming noises, whereas Stephen emits mainly high-pitched squeaks, so that the child's whistle becomes the final and most accurate figure of analogy.

Young Knowell in his new incarnation is thus a quite different figure from the Lorenzo Junior of the Quarto. Having cast off his poetical fervor, he ceases for the most part to be a spokesman for Jonson's ethical view of poetry. Having acquired, on the other hand, a mastery of ambiguous insult, together with his equally changed companion Brainworm, he becomes the satiric expositor engaged in the unmasking of fools. As Knowell and Brainworm now stand out more clearly than ever in the ranks of the witty, so the gulls recede further into the dim legions of the witless. The sentence against them may well be lighter this time, the penances of fasting and recantation removed, since through their own language and through the mordant commentary of their associates they have been so much more pitilessly exposed. The formal penalties and rewards, distributed by a justice more clement than ever, now take on the emblematic nature of the punishment of Tucca; the fools need no more crushing retribution, and the wits no further public sanctification. Folly has finally become its own worst punishment, as the wit of a Brainworm its own reward.

IV

Things of Sense

Aᴄᴛᴇʀ *Poetaster*, Jonson virtually abandoned the mixed prose-verse play. His doing so may indicate no more than a growing preference for concentration and singleness of effect. It may also, however, in ways to be suggested shortly, reflect his changing view of the theater and of his own role as playwright.

Sejanus [1] uses prose only once, in a fashion at once highly conventional and highly original: conventional, in that the use of prose for a letter read on stage was one of the oldest rules of thumb of Elizabethan dramaturgy; original, in that the reading of the letter — from Tiberius to the Senate — forms the climax of the action, precipitating Sejanus from his altitude of power into disfavor, degradation, and death. The language of the letter itself, moreover, dictates from point to point the theatrical progress of the scene, by its ambiguities provoking the waves of doubt, fear, and panic that seethe through the listening Senate. Tiberius' duplicity and back-tracking find their linguistic counterpart in the winding, shifting indirections of the loose period, in the casually appended "thoughs," "yets," "excepts," and "howsoevers," that seem in one clause to endorse Sejanus, in the next to suspect him, and end by destroying him altogether.

Volpone [2] employs prose more ambitiously, though at a less critical point in the action, in the long and brilliant mountebank scene in Act II. The scene affords the one instant in the play when the fierce intrigue going on between Volpone and his dupes impinges, if only obliquely, on the outside world. And it provides Volpone with a magisterial public role that allows him almost to wallow in the excesses of his own temperament, after the confining deathbed charade of the earlier scenes. By assuming the guise of an itinerant huckster, peddling his wares in a flamboyant spiel based on the improvisations of the *commedia dell'arte*, Volpone can satisfy his histrionic gifts, his linguistic virtuosity, his knavery, and his desire to see Celia, at one and the same time. The scene, with its lifelike market milieu, is the most realistic episode in the play, and also the most stylized. The monologue itself is a piece of bravura rhetoric, seasoned with Italian phrases and jawbreaking medical terms, in which Volpone contrives to use — and pervert — virtually every effect known to classic oratory. The lay public, represented by the credulous Sir Politic Wouldbe and the hardheaded Peregrine, breaks in from time to time with the kind of choric comment that focuses our attention on the excesses of Volpone's jargon. "Is not his language rare?" exclaims the dazzled knight. "But *Alchimy*, / I neuer heard the like: or BROVGHTONS bookes," returns the astringent Peregrine (II.ii.118–119), thus lumping Volpone's cant with the mumbo jumbo of the alchemists and the obscure rantings of the Puritan divine Broughton as a trio of exercises in verbal fraud. Language thus for one moment becomes an explicit object of satire, and Volpone's surcharged imagination achieves fully adequate linguistic expression. The rest of the play, as befits its basic antirealism and the hyperbolic nature of the visions that possess its characters, is rendered in the more incantatory medium of blank verse.

With *Epicene, or The Silent Woman*,[3] the scene is London, and the characters are recognizable London types: idle gallants, ladies of pleasure, a barber, a page, a henpecked captain. Their subjects of conversation are the fashionable topics of the day, and the plot itself depends strictly on the facts of the local setting. The milieu, in short, is realistic, and the language is prose.

Perhaps some comment should be made on the deceitful terms "realism" and "satire" and the slippery relations between them. Pure realism, if by it is meant absolute fidelity to nature or impartial transcriptions of the phenomenal world, is of course a will-o'-the-wisp. The mere act of finding details, choosing among them, ordering them into a new totality, forces the artist into a position of mastery over nature. The idiosyncrasies of human perception, the multiple zones and levels that constitute the "real," as well as the alchemy of the creative process, forbid, strictly speaking, any objective account of the world in art. They do not, of course, preclude a more or less skillful and convincing imitation of human experience, but this in itself is only a stratagem of plausibility and does not alter the fictive nature of the work of art. Realism can never be more than approximate: "Art cannot give us *la chose même* except by resorting to artifice; the theater has its trick mirrors, its optical illusions; the playwright, like the painter, manipulates techniques and calculates impressions." [4] Art, indeed, does not even really wish to give us *la chose même*. Artists proclaim their fidelity to nature, and then proceed to demonstrate, in their works, their fidelity to art. "Rodin parle toute la journée de la Nature, mais sculpte le *Balzac* et ne pense qu'à la sculpture." What artists describe as "Nature," is, in fact, what they themselves find in the world, what they take of it, and how they transform it: "Le génie n'a rien à voir avec la nature, sauf ce qu'il prend chez elle pour l'annexer à la sienne." Art, finally, cannot found itself on nature pure and simple; it sees nature through the screen interposed by the art of the past. "A Chartres comme en Egypte, à Florence comme à Babylone, l'art ne naît de la vie qu'à travers un art antérieur." [5]

Applying these axioms to Jonson, one may say that his celebrated "empiricism" [6] is only a stratagem, developed in protest against the wholesale improbabilities of Elizabethan romantic comedy; that his disenchanted eye sees in the visible world exactly what it wishes to see, what it wishes to transmute into art; and what it does see and what it plots to transmute into art is the visible and audible fact of universal folly. The moment we scratch the surface of "realistic" comedies like *Every Man in his Humour* or *Epicene*, we find fantasy clothed in plausibility, old comic formulas and satiric techniques renewed and freshened and given an air of naturalness by being planted in a half-recognizable environment. The touches of local color form not a realistic but a highly selective quasi-realistic context within which prance follies never before met with on sea or land. Like Mrs. Martin Johnson, Jonson cranks the camera as strange beasts lope across the horizon, but unlike Mrs. Johnson, Ben Jonson has called into being the very beasts he is filming, with the aid of the ancestral beasts of earlier literature. [7] Even more obviously is this true of the sound track. We do not need phonograph records of Elizabethan speech to tell us that no one ever talked like Sordido or Amorphus or Morose, just as no one talks like characters in the novels of Henry James or William Faulkner. What we are dealing with in each case is an artistic metamorphosis based on an imitation of heard speech, the imitation — through the strategies of the loose and curt styles, the infusion of fashionable cant — being no doubt closer in Jonson's case than in some others, but the metamorphosis no less decisive in transforming life into art. Even to Jonson, with his "graphic" realism [8] and his frequent importation of real noises into the mouths of his imaginary toads, we must apply Malraux's dictum that "les grands artistes ne sont pas les transcripteurs du monde, ils en sont *les rivaux*." [9]

To state the matter more practically, "realistic" details in Jonson are always chosen to illuminate moral deformities, exaggerated for purposes of ridicule, shaped according to the laws of comedy, and — one must add — unquestionably often invented rather than actually observed. But Jonson is rarely content to let the ludicrous assemblage of detail speak for itself. However loudly the grotesque exterior proclaims the inner vacuum, Jonson, especially in his early plays, insists on supplying direct moral comment as well. In such cases, the shifts between prose and verse become a rough counterpart to the shifts from a given situation to the comment upon it. Prose registers the folly embodied in palpable form, and verse affords glimpses of a positive moral norm from which the fools have strayed.[10] This distinction, evolving in the first two plays, but somewhat obscured by the reliance on Roman intrigue plots and technical clumsiness, crystallizes, in the comical satires, into a more or less stable technique and a uniquely Jonsonian vision.

"Realism," used in a homelier but not unrelated sense, often denotes the attitude of one who faces the facts of the world and accepts them. Realism of this sort runs somewhat counter to satire, which, if it faces facts, does so in order to change them. Jonson never quite became a realist in this sense. But the satiric tendency to insist on the gulf between things as they are and things as they ought to be wanes noticeably in the course of his career, and his attitude becomes more and more that of the man whose recognition of folly in himself prevents him from judging it too harshly in others. And this shift, in turn, may help to explain his abandonment of the mixed prose-verse form of the comical satires.

The comical satires, that is, supply not only a sharp and mordant image of a "real" world — in prose — but also a supra-real world of divine truth and justice by which the ordinary world is to be judged — this in verse. Over and above the follies of society stands the high court of Cynthia in *Cynthia's Revels* or the tribunal of Augustus in *Poetaster*, from which semidivine embodiments of virtue and justice pronounce sentence on the contemptible antics below. *Volpone*, too, has its court of high justice, but this is no longer represented as infallible. Though eager to find the truth and capable of recognizing it if it appears without disguise, the Venetian *Scrutineo* shares with the rest of the world a proneness to mistake vice for virtue, folly for wisdom, appearance for reality. Appropriately, then, Jonson makes no linguistic distinction between the language of the court and that of the other Venetians; the *avocatori* speak only a slightly more stilted, more ceremonious version of the verse common to the fools and knaves. In *Epicene*, the transcendent court has been discarded entirely, and with it the higher standards of justice to which the author could appeal. Again, therefore, the need for a special language to mark the apes from the sages has disappeared. The intermediary between the two worlds has likewise vanished. The satiric expositor, like Macilente, who belonged to a higher order of reality than the fools and who mixed with them only to deliver acrimonious judgment on them, has been absorbed into their world and transmuted into their boon companion, Truewit.

Truewit inhabits the same social and intellectual sphere as his fellows, and even formulates their own attitudes for them, while suggesting at the same time the possibility of other attitudes. He offers simultaneously a defense of the fashionable life and an awareness that this life does not exhaust the capacities of its votaries. The two ways of responding to the kind of reality projected by Jonson — the satirist's impulse to reject it with a cry of outrage, and the "realist's" impulse to embrace it or at least accept it with a cynical shrug — reach a kind of uneasy suspension in Truewit. If we take Truewit, however, as Jonson seems chiefly to have meant him, as a spokesman for things as they are, we find the antithetic attitude, the spirit of satire, alive and incarnate in the person of Morose, who is an Asper thrown amidst fools, a Crites unsupported by a Cynthia, a satirist himself the butt of satire, and a living object-lesson in the absurdity of looking for perfection in a corrupt world.

This antithesis, and the irresolutions it produces in the play, have been discussed elsewhere [11] in an analysis of Jonson's use of his two chief literary sources, Ovid's *Ars amatoria* and Juvenal's Sixth Satire, against women. Ovid, broadly speaking, is the realist of this pair (in the homely sense) and Juvenal the satirist. Jonson, though by temperament a Juvenal, allows Ovid to carry off most of the public honors in the person of Truewit, while the spirit of Juvenal is kept at bay and mocked in the figure of Morose. But at the same time, while Truewit, with the flag of Ovid nailed to his mast, sails grandly to victory, the tides and crosscurrents of the language are setting up a counterdrift that almost carries the ship into the wrong port. The result is a stalemate; what Jonson affirms on one level he denies on another. If *Volpone* represents an unequivocal triumph of "negative" comedy, of rejection over acceptance, *Epicene* represents the highly equivocal victory of acceptance of life, in which Jonson can exorcise the satiric spirit in himself only by magnifying it to monstrous proportions and then tormenting it beyond measure.[12]

As we might expect, Truewit and Morose form the central linguistic pillars of the play, but the pillars oppose each other across a very narrow span, and display an analogous roundness and polish. Critics have noticed that the prose of *Epicene* shows a high degree of artful balance,[13] appropriate, perhaps, in a play that makes such a strong plea for artifice as against "naturalness" and simplicity. On the other hand — again appropriate to a play with such ambivalent motivation — the prose of the spokesman for artifice, while polished to a degree, contains everywhere the disruptive effects of the baroque style, the sudden interpolations and afterthoughts and whimsical flourishes, whereas the prose of the champion of simplicity carries studied formality to pedantic extremes.

Truewit, the sophisticated defender of artifice, is the master of baroque style. We have already, in Chapter II, observed his characteristic manner, which sets in motion large-scale syntactic movements, based on recurrence of initial or final elements and some degree of equivalence between members, and then proceeds to vary the details so as to produce a maximum of syncopation without losing the symmetrical ground plan. The vitality of these periods consists precisely in the tension between implied symmetry and explicit irregularity, much as the prosodic vitality of verse depends on a tension between the ideal metrical beat and the actual irregular embodiment of that beat in words.

The case of Truewit illustrates rather fully another stylistic habit observed in Chapter II: the use of "balance" and "antithesis" of a peculiarly oblique, deceptive kind, where the rhythm and the sense (if one can so separate them) are asynchronous; where the two halves of an antithetic statement may have rhythmic identity without grammatical parallel, or the other way around; where there occurs, so to speak, an illusion of antithesis rather than the completely realized thing. In the following extract, Truewit, with feigned solicitude, is instructing Morose in his duties as a groom:

Would you goe to bed so presently, sir, afore noone? a man of your head, and haire, should owe more to that reuerend ceremony, and not mount the marriage-bed, like a towne-bul, or a mountaine-goate; but stay the due season; and ascend it then with religion, and feare. Those delights are to be steep'd in the humor, and silence of the night; and giue the day to other open pleasures, and jollities of feast, of musique, of reuells, of discourse: wee'll haue all, sir, that may make your *Hymen* high, and happy.

(III.v.43–52)

Each of the central periods here splits into an antithesis, and each term of each antithesis contains some doubling or compounding of elements. In both cases the rhythm produces a sense of balance; in neither case does the antithesis maintain itself with any rigor. "Not mount the marriage-bed, like a towne-bul, or a mountaine-goate" prompts us to expect parisonic equivalence in the answering phrases — "but stay the due season; and ascend it then like a courteous groom, and respectful squire" — or something that will fulfill the projected formula. Instead, "ascend it then with religion, and feare" defiantly departs from parison, shifts from the concrete (bull and goat) into the abstract (religion and fear), and ignores the interior elaboration of "*towne*-bul" and "*mountaine*-goate." The next sentence — but what we confidently expect to be the next sentence turns out to be merely a continuation of the present one. It starts with a parenthetic clause, "Those delights are to be steep'd in the humor, and silence of the night," which is, bizarrely, both related and unrelated to the clause that follows it: related in its antithetic pitting of night against day, and humor and silence against pleasure and jollities, but unrelated grammatically, a mere parenthetical interpolation, after which the series of verbs initiated earlier — "owe," "mount," "stay," "ascend" — resumes and concludes with "giue." "Humor, and silence of the night," moreover, prepares us for something like "open pleasures, and jollities of the day," instead of which, "day" is tucked in at the beginning as direct object of "giue," while the balancing phrase turns out to be "open pleasures, and jollities of feast," which has only rhythmic identity with its partner. After this, Truewit concludes his sermon with a characteristic flourish, in which the jollities expand to include music, revels, and discourse, and all that may make the "*Hymen* high, and happy."

In short, the balanced style of *Epicene* — of Truewit, at any rate — amounts to this: the doubling of elements — words, phrases, and clauses — causing a perpetual little dance in the language and a sense of rhythmic fullness, and at the same time a studious avoidance of exact congruence, creating an equally strong feeling of free-flowing spontaneity. Jonson's antitheses, at the same time that they satisfy rhythmically, catch us off balance grammatically. We glimpse them traveling eccentrically away from us, like the tail of a comet, or we are suddenly in the middle of one without warning, but we rarely get a full, steady, unobstructed view of one, as we do in Lyly or Shakespeare. Shakespeare, in his use of the disjunctive "though" pattern, characteristically places the subordinate clause first, so that it leads up to its own contradiction: "though honestie be no Puritan, yet it will doe no hurt" (L. 251; *Alls W* I.iii.97–98). The suspense created in the first clause is gratified in the second. Jonson, just as characteristically, places the main clause first, and then casually lets fall the other, so as to add an unexpected twist to an idea we might have supposed complete.

I, and he will know you too, if ere he saw you but once, though you should meet him at church in the midst of praiers. Hee is one of the *Braueries*, though he be none o' the *Wits*.   (I.iii.27–30)

If shee loue wit, giue verses, though you borrow 'hem of a friend, or buy 'hem, to haue good. If valour, talke of your sword, and be frequent in the mention of quarrels, though you be staunch in fighting. (IV.i.97–101)

The sense of negligence induced by this procedure would seem to be a fairly exact linguistic counterpart for Truewit as we see him altogether: a young man with a flair for elegance and at the same time a certain *sprezzatura*.

The fairly regular disintegration of sentences into units of equal length, however, implies a certain degree of logicality, and in fact Truewit develops his speeches more logically than most of Jonson's characters. His harangues and digressions usually start with some prefatory formula that stakes out the area to be explored: "I'll tell thee what I would doe" (I.ii.13), "I must tell you, all the perills that you are obnoxious too" (II.ii.65–66), "Men should loue wisely, and all women" (IV.i. 141–142). And he may conclude with an equally succinct formula of summary: "any way, rather, then to follow this goblin *matrimony*" (II.ii.31–32). Yet as in the case of Amorphus' soliloquy discussed earlier, the real interest and the real progress of the period lies largely in the details themselves, in their comic extravagance or their imaginative vividness, and not in their logical working out.

One of Truewit's common verbal mannerisms is the hypothetical proposition, usually introduced by "if." This is among other things a handy device of disjunction, and also a form of logical analysis that divides antecedent from consequent. It differs from other kinds of logical division in that it rests initially on a contingency or a chimera. As a mere expression of possibility it transcends reliance on verifiable data. It invents its own data, and may become as bizarre as the mind that imagines it. Truewit's hypotheses, as we might expect, verge on the fantastic.

Well, sir gallant, were you strooke with the plague this minute,
or condemn'd to any capitall punishment to morrow, you would
beginne then to thinke, and value euery article o' your time, esteeme it at the true rate, and giue all for't. (I.i.27–31)

. . . if you had liu'd in king ETHELRED's time, sir, or EDWARD the
Confessors, you might, perhaps, haue found in some cold coun-
trey-hamlet, then, a dull frostie wench, would haue been con-
tented with one man. (II.ii.36–40)

If, after you are married, your wife doe run away with a vaulter,
or the *Frenchman* that walkes vpon ropes, or him that daunces
the iig, or a fencer for his skill at his weapon, why it is not their
fault; they haue discharged their consciences: when you know
what may happen. (II.ii.60–65)

By offering such unlikely hypotheses, Truewit illuminates
a new tract of reality — that of the possible — for his listeners,
and tries to break them loose from the chains of probability
and habit. His exhortations of his friends to love and his de-
hortation of Morose from marriage are built up out of blocks
of such hypotheses; they construct microcosms of their subjects; they exhaust for the sake of argument a whole spectrum
of possibilities. From the fantasy that Clerimont will be stricken
with plague on the spot, or condemned to capital punishment
on the morrow, he elegizes on the waste of time. But by keeping the whole notion in the realm of possibility, he forestalls
any tendency to regard his morality as urgent. He offers the
glimpse of a world in which men are really governed by the
kind of edifying considerations he toys with, and then closes
the view as a mere contingency, ready from that moment not
only to allow but to encourage his friends in their dissipation
of time.

To dissuade Morose from wedlock he takes a sterner course,
giving the consequence of each contingency as necessary, in
order to wall off every avenue of escape. "If shee be faire,
yong, and vegetous, no sweet meats euer drew more flies; all

the yellow doublets, and great roses i' the towne will bee there" (II.ii.66–68), he starts, canvassing for the moment the proposition that the wife will be attractive, but that this will lead to disaster anyhow. From this point on he imagines a succession of unattractive wives who will actively study torment for their husbands: the foul and crooked, the rich, the well-born, the fruitful, the learned, the precise, each with her own instruments of torture. The last and most awful contingency presupposes that the husband is in love with his wife. From this premise alone unfolds a whole chronicle of torment. By the time Truewit has finished describing it, he has settled Morose's fate so inexorably that he can drop the sign of contingency, the "if," and go on to describe the wife's visit to her "cunning woman," her loathsome cosmetic practices, and the like, as absolute certainties. He returns to overt hypothesis only for his peroration, when he delivers a last warning against the wife who has already antedated her husband's cuckolding, or effects it on the wedding day. And having conjured up this nightmare world of contingency, he leaves a rope, as a symbol of the only possible escape from it, and departs.

Instructing his friends in the management of a seduction or paraphrasing Ovid on the varieties of feminine adornment, Truewit invokes hypotheses less grotesque but no less exhaustive. Many kinds of feminine beauty are enumerated, and even more kinds of ugliness. And each leads to an appropriate injunction: "If shee haue good eares, shew 'hem; good haire, lay it out"; "If shee bee short, let her sit much . . . . If shee haue an ill foot, let her weare her gowne the longer, and her shoo the thinner." Similarly, the differences in feminine temperament must dictate the varying styles of courtship: "If shee loue wit, giue verses . . . . If valour, talke of your sword." But the contingencies remain contingencies, mostly unrealized in action. The fearsome diatribe against matrimony only prompts Morose to hasten his wedding plans. The lessons in courtship ignore the fact that the only available women, the collegiate ladies, tend to take courtship brazenly into their own hands. As for the rhapsody on cosmetic, its only positive result is to reconcile Clerimont and Dauphine to the face-painting of the collegians so that they may be all the more bleakly disillusioned by the collegians themselves.

Another of Truewit's recurrent figures is the claim of uniqueness:

If shee be faire, yong, and vegetous, no sweet meats euer drew more flies. (II.ii.66–67)

If learned, there was neuer such a parrat. (II.ii.76)

If euer GORGON were seene in the shape of a woman, hee hath seene her in my description. (II.iv.15–17)

. . . there was neuer poore captaine tooke more paines at a muster to show men, then he, at this meale, to shew friends.
(II.iv.107–109)

No Anabaptist euer rail'd with the like licence. (III.ii.15)

There was neuer fencer challeng'd at so many seuerall foiles.
(IV.v.114–115)

Since these claims usually serve to expose the exemplary foolishness of the gulls or to carry to its extreme some imagined contingency, they may be classified as variations, or heightenings, of the hypothetical proposition, or in short as another form of Truewit's verbal prankishness.

If the knack of peopling the air with imaginary creatures produces, on the verbal level, the hypothetic formula and the "nonpareil," [14] it issues, on the level of physical action, in the practical joke. The hypothetical proposition resembles the daydream of a child as it creates its fantasy world. The practical joke simply translates the fantasy into actuality. The more vivid the fantasy, the more effortlessly it passes into act and imposes itself on its surroundings, but the act retains its verbal basis. Truewit's weapon in his pranks, like that of Saki's romancing heroes, is the word, the quip, the metaphor, the linguistic construct with which he batters down the walls of normality. Speaking more or less *in vacuo*, he urges ladies to repair the ruins of time and their own defects with cosmetic, and so defeat the prosaic realities of the flesh. When, transmuting precept into act, he invents for Morose a cosmos of matrimonial terror, for Daw and La Fool a nightmare of reciprocal pugnacity, and for Morose again a purgatory of clamorous dispute between the civil and canon law, he scores in each case a triumph for his make-believe world over the prosy facts of the "real" world. Unlike other Jonsonian characters of comparable linguistic talent who improvise with equal zest, Truewit does so disinterestedly, unmotivated by the itch for gain or by moral fervor. And unlike Volpone, Morose, Overdo, and the rest, who fall victim to their own language and to the strange worlds they have created with it, Truewit remains master of his, because he never ceases to keep one foot planted solidly in the real world.

Truewit thus becomes a kind of surrealist. His imagination discloses so many planes of possibility to him at once that he can scarcely choose between them. He embraces all with an Olympian impartiality. He can welcome the shortcomings of ordinary existence without blinking the fact that they are shortcomings. He can philosophize on time at one moment and deprecate his own philosophy in the next. He can praise feminine artifice and undermine it in one breath. He can describe the Ovidian life of seduction as an ideal, and then expose the embodiments of that ideal — the collegiates — as shams. And as he shifts his attitudes, so he shifts his style of speech, adopting a kind of elegiac wistfulness when chiding his friends for their frivolity, and an astringent dryness as he expounds the rules of amorous conquest, deluging Morose under cataracts of huge, rolling periods at one moment, and growing all agitation and distraction in the next, when presiding over the comedy of confusion between Daw and La Fool. If the common denominator through all of these numerous rhetorical postures remains that of the negligent young wit, disdainful of excessive linguistic precision, it is nevertheless true that Truewit speaks through so many masks that one is not sure when, if ever, he is speaking *in propria persona*. He resembles a disembodied intelligence flickering over the action and lighting up its dark corners. And if this intelligence triumphs over the fixations of Morose, it is due to the energy of the language through which it operates.

2

Morose, on the other hand, is always himself. His speech reflects personality much more directly than Truewit's because, unlike Truewit, and very much like the humors characters of the early plays, he remains trapped within the confines of his own personality — end-stopped, to borrow a term from a recent critic.[15] His language includes roughly two modes: first, his normal style of self-congratulation, in repose, and then the highly agitated idiom of distraction to which he is goaded by the various torments arranged for him.

The former, not unnaturally, is more closely planned and fully organized. In fact, it is probably the fussiest style used by any Jonsonian character. Truewit's breezy way of initiating antitheses that he does not bother to round out reflects the carelessness of the young gallant about town, indifferent to niceties of phrasing. Perhaps it reflects as well the tentative quality of one who is still experimenting with a variety of attitudes and has not yet allowed any to take full possession of him. In any case, it is a sign of grace, for in Jonson, as in Seneca, "Too much pickednesse is not manly" (*Disc.* 1422), and linguistic affectation always betrays moral weakness. Morose, by contrast, is a mass of affectation, and exhibits an old-maidish pickedness in his choice of phrase.

When Truewit says "let me play the mounte-bank for my meate while I liue, and the bawd for my drinke" (IV.i.151–152), he not only interposes an adverbial qualifier between the two objects of "play" so as to hide the symmetry, he is setting up a pair of matched phrases rather than an antithesis. Meat and drink, proverbially bracketed, one solid, the other liquid, may pass as antithetic, but there is no necessary opposition between bawd and mountebank, nor any reason why "mounte-bank" should go with "meate" rather than "drinke," or vice versa, except considerations of euphony. Morose, however, licks every antithesis into shape with maternal solicitude.

Cannot I, yet, find out a more compendious method, then by this trunke, to saue my seruants the labour of speech, and mine eares, the discord of sounds? (II.i.1–3)

The phrases here, perhaps better described as complementary than antithetic, match exactly. The labor of speech undergone by the servants produces the discord of sounds suffered by the ears; one a spoken noise, the other a heard sound, both fork off from the zeugmatic verb "saue," and except for an extra syllable in "seruants," maintain perfect syllabic correspondence. Morose infrequently carries his antitheses to great lengths, but he never allows them to be less than rigidly logical.

. . . answere me not, by speech, but by silence. (II.i.9)

This is not, onely, fit modestie in a seruant, but good state, and discretion in a master. (II.i.14–16)

The knaue hath exceedingly wel fitted me without: I will now trie her within. (II.v.19–21)

As it is bounty to reward benefits, so is it equity to mulct iniuries.
(III.iv.16–17)

The key terms are squarely antithetic: "speech" and "silence"; "seruant" and "master"; "without," "within"; "benefits," "iniuries." And they occur within the kind of highly logical formula we have discovered to be normal in Shakespeare: "not by X, but by Y," "not only X, but Y," "as . . . so." As we have also discovered, these are danger signals in Jonson.

They imply what is made perfectly obvious in other ways, an affected and unnatural language drawn largely from books. Morose's studied singularity of diction and gratuitous floridity emanate fittingly from one who has shut himself off from the sound of the human voice and must rely upon memory and reading. Morose keeps insisting, ironically, that he is "courtly"; his diction confirms that he is at least pseudocourtly. Specifically, he commits the linguistic sin of "complement," that is to say of an affected style oriented stylistically rather than socially, tending toward pedantry more than foppery. Arthur H. King's study of *Poetaster* enables us to determine with some precision the various strands of compliment [16] woven into Morose's style. It consists of a complex of vices: magniloquence (big words), hyperbole (strong words), and expletives (surplus words). Magniloquence in turn breaks down into excessive alloquialism (modes of address), ornate usage in preference to simple, and pedantry.

The scene in which Morose examines his future bride affords a useful testing point. His language brims over with alloquial formulas: "Deare lady," "good ladie," "faire ladie," "faire gentlewoman." Used by a man addressing a woman, "lady" is always affected in Jonson, while "deare" and "faire" are expletives of fake politeness. Morose's ornateness appears in his genius for periphrasis, as in the stagey piece of rhetoric with which he greets Epicene:

As I conceiue, CVTBERD, this gentlewoman is shee, you haue prouided, and brought, in hope shee will fit me in the place and person of a wife? Answer me not, but with your leg, vnlesse it be otherwise: (——) very well done CVTBERD. I conceiue, besides, CVTBERD, you haue beene pre-acquainted with her birth, education, and quallities, or else you would not pre-ferre her to my acceptance, in the waighty consequence of marriage.

(II.v.5–13)

The quasi-legal redundancy of "place and person of a wife," the quaintly circumlocutory "pre-ferre her to my acceptance, in the waighty consequence of marriage" illustrate the complacency with which the speaker hearkens to the sound of his own voice.

The same taste for decorative phrasing appears in his use of perfumed and pedantic words. Gems of polite parlance like "diuine," "felicity," "I conceiue," cast their glitter everywhere, together with even more dazzling terms like "aemulous" (II.v.75), "transcend" (II.i.37), "exquisite" (II.i.34), "facinorous" (II.ii.54), "vitiated" (II.ii.51), and "impulsion" (II.i.29). Some of Morose's precious words sound even more mannered as a result of the unidiomatic way in which they are used: "frugal" ("a frugall, and comely grauitie" [II.i.21]), "audacious" ("courtly, and audacious ornaments" [II.v.33]), "impaire" ("a most desperate impaire" [II.v.51]). His iteration of "courtly" carries a tinge of etymological pedantry, by its juxtaposition with "curt-sie" and "court-lesse." And his sudden introduction of two Anglo-Saxon words, "bedpheere" and "heicfar" (II.v.50, 69), as learned synonyms for "wife," produces at the same time a sense of stilted unreality and a slight shock effect as from strong biblical language.

Under "hyperbolical" usage King [17] includes verbs too strong for their context, for example the courtly clichés "entreat" and "beseech," and disproportionately emphatic adverbs and adjectives like "exceeding" or "diuine," all of which enter

repeatedly into Morose's speech, together with such private addictions as "desperate" and "speciall" with their own added quality of exaggeration. King's subdivision of amatory hyperbole is also relevant here. Morose, in his testing of Epicene, is acting out a scene of courtship according to his own unreal notions of courtliness, and much of his florid verbiage is intended as gallantry. Since Epicene remains mute, Morose demands to know whether she has not begun to feel symptoms of passion, as he has: "I beseech you, say lady, out of the first fire of meeting eyes, (they say) loue is stricken: doe you feele any such motion, sodenly shot into you, from any part you see in me? ha, lady?" (II.v.26–29). The "they" of the parenthesis can of course refer only to the sonneteers, playwrights, and authors of romantic novels. Morose's absurd attempt to translate an amatory conceit into a literal event, and that between his own elderly self and a girl whom he is virtually buying for her silence, marvelously characterizes the distorted knowledge of the world that he has purchased with his reclusiveness. His parting salute, "Let me now be bold to print, on those diuine lips, the seale of being mine," conveys the same strange impression, that the speaker is airing courtly clichés he has found in love poems but never heard from a human voice. If Morose parrots the language of amatory literature, it is partly from affectation and partly from ignorance of how live people talk. His style, with its old-fashioned bookishness, its starched formality, seems frozen in a variety of antique postures, and one imagines their speaker constantly striking attitudes of self-approval or condescension as he moves about haranguing his household or inspecting his chosen bride.

The conclusion of this scene provides one of those sudden illuminations of character that defy any prediction from Jonson's theory of comedy, still more any attempt to project the "humor" doctrine beyond its proper sphere in the comical satires. The betrothal has been sealed by a kiss, Cutbeard has left in search of a parson, and the mute has conducted Epicene into an adjoining room. Morose, alone now on the stage for the first and only time in the play, drops the egregious style of civility he has been practicing, and bursts into a cry of triumph at the prospect of revenge against his nephew. All of his archaic courtliness, all of his spinsterish phrasemaking evaporates as he launches into a vindictive prophecy of the humiliations — the poverty, beggary, and ostracism — he hopes to inflict on Dauphine by disinheriting him. The vocabulary now concerns twelve-penny ordinaries, term time, borrowing letters, London taverns, commodities of pipkins, bakers' wives, and the whole paraphernalia of London life from which Morose has excluded himself. The syntax, except for one local antithesis, marches steadily forward in a series of simple clauses organized about the recurrent key terms "kinsman," "its knighthood," "it knighthood," and finally "it." The kinsman's knighthood becomes a personified thing, powerfully imagined in a series of progressively more degrading circumstances, ending with "its" marriage to a prostitute to stave off starvation.

Though we have often in Jonson found characters giving themselves verbal airs in order to impress others — Chloe, for instance, when she turns from rebuking her husband to greeting her courtly friends — we have never before seen the mask of affectation stripped off so totally. With the impostors of the comical satires, the affectation *is* the character; the two have no independent existence, but live and die together. Fallace and Sordido, in soliloquy, remain more than ever caught in the grip of their obsessions. But Morose is capable of discarding some of his verbal shamming and speaking from a deeper level of himself — almost from an infantile level, to judge from his reversion to the neuter genitive "it" — under the pressure of strong feeling. The discovery of this deeper level turns the outer layer of stylistic affectation into a kind of vocal disguise, but in the case of Morose, at least, it is a disguise over which he has little control. If Truewit (and Epicene) can vary their accents so as to dissemble their "real" voices, Morose is very much at the mercy of his own disguise.

For the moment, the disguise cracks because Morose is alone and caught up in an exultation of gratified revenge. But the disguise has begun to slip in public, too, and well before the play ends it has been cast aside entirely. The Morose wedded and assaulted by noise and hounded up into the eaves of his own house, muffled in nightcaps, is a very different creature, linguistically, from the Morose who courts Epicene in the stillness of a triple-walled chamber. Inklings of his later manner occur almost from the beginning, from the moment when he protests against Truewit's strong-arm entry into the house, in a barrage of furious short questions that succeed each other in ascending order of vehemence.

Good sir! haue I euer cosen'd any friends of yours of their land? bought their possessions? taken forfeit of their morgage? begg'd a reuersion from 'hem? bastarded their issue? what haue I done, that may deserue this? (II.ii.43–47)

Speeches that follow display similar turmoil. Although the inkhorn vocabulary, for the moment, waxes even more outlandish than usual, suggestive of the continuing element of exhibitionism, syntactic artifice reduces itself almost wholly to strings of series. Goaded finally beyond endurance, Morose breaks out into the lamentation in duplicate that hereafter becomes his capital way of expressing misery: "O, what is my sinne! what is my sinne?" (II.ii.90). Throughout his long day of affliction, whenever he groans, he groans twice: "O, my torment, my torment!" (III.v.53), "O, 'tis decreed, 'tis decreed of mee" (III.vi.15–16), "Complement! Complement!" (III.vi. 27), "O, a plot, a plot, a plot, a plot vpon me!" (III.vii.3), "O, redeeme me, fate, redeeme me, fate" (IV.iv.145), "O no, it was too voluntarie, mine: too voluntarie" (V.iii.145). There is irony in the fact that Morose, pathologically sensitive to the smallest repetitions in the speech of others, should himself sin through constant repetition. Epicene's concise question, "How doe you, sir?" is answered with a furious series of exclamations that insist that the question was unnecessary: "Did you euer heare a more vnnecessary question? as if she did not see! Why, I doe as you see, Empresse, Empresse"; Epicene's further interrogation, "You are not well, sir! you looke very ill! something has distempered you" draws from Morose an enraged redundancy against the redundancy of the questioner: "O horrible, monstrous impertinencies! would not one of these haue seru'd? doe you thinke, sir? would not one of these haue seru'd?" (IV.iv.30–38).

The disintegration of Morose's nicely wrought antitheses into these bleats of despair is accompanied by a rise in metaphoric temperature. Except for the posies of gallantry offered to Epicene in the trial scene, Morose, in moments of calm, does not cultivate figurative speech. But his self-possession is precarious from the start. A single off-stage blast of Truewit's trumpet goads him to fury: "How now? oh! oh! what villaine? what prodigie of mankind is that? looke." A second blast unleashes homicidal impulses: "Oh! cut his throat, cut his throat: what murderer, hell-hound, deuill can this be?" Finally, the timid reply of the servant, "It is a post from the court — " provokes an enraged pun, "Out rogue, and must thou blow thy horne, too?" (II.i.38–43).

The pattern merely amplifies itself when the torments have started in earnest. The language of compliment crumbles away, and to replace it Morose dips into a seemingly inexhaustible well of vituperative epithets and similitudes of suffering. His tormentors become "Villaines, murderers, sonnes of the earth, and traitors" (IV.ii.70–71), "Rogues, Hellhounds, *Stentors*" (IV.ii.124); Epicene is "a PENTHESILEA, a SEMIRAMIS" (III.iv.56–57), Mrs. Otter "that *Gorgon*, that *Medusa*" (III.vii.21). The wedding guests resemble "another floud! an inundation!" (III.vi.2–3); the music sounds "worse then the noyse of a saw"; and for himself, he is "their anvile to worke on," whom they will "grate" asunder with their noise (III.vii.4–5).

The language of most sustained imaginative force — though not, strictly speaking, metaphoric — coincides with the moment of greatest emotional upheaval, when Morose, stunned by the treachery of his henchman Cutbeard, joins Truewit in cursing him in a litany of retributive torments that grows steadily more sadistic. The syntax builds on simple anaphoral series; occasional antithetic or chiastic details have a savage chop to them that suggests desperation rather than complacency. Blunt, crushing monosyllables of native origin replace the involute Latinisms, and vulgarisms like "itch" and "lousy" replace the scented terms of compliment.

No, let the wretch liue wretched. May he get the itch, and his shop so lousie, as no man dare come at him, nor he come at no man.   (III.v.74–76)

His chaires be alwaies empty, his scissors rust, and his combes mould in their cases.   (83–84)

Let there be no baud carted that yeare, to employ a bason of his: but let him be glad to eate his sponge, for bread.   (87–89)

May all the botches, and burnes, that he has cur'd on others, breake out vpon him.   (97–98)

Sounds play a cardinal role here. The hard consonants of

"wretch," "itch" and "botches"; "combes," "come," "cases," "cur'd," "carted"; "baud," "bread," "bason," are spat out with a tooth-breaking violence that is all Morose retains of his earlier verbal mastery. The extent to which his language now registers the collapse of his virtuoso elegance may be measured by comparing these curses with his earlier utterances: "As I conceiue, CVTBERD, this gentle-woman is shee, you haue prouided, in hope shee will fit me in the place and person of a wife."

The invasion of Morose's privacy, in short, has put an end to his linguistic preening as forcibly as it has shattered his cork-lined chamber. For the first time, he is actually communicating with those around him, in a language not so much curiously spun by him as wrung from him. The events of the action have humanized him by forcing him into situations where the complacent, bookish attitudes implied by his earlier style of expression will no longer serve. And with the abandonment of his affected language goes a good deal of his moral culpability. Morose, initially repugnant, comes to command a kind of furtive sympathy from us, and the Jonsonian atonement suggested by his reformed speech makes the final scene, with its harsh dismissal of him, taste more bitter than Jonson evidently meant it to.

3

Around the linguistic blocks formed by the big set pieces of Morose and Truewit, the language of the rest polarizes itself. The polite social level and the intimacy among the members of the group lend a certain homogeneousness of style to all the speakers. Clerimont, Dauphine, and a Lylian lapwing of a page employ a quasi-balanced idiom akin to that of Truewit in his quiet moments, while the carefully rubbed speech of the collegians differs chiefly in its lack of irony and its heavier freight of "compliment." One can imagine the delight with which the Blackfriars audience listened while the Children of the Revels prattled, in a style too sophisticated for them, about matters beyond their understanding. Even more than *Cynthia's Revels*, also written for the children's troupe, *Epicene* is shot through with sexual *double-entendre* and deliberate exploitation of varying mixtures of masculinity and femininity. Most of the language falls into the kind of patter that would lend itself to the voices of precocious children. But, in contrast to *Cynthia's Revels*, the prevailing harmony of style does not grow wearisome, for one thing because it is in itself freer and suppler, and for another because against it are counterpointed the comic cacophonies of Daw, La Fool, and the Otters. These four make successive appearances at strategic moments, and, somewhat like operatic characters, each follows his entrance with a major aria after which he subsides back into the cast as a member of the ensemble. Otter's big scene is deferred until Act IV, because on his first entrance, Mrs. Otter does all the talking.

Sir Amorous La Fool enters after some idle conversation between Truewit, Clerimont, Dauphine, and the page. Clerimont has furnished us with a thumbnail portrait of the knight, and vowed to make him tell the rest "his pedegree, now; and what meat he has to dinner; and, who are his guests; and, the whole course of his fortunes: with a breath" (I.iii.53–56). Needless to say, the promise proves a prophecy. No sooner has the discussion touched on Sir Amorous' family than he uncorks his breathless recital, in which pedigree and dinner plans are mingled with a superb disregard for relevance.

They all come out of our house, the LA-FOOLES o' the north, the LA-FOOLES of the west, the LA-FOOLES of the east, and south — we are as ancient a family, as any is in *Europe* — but I my selfe am descended lineally of the *french* LA-FOOLES — and, wee doe beare

for our coate *Yellow*, or *Or*, checker'd *Azure*, and *Gules*, and
some three or foure colours more, which is a very noted coate,
and has, some-times, beene solemnely worne by diuers nobilitie of
our house — but let that goe, antiquitie is not respected now —

(I.iv.37–46)

By punctuating the entire long speech with dashes and commas, Jonson manages to suggest the continuousness of the
knight's discourse, like a strip of tape forever unrolling, where
no divisions are marked, and cadences are lacking even when
the grammatical logic would allow them. Between the main
sections, where a dash indicates a self-interruption and a sudden plunging off into a new direction, Sir Amorous piles up
details in series, with or without "and's," in such a way as to
suggest the tongue rattling on automatically, almost without
the cooperation of the brain. The rehearsal of the pedigree
allows Jonson to score his familiar point concerning the omni-
presence of folly (east and south, north and west), its antiquity ("as ancient a family, as any is in *Europe*"), and to intimate, by conferring heraldic honors on it,[18] how often it has
been mistaken for wisdom and revered accordingly. At the
same time, the litter of detail reveals the magpie mind that must
say everything about everything. La Fool not only recapitu-
lates his lineage, but the colors of his coat, and adds his opinion
on that. He enumerates all the game he will serve at his feast,
all the guests he will invite, all the merriment he hopes to
promote, and concludes with a survey of his own madcap
youth. Unlike a good many passages already discussed, this
one does not depend for its comic force on the piquancy of the
details themselves, which matter little. What matters is the
patchwork way they are sewn together to form the substance
— such as it is — of Sir Amorous' discourse, their value con-
sisting for Sir Amorous in their sheer exhaustiveness, in the
catharsis they afford him, and for his friends, in the ease with

which the shallow bucket of his mind can be overturned and its contents emptied out at one stroke.

A little while later, the mind of Sir John Daw, the archfool of the play, is emptied with equal ease of its stupid verses and its collection of authors' names. The speech rhythms in this case acquire some of their childish petulance from being based on the model of the curt period: short, disconnected members, of irregular formation, drumming along and stopping.

> The *dor* on PLVTARCH, and SENECA, I hate it: they are mine owne imaginations, by that light. I wonder those fellowes haue such credit with gentlemen! (II.iii.45–47)

> Graue asses! meere *Essaists!* a few loose sentences, and that's all. A man would talke so, his whole age, I doe vtter as good things euery houre, if they were collected, and obseru'd, as either of 'hem. (49–52)

As Daw warms up, he drops names more freely, till at length he unbuckles his whole "sacke full" and spills it out in a heap. This done, and his *"madrigall* of procreation" (II.iii.138) to Epicene recited, he, like La Fool, has exhausted the small contents of his no mind, and both now subside into the ensemble to await the more devastating exposure of the mock duel and the slander scenes of the last acts. The careful arrangement is worth noting: Jonson shows first their verbal inadequacies, their pretentiousness of speech, and then develops the more specifically moral indictments of slander and cowardice. One obvious indication that these two belong to an older generation of Jonsonian types is that they command no language beyond the one that registers their folly; they are Johnny One Notes, incapable of inflection or change until silenced at the end.

Act III introduces us to Captain Otter and his terrible lady, and provides the latter with an extended exercise in objurgation. In Fallace, of *Every Man out of his Humour*, and Chloe, in *Poetaster*, Jonson had already dramatized the termagant wife mated to a servile husband. Mrs. Otter, like Fallace and Chloe, nurses rather crude social ambitions, the chief obstacle to the consummation of which she imagines to be her husband's lack of breeding. Her tyranny over the captain is aggravated by the fact that she has brought him a large dowry and so rescued him from poverty. By putting him on an allowance she ensures his obedience, and gives herself license to bully him.

The verbal idiom has already been worked out for Fallace and, especially, Chloe. It consists chiefly of a series of scolding rhetorical questions, often heavily tinged with sarcasm. Chloe demands to know what Albius is thinking of, to act like master in his own house.

> In sinceritie, did you euer heare a man talke so idlely? You would seeme to be master? You would haue your spoke in my cart? you would aduise me to entertaine ladies, and gentlemen? because you can marshall your pack-needles, horse-combes, hobby-horses, and wall-candle-stickes in your ware-house better then I; therefore you can tell how to entertaine ladies, and gentle-folkes better then I? (*Poet.* II.i.46–53)

On the other hand, when she finds herself among her social superiors, Chloe works hard to eliminate from her speech such citified expletives as "in sinceritie" and to replace them with what she fancies to be courtly phrases. The result, of course, is a hodgepodge of vulgarism and pseudo elegance.

The same traits reappear in the language of Mrs. Otter. Again there is the insistent rhetorical question, the ear-bruising reprehension on the score of ingratitude:

> Is this according to the instrument, when I married you? That I would bee Princesse, and raigne in mine owne house: and you would be my subiect, and obay me? What did you bring me, should make you thus peremptory? Do I allow you your halfe-

crowne a day, to spend, where you will, among your gamsters, to vexe and torment me, at such times as these? Who giues you your maintenance, I pray you? who allowes you your horse-meat, and mans-meat? your three sutes of apparell a yeere? your foure paire of stockings, one silke, three worsted? your cleane linnen, your bands, and cuffes when I can get you to weare 'hem? 'Tis mar'l you ha' 'hem on now.   (III.i.32–44)

The situation becomes progressively more comic as Mrs. Otter descends, in her enumeration of benefits, from the daily allowance to the two kinds of meat to the number of suits, pairs of stockings, and kinds of stockings per year. As her voice grows shriller, the benefits she is holding up for gratitude grow one by one more ludicrously petty, until the final item turns out to be a benefit that Otter has had thrust upon him in order to preserve the dignity of the rank to which his wife aspires. The barrage of accusations collapses into absurdity as soon as it becomes plain that Mrs. Otter simply uses her captain as he uses her: unable to find a husband except by buying one, she has converted her purchase into a household fixture designed to help consolidate her social position. Even Mrs. Otter, it may be noticed, speaks in balanced phrases and clauses: "Princesse" and "subiect" submit to antithetic expansion; the meat splits into "horse-meat" and "mans-meat" — suggesting the kind of status Otter occupies in his wife's household — while the four pairs of stockings break down into "one silke, three worsted."

After this lesson in home economics follows the inevitable claim that the marriage has been socially profitable for him. Just as Chloe's mind runs continually, and fretfully, on the vulgar mercantile trade her husband is engaged in, so Mrs. Otter cannot forget that the Captain's career originated in the bear-garden. And the fury with which each recalls the uncourtly antecedents of her spouse is matched only by the languishing mellifluousness with which she addresses herself to the visiting gentry.

The effectiveness of this simple device, the series of irate questions, to characterize the shrewish wife may be judged not only by Jonson's successes with it but by the echoes of it that still haunt the drama a century later. In Lady Pliant, Congreve recreates the Jonsonian termagant, and when he wishes her to fly into a rage at her uxorious husband, he merely unleashes the stream of rasping questions.

Gads my Life, the Man's distracted, why how now, who are you? What am I? Slidikins can't I govern you? What did I marry you for? Am I not to be absolute and uncontrolable? Is it fit a Woman of my Spirit, and Conduct, should be contradicted in a Matter of this Concern? [19]   (*The Double-Dealer*, II.iv.23–28)

Even the addiction to shopkeepers' oaths remains unchanged, Lady Pliant merely exchanging for Mrs. Otter's "By that light" and "By my integrity" her own more up-to-date expletives "Gads my Life" and "Slidikins."

Otter himself figures only passively in the scene in Act III, confining himself to a few feeble gestures of protest and conciliation. Truewit, however, has forewarned us that Otter grows defiant as soon as his wife is away, and that then "No Anabaptist euer rail'd with the like licence." In the following act, we hear a specimen of his railing. Otter's range of conversation is limited to two subjects: his drinking mugs and his wife. In defense of the former, his bull, bear, and horse, he marshalls classical precedent and quotes Latin phrases. In attacking the latter, he reduces her, too, to the level of an animal: "Wiues are nasty sluttish *animalls*" (IV.ii.56), "A wife is a sciruy *clogdogdo;* an vnlucky thing, a very foresaid beare-whelpe, without any good fashion or breeding: *mala bestia*" (IV.ii.74–76). It is charming to hear Otter complain that his wife lacks "fashion" and "breeding." When he comes to dissect her appearance, he provides the antidote to Truewit's praise of face-painting. Truewit had likened a well-dressed woman to a delicate garden; Otter finds all the most degradingly commercial equivalents for the details of his wife's toilet. Her peruke is "like a pound of hempe, made vp in shoothrids"; she spends "fortie pound a yeere in *mercury*, and hogs-bones" for her facial ointments; "Euery part o' the towne ownes a peece of her," whether it be her black teeth, stringy eyebrows, or grey hair, and after she has disassembled herself at night into some twenty boxes, she must be put back together again the next day "like a great *Germane* clocke" (IV. ii.88–99). For the most part, Otter's syntax, like his diction, is plain and without varnish. Whatever his defects, he does not suffer to any noticeable degree from wantonness of language. As a result, being free from affectation, he is also exempt from any dramatic reversal more important than a beating from Mrs. Otter, and can be used by Truewit in the final scene as a member of the panel that "tries" Morose's matrimonial case.

It might be added that Otter's Latin, like Cutbeard's, has the air of having been deliberately planted so as to make him available for the last scene, where he masquerades as a canon lawyer. There is a certain piquancy in hearing an ex-bearward and a barber rattle off scraps of Latin, but in neither case does it signify much or bear very meaningfully on the rest of their behavior. And one trouble with the final scene itself is the opaqueness of the verbal disguise of these two. They virtually cease to be Otter and Cutbeard, and become merely a pair of dummies wired for sound, grinding out legal jargon at ear-splitting volume, exchanging no recognition with each other or with the rest and displaying no gleams of their former selves. And this erasure of their personality, while it lightens Truewit's task, robs the scene of the kind of richness that Jonson achieves when disguised characters like Brainworm or

Volpone play themselves at the same time that they are posing as begging soldiers or traveling charlatans.

4

Instead of continuing to pursue linguistic details, we may conclude by glancing at some of the major themes of the play as they unfold in all of the language, especially in the opening scene. The opening scene itself breaks down into three or four cleanly defined blocks of conversation between the young men, characteristically not meshed together by causal logic or narrative necessity, but simply juxtaposed, as the members of the curt period are juxtaposed. One topic of conversation does not "lead into" or "grow out of" another, but twice in the course of the scene Truewit brusquely changes the subject, producing the kind of shift of stance that occurs from one member to the next of a curt period. There is evidently an asyndetic manner of composing a dramatic sequence, as there is an asyndetic manner of forming a single period, and the chunks of talk that enter into the former display the kind of thematic "hovering" characteristic of the latter. In both cases, connections remain implicit, oblique, and must be sought by the listener. And as, in the last analysis, the more casual, lifelike pausing and lurching of the *stile coupé* will demand greater attentiveness than the strict parallels of a logical style, so too will the lurches and pauses of the *scène coupé*.

Clerimont has been learning some of the mysteries of Lady Haughty's closet from the page when Truewit enters to deliver, half seriously and half mockingly, the reflections on time in which he reminds Clerimont that his fashionable pursuits do not really satisfy him but merely dull him to reality. But when Clerimont inquires, "what should a man doe?" Truewit declines to implement his academic strictures with practical therapy. He offers instead the kind of advice that Clerimont will listen to: "Why, nothing: or that, which when 'tis done, is as idle. Harken after the next horse-race, or hunting-match; lay wagers, praise *Puppy*, or *Pepper-corne*," continuing with an itemized list of the polite follies of gentlemen — betting, visiting, ostentatious spending — and concluding, ambiguously, "These be the things, wherein your fashionable men exercise themselues, and I for companie" (I.i.33–41). The tone of this last remark suggests that although Truewit is in the world of fashion, he is not of it. The recital of worldly diversions represents a good-natured descent from high Stoicism to an acceptance of things as they are, and the descent is made more decisively a moment later, when Truewit, having actually quoted Seneca and been rebuked by Clerimont for his tedious "*Stoicitie*," abandons his warnings and drops the whole subject: "Well, sir. If it will not take, I haue learn'd to loose as little of my kindnesse, as I can. I'le doe good to no man against his will, certainely. When were you at the colledge?" (I.i.67–69).

This interchange, since it leads nowhere in terms of action, must be read thematically. (Achard, of course, suppresses it outright in his version.) Its obvious purpose is to set the tone of the play, and to establish the position of Truewit toward subsequent events, a position to some extent purposely ambiguous. Truewit's advice to Clerimont to pursue the fashionable follies of his class contains evident irony, but how mild and stingless the irony is we may judge by comparing it with the acrid blasts vented elsewhere by Jonson against gentlemen who shun edification in favor of amusement. Audiences, he complains in the *Discoveries*, enjoy a scurrilous play immoderately,

. . . whereas, if it had savour'd of equity, truth, perspicuity, and Candor, to have tasten a wise or a learned Palate, spit it out pres-

ently; this is bitter and profitable, this instructs, and would informe us: what neede wee know any thing, that are nobly borne,
more then a Horse-race, or a hunting-match, our day to breake
with Citizens, and such innate mysteries? [20]   (*Disc.* 2669–75)

We may even better assess the difference in tone between
this and Truewit's playfully ironic advice when we consider
that Clerimont, after all, typifies precisely the indolent gallant
against whom Jonson is fulminating in the quoted extract.
Instead of being held up to scorn, Clerimont is condescended
to by the satiric expositor, and becomes, in his own right, one
of the instruments of exposure of the gulls, while the expositor Truewit, having canvassed the philosophical realities
of the situation, climbs down from his high horse and joins
Clerimont on his own level.

   Truewit's descent has its counterpart in the descent of Jonson himself. One might say that Jonson, having tried, in a
series of increasingly bitter and powerful plays culminating
with *Volpone*, to educate his audience, to "instruct" and
"informe" it, has decided this time to lose as little of his kind-
ness as he can, to do good to no man against his will, to relax
his moral stringency and accept the limitations of the society
in which he finds himself. Both prologues accept the necessity
to entertain:

> Our wishes, like to those (make publique feasts)
> Are not to please the cookes tastes, but the guests.
>   (*Prologue* 8–9)

> The ends of all, who for the *Scene* doe write,
> Are, or should be, to profit, and delight.   (*Another* 1–2)

For the first time Jonson explicitly subordinates the "utile"
to the "dulce" of the Horatian duo. In the first prologue, indeed, he goes out of his way to dissociate himself from a
"sect" of writers who scorn popular approval and cater to a

fastidious minority. Evidently if *Epicene* is to be "bitter and profitable," it is to be so only in the sense in which Nashe commended plays: "they are sower pils of reprehension, wrapt vp in sweete words." [21]

Truewit, then, like Jonson, speaks from a higher altitude of perception than his friends, but is willing to descend to their level and even to become a spokesman for their world. The descent, however, in both cases remains tentative. Jonson is still engrossed with the scourging of folly; Truewit still acts as the satiric expositor, maneuvering Daw, La Fool, and the collegiates into situations that will reveal their shallowness, and formally sentencing them to derision. It is not until *The Alchemist* that Jonson can dispense with an expositor, and not until *Bartholomew Fair* that, in a last reversal, both expositor and justicer can be actively ridiculed themselves and so brought within the circle of fools. In *Epicene*, the exhibitor keeps his distance from his exhibits. Truewit stalks folly purely for the pleasure of the chase, staking nothing but his wit. On the verbal level, the elusive skepticism of his remarks, his refusal to take an unequivocal position, his way of playing both ends against the middle, suggest a suspension of strong conviction on the part of Jonson himself. It is not for nothing that Truewit deals so lavishly in hypotheses: the play itself is a hypothesis struggling to become, and never quite becoming, a thesis. Truewit, who sees the vanities of life as plainly as Morose, differs from Morose in that instead of recoiling furiously from them, he accepts them as a game that men are doomed to play. And if Jonson packed his darker misanthropy into the figure of Morose, he made of Truewit an ideal of equivocal detachment, equally unable to commit himself wholeheartedly to the world and to let it alone.

Looked at another way, Truewit's moralizing on time merely restates, in terms appropriate to polite society, the Renaissance dread of mutability. Heedlessness of time, "our common disease," has its roots in the fact that time is "an incorporeall thing" and "not subiect to sense" (I.i.51–57). But by dropping the subject so casually, Truewit acknowledges that if men cannot escape the pressure of the incorporeal, still less can they ignore the corporeal, the things of sense of which lives are composed. And this admission of the claim of sensible things constitutes Jonson's first major concession to them also, as the fate of Morose will demonstrate. It is less hurtful to immerse oneself in the here and now of the senses (Clerimont) than to attempt a retreat from them (Morose). The ideal is an attitude at once submissive, sympathetic, and skeptical (Truewit).

The transition from Truewit's desultory stoicizing to the gossip about the college may seem haphazard, but the two subjects are thematically related. The collegians share a preoccupation with the passage of time that will consume their youth. They are as conscious as Truewit of the ticking of the clock, but they draw Clerimont's moral, that youth is meant for indulgence, and old age for fasting and praying. Their efforts to arrest time may seem as vain and pointless as Clerimont's refusal to concern himself with it, yet they win the endorsement of Truewit himself. Paradoxically, it is Clerimont, the slave of fashion, who inveighs against the cosmetic practices of ladies, and Truewit, the satirist of fashion, who defends them. Clerimont, an inhabitant of the world of affairs and a suitor to Lady Haughty, upholds the sentimental notion that unadorned simplicity surpasses artful beauty, while Truewit, with one eye on a higher standard, and uninvolved with the collegians, takes the hardheaded Ovidian view that expert grooming improves any woman, beauty being nature to advantage dressed. Truewit, that is, expounds the assumptions by which Clerimont's world actually lives, while Clerimont clings to the older, more familiar Jonsonian distrust of decorated surfaces. Jonson, for his part, by setting up such a paradoxical crisscross of attitudes, indicates an awareness both more complex and more unstable than that of the sharp dualities that reigned in the early plays. If the ethical rage of the comical satires has by no means wholly subsided, it has begun to be sophisticated, at least, with a keener appreciation of the pull of solid things, of the value, in and for itself, of physical attractiveness, even if this no longer serves as an index to moral excellence. That a playwright, even an ethical traditionalist like Jonson, suspicious of appearances, should come to attach a certain value to artful surfaces, is scarcely surprising, nor that he should associate such surfaces, tentatively at least, with his own art and its proverbial need to externalize. The Elizabethan drama, with its What You Will's and As You Like It's, its pomps and masquerades, did not need a Pirandello to discover the paradoxical identity between reality and appearance.

In the present case, Clerimont's lazy pursuit of fashion leads to an equally facile espousal of an inconsistent ideal, that of simplicity, of "life" in preference to "art." Because he has no real moral standards at all, Clerimont reaches for the nearest platitude and pins it in his buttonhole. Truewit, by contrast, capable of seeing the things of sense in wider perspective, can value them for what they are. His disenchanted view of life ends not in hardness or cynicism, but in a sharper appreciation of the possibilities of life. It is Clerimont who frequents the college, and Dauphine who falls fatuously in love with all the collegians, but it is Truewit who can state with finality the case for artifice over naturalness in one moment, and in the next expose the collegians for the frauds they are. Clerimont, who sentimentalizes over simplicity, and Dauphine, the bashful lover, may heartlessly propose to lop off Sir John Daw's left arm as a prank, but it is the unsentimental Truewit who reacts with humane horror to the suggestion: "How! Maime a man for euer, for a iest? what a conscience hast thou?" (IV.v.135–136).

Lady Haughty, according to Truewit, is a "graue, and youthfull matron," but Clerimont is struck by her "autumnall face" (I.i.83–85). Though time itself may be incorporeal, its effects are evident enough, in man and nature. A recent critic has pointed out the frequence in *Epicene* of metaphors drawn from nature; [22] most of these concern the rotation of the seasons and the withering of the year, and the equivalent processes in human life. The passage of time, in *Epicene*, seems to lead inexorably into the final stage of the seasonal cycle, the cold, dead heart of winter, with its attendant barrenness and loneliness, and all the scattered associations in the language that imply this drift into death are gathered up and concentrated in the person of Morose. [23]

Appropriately enough, then, when Truewit, having canvassed first the ruins of time and then the repairs of art, changes the subject once again, he introduces the third chief theme of the play, the torments of Morose. Again the conversation seems to bolt from one topic to a wholly unrelated one, as though by chance. But again the new topic discloses multiple thematic relations with its predecessors. If in Clerimont we see the young gallant, oblivious of the pressure of time, throwing himself too mindlessly into the traffic of life, and in the collegians ladies haunted by the fear of age and trying vainly to arrest the world, in Morose we find old age, sterile and solitary, spurning life with such fury that it retaliates by breaking the dike he has built against it and inundating him in its flood. Morose complains that the usual polite phrases of society are a way to "weare out time . . . vnfruitfully" (V.iii. 26), but no one has worn it out more unfruitfully than he, in the solitude of his triple-walled chamber. His attempts to redeem it by a belated marriage, undertaken in spite, end only in frustration and continued sterility. The silence with which he attempts to shield himself from the world ends by becoming — as critics have seen — a symbol of impotence.

The impotence extends beyond Morose himself to the atmosphere of the entire play, in which natural functions are repeatedly frustrated, or referred to as frustrated. The collegiate ladies with their contraceptive remedies, La Fool's painful sojourn in a closet with a full bladder and no chamber pot, the emblematic forfeiture of potency on the part of both the doltish knights in the mock duel, the feast that is no feast and the marriage that is no marriage, leading up to the final scene with its climax of annulment, all create an ambiance of sterility and impotence, at the center of which stands the epicene figure of the title page, a person both less than a man and less than a woman, whose exposure in the final moments amounts to little less than the exposure of the impotence of everyone else in the play.[24]

The talk about the collegiates, by likening human life to the seasons, has prepared us, so to speak, for the arrival of winter. The ensuing conversation, on Morose, goes a step further by identifying living people with cold inorganic substances. The lady dressing herself in her closet has already been compared to city statues made of "rude stone" (I.i.124), subsequently painted and burnished, and she evidently shares some of the stony quality of the statue she resembles. Jonson now expands Libanius' mention of silversmiths and ironworkers to include braziers, armorers, a pewterer's apprentice, and virtuosi on various brass instruments, and, like the broom men, who "stand out stiffely" (I.i.153), each of these tradesmen seems to acquire some of the hardness and imperviousness of the metal he works with. Morose, above all, is thought of as something hard, unyielding, and inorganic, and the cause of these qualities in others. Merely listening to tales of this "stiffe peece of formalitie," Truewit declares himself "strooke into stone" with wonder, but after he has visited him, the case is altered.

I had no other way to get in, but by faining to be a post; but when I got in once, I prou'd none, but rather the contrary, turn'd him into a post, or a stone, or what is stiffer, with thundring into him the incommodities of a wife, and the miseries of marriage. If euer GORGON were seene in the shape of a woman, hee hath seene her in my description. (II.iv.11–17)

Morose thus turns others to stone, or can be so turned himself; he intimates as much when warned of the approach of Mrs. Otter: "Is that *Gorgon*, that *Medusa* come? Hide me, hide me" (III.vii.21–22); a moment earlier, he has thought of himself as an "anvile" whom the raucous guests will grate asunder with their noise (III.vii.4–5).

The persistence with which living creatures are identified with blocks of stone and metallic artifacts corresponds to a certain frigidity at the heart of the play. Morose's silence is linked not only with death, but with that which has never lived at all, a mere frozen replica of life. The stiffness of texture of his language is not deceptive: it is a kind of linguistic *rigor mortis*. The "contagion by the senses" [25] that prevails in the streets is counterbalanced by the sepulchral coldness in Morose's chamber. The chatter about feasting leads to a wedding banquet that is primarily a torment; various aimless sexual impulses on the part of some of the characters appear mainly as hypotheses. Daw's madrigal of procreation and Truewit's advice to Morose on the proper awe for the marriage bed both refer to a realm of contingency that proves at length to be a realm of impossibility, since the object in each case is Epicene. More characteristic in tone is Dauphine's complaint that Truewit's meddling has "blasted in a minute" all

that he has been plotting and "maturing," and that his hopes
are "vtterly miscarried" as a result of the other's officious interference (II.iv.37–46).

As it happens, of course, Dauphine's talk of abortion proves
premature. It is Morose whose plans ultimately miscarry. And
long before he has appeared on the stage, Morose has been introduced verbally in the posture of frustration.

This youth practis'd on him, one night, like the Bell-man; and
neuer left till hee had brought him downe to the doore, with a
long-sword: and there left him flourishing with the aire.
$$(\text{I.i.163–166})$$

It is in such attitudes, "flourishing with the aire," that Morose
will appear throughout, quixotically bidding the world remove itself from his doorstep, and finding the world dissolve
into "aire" — words — at which he can only flail helplessly.
From this point on, the emphasis on torment is almost continuous. "Torment," "plague," "vexation," "affliction," "pur-
gatorie," "martyr," "suffer"; the vocabulary of pain, with all
its varieties and changes, becomes a "perpetuitie of ringing"
(I.i.183–184) in the language of the victim and his captors.

Noise, of course, is for Morose the primary torment. And
his horror of it implies a horror of all strong sensory experience, and thus, by extension, of all human engagement.
If silence in this play stands for impotence and death, then
noise becomes the emblem of life, the inescapable ingredient
of which normal existence is composed. In itself, it is made
neither comforting nor attractive. The strident clatter of the
collegiates and the empty word-spinning of the two knights
have little enough to recommend them. But, like the plague
that rages in the city, they are symptoms of a *common* disease,
against which no prophylaxis is possible.

Morose, symbolically isolating himself from his kind, hence

displays a pathology more desperate than the plague he is fleeing. A later avatar of such contemners of the world as Asper and Crites, he differs from them in having no world of transcendent virtue and timeless truth into which to retreat, and in the fact that his satirical rages are shown up, finally, as perverse modes of selfishness. Morose's only escape is into the unfruitful miseries of solitude. The moral of the noisy retribution that overtakes him is that to try to insulate oneself from ordinary concerns — for whatever excellent philosophic reasons — is to ignore reality even more fatally than by plunging into its trivia. The only road past the world of flux leads through it. Satire is thus turned inside out, as the misogynist and misanthrope, the one who recognizes the futility of existence and can penetrate the painted disguises of ladies, becomes himself the victim of disguises and the object-lesson in futility. The world of folly triumphs, however ambiguously, over the world of higher wisdom. We are faced, thus, at the end of *The Silent Woman*, with a situation analogous to that at the close of *Gulliver's Travels*, when Gulliver, a satirist and misanthrope in his own right at last after his stay among the Houyhnhnms, ends by cutting a more ridiculous figure than any of the absurd fellow creatures he has learned to despise in the course of his voyages.

Unfortunately, the turn of the screw that enables Swift to turn his satire against himself serves Jonson less well in *Epicene*, which attempts, for the most part, to assert life values more positively, and to recommend folly, within limits, as the only wisdom. Sheer noise is, in itself, too much of a pleasure-pain mixture to symbolize the desirability of life, and in this play especially, it is too closely associated with suffering to fill such a role well. Most of the noise emanates from imbeciles whose only itch is to exhibit themselves. Dauphine, the nominal hero of the play, pushes his path through the obstacles raised by Morose in order to secure — not, as one might expect, the girl of his choice — but a steady income and an inheritance. The crassness of the motivation does not augur well for a brave new world, and Dauphine's heartless dismissal of the old man, after triumphing over him in such a question of mere commodity, stifles further any tendency to rejoice.[26] If Jonson did borrow the main device of his plot from Aretino's *Il marescalco*, as seems likely,[27] he intensified the sadism of it. The Marescalco, after all the perturbation he endures, ends by being delighted with his boy-bride, and by marching happily off to a feast with his erstwhile tormentors. But there is no reconciliation, no joining of hands, for Morose, only a return to the old miseries of hatred and solitude. Instead of release, for which the nature of the plot prepares us, the end brings constriction. Jonson's real praise of folly is still to come, in *Bartholomew Fair*.

Nevertheless, *Epicene* remains a huge achievement. In its grace, its verve, its hard-won realism, and its appeal to the coterie instincts of a social elite, it became almost a model for future English comedy. Dryden merely ratified the enthusiasm of his generation when he accorded it the place of honor among English comedies of the giant age.[28] Although, in keeping with the changing style of gentlemanliness, Dryden complained that Truewit's speeches smelled too strongly of the lamp, he did not hesitate to prefer Truewit to any other Jonsonian character.[29] And it is Truewit, clearly, and the courtly values for which he is made spokesman, that exerted the fascination on later playwrights. Truewit's descendants may be traced in the innumerable tribe of rakish young wits who conduct amorous intrigue between bouts of elegant conversation. And Truewit's speeches themselves, in their combined preciosity and negligence, their taste for paradox, and their cool appraisal of the facts of society, supply the model for the endless chatter about love and sex and female temperament that engrosses his descendants.

Morose, a more turbulent and unmanageable spirit, represented all the antisocial impulses most feared by Restoration society. The "blocking characters" [30] of later comedy depart less preposterously from approved behavior, pose a feebler threat to the hero's success, than does Morose with his passionately retrograde instincts. What we remember, in Restoration comedy, is the voice of the hero, languidly spinning witticisms on seduction in a "Senecan amble" adapted from Truewit. The occasional tantrums of an outraged mistress, a jealous husband, or a heavy uncle are lost in the chorus of self-congratulatory rejoicing that concludes the action. But Morose, playing the cavalier before his silent woman, or shivering with agony under the impact of "so much noise," fixes once and for all a state of frantic regression that mere defeat cannot dispel. His formal style, like the starched ruff or purfled sleeve it seems to suggest, or his cry of pain like that of the stricken elephant, remains in the ear like a nightmare voice which later generations ignored only at the cost of a loss in self-knowledge. [31]

V

Flesh and Blood

I T will perhaps be evident by now that if prose rhythm in Jonsonian comedy is attended by a certain degree of realism — using that term in a relative sense — it is also characteristically coupled to linguistic satire. Fallace, in *Every Man out of his Humour*, displays her vanity and ill temper on all occasions, but it is only when she speaks prose that her stupid expletives and her parroting of modish phrases — her linguistic vices, in short — betray the full extent of her vulgarity. The use of prose does not in and of itself signify linguistic viciousness, but where the chief stigma of folly is mimicry, as it is with most of the gulls in the early plays, prose is the normal vehicle. The return to verse in *Volpone*, hence, marks a momentary shift of Jonson's attention away from specifically linguistic caricature. Sir Politic Would-be differs from many of Jonson's previous fools in that while he sedulously apes Venetian customs, he does not, in his speech, mimic a language other than his own, nor does the texture of his speech in itself imply falsity. In the mountebank scene, he falls victim to a false rhetoric, but he is not the perpetrator of it. In *Epicene*, prose rhythm once again reasserts itself, transposing the high-strung Venetian fantasies back into a lower, minor key, and making fresh conquests of the deranged linguistic worlds of Morose, Daw, La Fool, and the Otters.

With *The Alchemist*,[1] the fantasies are again screwed up to an unnatural pitch, and this time they vibrate with all the strange resonances of an occult jargon. For the first time, in this play, verse becomes the basis for a full-scale linguistic anatomy. The cozening tongues of Face and Subtle drip with deceitful honey. The satire, however, as in the mountebank scene of *Volpone*, is directed less against those who practice the deceit than against those who are seduced by it. By its sheer virtuosity, the knavery of the tongue compels a certain respect, whereas the folly of the ear, the deafness that can filter out the hypocrisy and hear only the siren promises, earns contempt. As more than one critic has noticed, the philosophers' stone resembles Volpone's voluptuous daydreams in that both are impossible of attainment.[2] In both plays the object of the quest proves a vacuum; and a vacuum, being abhorred by nature, can be rendered only in a correspondingly fabulous surrealistic language. The radically illusory nature of the hopes nursed by rogues and fools alike — Dapper's dream of a familiar spirit to bring him luck at play, Drugger's scheme to ensure the success of his shop through necromancy, the power-visions of the silenced saints, the "perpetuitie / Of life, and lust" (*Alch.* IV.i.165–166) fantasied by Volpone and Sir Epicure Mammon — all require Jonson's most radically hyperbolic blank verse incantations.

I

With *Bartholomew Fair* [3] we return to a world where the objects of desire are once again familiar and available and concrete. Prose, of a realistic density uncommon even in Jonson, becomes once more the dominant rhythm. Satire on language takes new forms. Two of the dramatis personae are mimics, but of a rather special sort, different from those so far encountered. The rest abuse their mother tongue not by standing on tiptoe and pursing their lips so as to sound genteel, but by slouching about on bare horny feet and drawling out of the corner of their mouths with a reckless disregard for elementary grammatical accuracy. *Epicene* portrayed a closely woven social community with a shared style of speech, from which only slight deflections were needed to produce the sense of derangement. *Bartholomew Fair*, by contrast, cuts a deep cross section through almost the whole social hierarchy, and dissects out the fibers of weird jargon that compose its linguistic tissue. Instead of the tight little coterie of gentlemen, *Bartholomew Fair* collects onto the stage a loose aggregate of social types, ranging from two gentlemen through the various strata of the citizenry represented by a proctor and his wife, a Puritan elder, and a city magistrate, to the polyglot swarm of swindlers who inhabit the Fair and prey on its visitors. The largeness of the milieu, the expansiveness of the plot, its freedom of gesture, are all reflected in the prevailing irregularity of the language, just as the tightness of the milieu, the inhibited gesture, and the strict plot of *Epicene* are reflected in the comparative formality of the language of that play.

The presence of two gentlemen, Quarlous and Winwife, affords a useful point of departure, since we may compare their utterances with those of their social peers in *Epicene*. Quarlous — one can only judge by the company he keeps and the kinds of diversion he prefers — in gentility cannot quite rival Clerimont, who has just come from court when *Epicene* opens. Still, the social difference between the two is negligible, whereas the linguistic difference is enormous. If we look first at Clerimont's description of Sir Amorous La Fool, we notice that it breaks down into a series of manageable units.

Hee is one of the *Braueries*, though he be none o' the *Wits*. He will salute a Iudge vpon the bench, and a Bishop in the pulpit, a

Lawyer when hee is pleading at the barre, and a Lady when shee is dauncing in a masque, and put her out. He do's giue playes, and suppers, and inuites his guests to 'hem, aloud, out of his windore, as they ride by in coaches. He has a lodging in the *Strand* for the purpose. Or to watch when ladies are gone to the *China* houses, or the *Exchange*, that hee may meet 'hem by chance, and giue 'hem presents, some two or three hundred pounds-worth of toyes, to be laught at. He is neuer without a spare banquet, or sweet-meats in his chamber, for their women to alight at, and come vp to, for a bait. (I.iii.29–41)

Despite all of its freedom of detail, the speech observes a fairly regular pattern. Sir Amorous himself is the subject of every sentence, and in every case is represented as thrusting his attentions upon others. The repeated "he" acts as a rhetorical binder, linking the sequence firmly together, and the various victims of Sir Amorous' impertinence are ranged in a scale of descending social importance from the judge to the waiting women. The first two periods submit to antithetic elaboration; the rest acquire coherence from their steady focus upon a single scene, Sir Amorous' lodging in the Strand, from which and in which he performs a series of increasingly desperate and absurd social maneuvers. Interior doublets like "playes, and suppers," "the *China* houses, or the *Exchange*" contribute to the effect of rhythmic fullness that, as we have already seen, is characteristic of the prose of this play.

Quarlous' sketch of Zeal-of-the-Land Busy, by contrast, borders on anarchy. It is punctuated, after an initial brief statement, as one continuous period.

A notable hypocriticall vermine it is; I know him. One that stands vpon his face, more then his faith, at all times; Euer in seditious motion, and reprouing for vaine-glory: of a most *lunatique* conscience, and splene, and affects the violence of *Singularity* in all he do's: (He has vndone a Grocer here, in Newgate-market, that broke with him, trusted him with Currans, as errant a Zeale as he, that's by the way:) by his profession, hee will euer be i' the state of Innocence, though; and child-hood; derides all *Antiquity;* defies any other *Learning,* then *Inspiration;* and what discretion soeuer, yeeres should afford him, it is all preuented in his *Originall ignorance;* ha' not to doe with him: for hee is a fellow of a most arrogant, and inuincible dulnesse, I assure you; who is this? (I.iii.135–148)

The convulsive quality of the passage springs almost entirely from its syntactic licentiousness. Within the first few moments, Quarlous contrives to refer to Busy in four different ways: by the neuter pronoun "it" (belatedly affixed to its predicate nominative), the masculine "him," the impersonal "one," and finally by the absence of a pronoun. The parallel phrases commencing with "Euer in seditious motion" exhibit the most captious variety of structure, ending with a phrase that is not a phrase at all but a new clause treated as though it were a phrase, with its own subclause ("he do's") tucked away inside it. Quarlous, that is, is busily laying down side by side, as though they were perfectly matched, grammatical bricks of differing size, shape, and texture. And where the bricks chance to fit each other grammatically, they remain queerly assorted semantically — "conscience, and splene" — unlike the smoothly mated doublets of Clerimont, "banquet, or sweet-meats," "playes, and suppers."

The parenthesis, by which Quarlous interrupts himself to recall the misadventures of a grocer who trusted Busy with currants, dislocates the eccentric period even further, and it shares some of the spasmodic quality of the whole, since the appositional phrase "as errant a Zeale as he" floats far from its moorings, the grocer to whom it is grammatically tied. And when the period has recovered from this digression, it continues to proceed in the same freakish fashion, until it is dropped, with total casualness, with a "who is this?" as Wasp buzzes onto the stage.

The lumpy, grainy lava of Quarlous' style, in short, makes Clerimont's portrait of Sir Amorous look like a quartz crystal of precision. And the cool translucence of the latter accords well with the young gentleman whose chief activities consist in conversations with other young gentlemen, visits to ladies' boudoirs, and fashionable gaming, while it is no less appropriate that the hectic tangle of Quarlous' speech should serve to characterize the young gentleman who frequents low haunts like Smithfield, goes on drunken binges with citizens, gets into brawls, and disguises himself as a madman in order to snare a rich widow in marriage. The contrast between these two styles extends, by and large, to the plays in which they appear: urbane foolery in the one, self-forgetful excitement in the other.

We notice further, in the character-sketches just cited, that the pronoun "I," absent from Clerimont's speech, intrudes twice into that of Quarlous. The trifling detail hints at a differing degree of personal involvement, which further investigation confirms. If we compare Quarlous' comic diatribe against widows with Truewit's lectures out of Ovid, we discover the latter to be relatively impersonal in tone. Truewit, though by no means self-effacing, presents his counsel in the form of generalized wisdom. He stands aside from his subject and contemplates it sardonically. Quarlous, on the other hand, repeatedly thrusts himself and his private feelings into his admonitions. The frequent interpolation of the personal pronoun gives the invective against widows a strong personal slant: "I feare this family will turne you reformed too," "Well, I will forbeare, Sir," "I'll be sworne," "we shall ha' thee," "I would endure to heare fifteene Sermons aweeke for her," "I would een desire of Fate, I might dwell in a drumme" (I.iii.58–86). The effect is to emphasize the speaker's close engagement with those around him, his tendency to identify himself with his friend and his friend's affairs, with the *ad hoc* situation rather than with the abstract maxims that may be drawn from it. Truewit cares nothing about Lady Haughty, but a great deal about the philosophy of cosmetics. Quarlous cares nothing, one way or the other, about widows in general, but does not want to lose Winwife's companionship.

At the same time, Quarlous' rapid-fire style carries to one extreme the power of baroque rhetoric to suggest incipient rather than finished thought, the ideas seeming to leap and tumble at random from the tongue, scarcely half formed in the brain beforehand. Even when he sets up a sequence of parallel members, each dependent on the same verb ("thinke") and connected by "or," he varies the interior construction of them wildly.

Dost thou euer thinke to bring thine eares or stomack, to the patience of a drie *grace*, as long as thy Tablecloth? and droan'd out by thy sonne, here, (that might be thy father;) till all the meat o' thy board has forgot, it was that day i' the Kitchin? Or to brooke the noise made, in a question of *Predestination*, by the good labourers and painefull eaters, assembled together, put to 'hem by the Matron, your Spouse; who moderates with a cup of wine, euer and anone, and a Sentence out of *Knoxe* between? or the perpetuall spitting, before, and after a sober drawne *exhortation* of six houres, whose better part was the *hum-ha-hum?* Or to heare prayers groan'd out, ouer thy iron-chests, as if they were *charmes* to breake 'hem?   (I.iii.87–99)

Part of the curiously opaque quality of these lines stems from the restless changes in metaphor, the way figures are jammed together in stretto, so to speak, introduced without warning and then dropped without ceremony and then resumed without prior notice. On top of the colloquial and puzzling locution that "brings" ears or stomachs "to" the "patience" of something, we have a double auditory and digestive image compressed into the phrase "drie *grace*." The grace is dry because delivered in a harsh, rasping voice, so that it causes a drought in the ear; but since eating and drinking must be postponed till it is over, it causes a gastric drought as well. It is also intellectually barren, and hence an arid diet for the mind. But no sooner have we grasped this figure when in the next phrase the grace is likened to something wholly different, a tablecloth, and likened to it, moreover, in respect to its least obvious quality, its length, requiring us to make the leap from spatial length (the tablecloth) to temporal duration (the grace) in an instant, and then to forget it. Characteristically, Quarlous puts the next phrase, "droan'd out by thy sonne, here," in parallel relation to the previous phrase, "as long as thy Tablecloth," with which it has nothing in common except a common reference in "grace." The parenthesis alludes *en passant* to the relative ages of Winwife and Littlewit, and leads into a figure that animates the cooling meat on the board and imagines it as "forgetting" it was that day in the kitchen, while the grace drones on and on. The period that follows (if it is a new period) continues to fuse auditory and gastric images, "brooke the noise," for example, still keeping, at this date, its literal sense of "digest the noise." Throughout, in the rapid current of metaphor, the figures tend to pile up and swirl on top of each other, to mingle with half figurative or literal statement, and to be embroiled in the tightly twisted syntax so that we lose all sense of spatial location.

And these qualities of Quarlous' language — its heatedness and syntactic density — reflect the increasingly close identification of the satiric commentator with the world on which he comments, the increasing abandonment of his special position. Quarlous and Winwife retain something of the function of the expositor, since it is chiefly through their agency that the procession of fools who visit the Fair is effectively ridiculed. During the first act they keep up a sort of witty duologue with each other concerning the visitors in Little-wit's house. They go to the Fair in order to witness "excellent creeping sport," and they think of the misadventures of Cokes as a play in five acts with a prologue, to be acted for their amusement. Once at the Fair, however, they become more the victims than the manipulators of circumstances. Their role as bystanders melts rapidly, until, by the time the sun is high, they are dueling for the hand of Mistress Grace, en-listing the madman in their projects, using the professional services of the cutpurse Edgeworth, ending, in short, as two more human atoms tossed about in the flux of Smithfield. The final reckoning, at the comic tribunal of the puppet play, finds them with almost as much to answer for as the rascals of the Fair itself.

2

One symptom of the authentic geniality of *Bartholomew Fair*, compared to Jonson's earlier comedy, is its indulgent treatment of the citizen couple whose longing for roast pig provides the "motive-passion" [4] of the plot. Jonson's previous specimens of this type are satirized with a ferocity that makes it seem as though only the need to objectify his material kept him on this side nausea. The earlier husbands are either in-sanely jealous or slavishly uxorious; the wives are aggressive, lecherous, and spiteful. The Littlewits, surprisingly, live to-gether in an unctuous harmony symbolized by Mrs. Little-wit's pregnancy. Instead of comically exaggerated incompati-bility, they exhibit a gluey fondness for each other, and the satire is directed against the billing and cooing that goes on between them, the immodesty with which they wash their clean linen in public. Instead of panting after social distinc-tion, they bask in their bourgeois status. Win's desire to "haue a fine young father i' law, with a fether: that her mother might hood it, and chaine it" (I.ii.25–26) reflects no thirst for gentility, but merely the hope of becoming a somebody among the citizenry, like the 'prentice's fantasy of becoming Lord Mayor of London. When Littlewit wishes to find a suitable comparison for his wife's new gown, he likens it not to the apparel of courtier's mistresses, but to that of the players' wives.

One does not, therefore, detect in Littlewit's language the pseudo-elegant vocabulary or the mincing formulas of compliment by which the Chloes and the Mrs. Otters advertised their precarious courtliness. Instead, Littlewit and Win speak a cozy citizens' idiom, full of useless pleonasms and empty expletives and comfit-maker's oaths, and only here and there a word that might have found its way — unknown to them — from court to city. Littlewit's apparent addiction to "apprehend" amounts to little more than a minor fixation on the part of a simpleton who must husband the few big words in his word-hoard for fear of becoming inarticulate. The absence of sarcastic comment from Winwife or Quarlous suffices almost in itself to absolve him from the imputation of mimicry.

The true vice of Littlewit's speech is garrulity, and it has come to him from nature, not from art. He crams his sentences with senseless expletives, "la," "indeed," "tut," "fie," "forsooth," "I warrant you." He waters down his verbs with auxiliaries, so that they go limp and flaccid: "this Cap do's conuince" (I.i.19–20), "They doe apprehend, Sir" (I.iv.68), "I doe feele conceits comming vpon mee" (I.i.32), "hee do's dreame now, and see visions" (I.iii.119–120); and he has a particular fascination with the auxiliary "would," and its variant "would faine": "I would faine see thee pace, pretty *Win!*" (I.i.24–25), "*Win* would faine haue a fine young father i' law" (I.ii.25). His most obvious and certainly his most imbecile mannerism consists of the continual hopping up and down on his wife's name, almost as a mark of punctuation: "*Win,* Good morrow, *Win.* I, marry, *Win!* Now you looke finely indeed, *Win!*" (I.i.18–19). Quarlous, alert as expositor, picks up this bit of verbal silliness and mocks Littlewit by mimicking it: "before *Truth,* if you haue that fearefull quality, *Iohn,* to remember, when you are sober, *Iohn,* what you promise drunke, *Iohn;* I shall take heed of you, *Iohn*" (I.iii. 32–35) — a more effective means of ridicule, it might be added, than Jonson's usual practice of direct comment. The only other linguistic trait of Littlewit's worth mention is his obsession with his own wit, his determination to find "conceits," such as the pretty thought that Bartholomew Cokes has come to visit Bartholomew Fair on St. Bartholomew's Day, and his dreary magazine of puns on his wife's name.

Littlewit and Win represent Jonson's triumph in the difficult art of making pure vapidity interesting; their language shows a far severer application of realistic technique than that of the Punch and Judy couples of earlier plays. Nevertheless, even without considering their relation to the rest of the plot, one can see in their concentrated emptiness, so to speak, a fictive distillation, a heightened projection, of a whole cavernous underworld of aimless folly. The inanity of the one and the simpering coyness of the other reduce *homo stultus* to his most ineffectual, most nondescript, and most faceless.

3

With Zeal-of-the-Land Busy, on the other hand, we are back on the highroad of linguistic caricature, where every cobblestone, every pebble, shrieks affectation, and the whole gives off a lurid phosphorescence more like that of a Martian than an earthly landscape. Jonson had already essayed the portrait of the canting Puritan with brilliant success in Ananias, in *The Alchemist*. Some of Busy's clichés appear in germinal form in Ananias' speeches, but not in such quantity as to make their speaker grotesque or to prevent his verse from blending smoothly with that of the others at most points. The prose of *Bartholomew Fair* enabled Jonson, as the verse of *The Alchemist* had not, to create an idiom so saturated in cant that the speaker might be identified by his least syllable.

Busy's speeches contain an abnormally high percentage of devices of repetition, and it is these more than anything else that give them their distinctive incantational hum. Characteristically, Busy combines repetition with apposition. A noun will be repeated in apposition with itself, but on its reappearance it will acquire a modifier, or if it already had one, it will acquire a new one, and if repeated a second time, two new ones. There is thus a constant return to some basic element: "an X, a something X, a something and something X," that gives one the odd sensation of being tied to a stake: "a disease, a carnall disease" (I.vi.48–49), "an Idoll, a very Idoll, a feirce and rancke Idoll" (III.vi.56–57), "obstinacy, great obstinacy, high and horrible obstinacy" (III.ii.81–82).[5] That this was a cliché associated with the Puritan lunatic fringe one may judge from its appearance in writers like Phillip Stubbes: "a lustful loue, a venereous looue, a concupiscencious, baudie, & beastiall looue." [6]

With the same technique one can construct pyramids of verbs, adverbs, or adjectives, with their appropriate modifiers, and Busy rings most of the possible changes: "troubled, very much troubled, exceedingly troubled" (III.vi.90–91), "not much, not very much" (I.vi.72), "naturall, very naturall" (I.vi.50), "Very likely, exceeding likely, very exceeding likely" (I.vi.102). Or, by using anaphora, he varies the interior element while keeping a bulldog grip on the initial one: "thy basket of Popery, thy nest of Images" (III.vi.73), "this Idolatrous Groue of Images, this flasket of Idols" (III.vi.98–99), "those superstitious reliques, those lists of Latin" (IV.vi.105–106).[7] The purpose, of course, is oratorical in the worst sense: to lull the listener into a narcotic doze. The repeated words set up a trancelike rhythm that conceals the vacancy of meaning beneath.

Such language, it need scarcely be said, traces its genesis through the Puritan preachers and pamphleteers back to the English Bible itself. The use of "synonymous, or almost synonymous phrases in apposition as in 'rebuke me not in thine anger' and 'neither chasten me in thy hot displeasure,'" which found its way into later English prose through the Authorized Version,[8] had already established itself as a biblical mannerism in the sixteenth century. Jonson, taking up in comedy where formal apologists like Hooker left off in rational dispute, is burlesquing the notorious Puritan habit of talking from the Bible. Busy's most trifling remarks swell with the ostentatious loftiness of a sermon. When he does not place his synonymous phrases in apposition, he couples them with "and's": "haue a vaile put ouer it, and be shaddowed" (I.vi.69–70), "to puffe vs vp, and make vs swell" (III.vi.31–32), "the opening of the merchandize of *Babylon* againe, & the peeping of *Popery* vpon the stals" (III.vi.91–93).[9] He displays an egregious fondness for the genitive phrase — two nouns linked by "of" — and here, as in the examples already cited, he takes care to echo the diction as well as the syntax of biblical language: "the vanity of the eye," "the lust of the palat" (I.vi.78), "the tents of the wicked" (I.vi.71–72), "the shop of *Satan!*" (III.ii.42), "the wares of diuels" (III.ii.41), "the bells of the Beast" (III.ii.48).[10] Alliteration often lends added emphasis to such phrases ("the peeping of *Popery*" [III.vi.92], "the Page of *Pride*" [V.v.81–82]), and so does assonance ("the seate of the Beast" [III.vi.44–45]), but more

199

important is the stress pattern. The nature of the construction makes it fall readily into the formal cadences inherited from classic oratory and still prized in Elizabethan pulpits.[11]

cursus planus ′x x′x   "smóake of tabácco" (III.vi.32)
"lúst of the pálat"
"ténts of the wícked"
"fúll of those bánners" (III.vi.29)

cursus tardus ′x x′x x   "spíce of *Idólatry*" (I.vi.55)
"básket of Pópery"
"légend of gínger-worke"
(III.vi.73–74)

The third *cursus, cursus velox* (′x x′x′x), occurs seldom, but what Morris Croll has called the native English cadence (′x x′) abounds, as in many of the examples already quoted, and as in

"Énsigne of príde" (III.vi.28–29)
"séate of the Béast"
"sínne of the *Fáire*" (III.vi.77)
"píkes of the Lánd" (III.vi.110)

That Jonson identified this genitive formula with Puritan cant may be seen from the frequency of its occurrence on the tongue of Ananias: "ruffe of pride" (*Alch.* IV.vii.51), "Child of perdition" (IV.vii.58), "seed of sulphure," "sonnes of fire" (V.iii.44), "marke of the *Beast*" (III.i.8), "cage of vncleane birds" (V.iii.47). What warrant he had for so doing may be judged from the writings of the Puritans themselves, both wise (Perkins: "ensigne of pride," [12] "the very bellowes of lust and vncleanes") [13] and foolish (Stubbes: "the ensigne of Pride, and the [standerd] of wantonnes," "cesterns of iniquity, & pittes of aduersity"; [14] or, anonymous, "the Schoolehouse of Satan, and chappel of il counsel").[15]

Busy possesses a whole wardrobe full of false biblical feathers. One other is his mode of exhortation. Admonishing his little flock to shun the temptations of the Fair, he places the negative particle after the verb, uses the coupling conjunction "neither," and alternates direct imperative with hortatory subjunctive. The effect of sham biblicality is pronounced:

So, walke on in the middle way, fore-right, turne neyther to the right hand, not to the left: let not your eyes be drawne aside with vanity, nor your eare with noyses. (III.ii.30–32)

Elsewhere he employs the pseudoscriptural subjunctive "were" in place of the conditional "would be":

. . . should she goe there, as taking pride in the place, or delight in the vncleane dressing, to feed the vanity of the eye, or the lust of the palat, it were not well, it were not fit, it were abominable, and not good. (I.vi.76–79)

A protasis so intricately subdivided requires an apodosis to match, and Busy fills out the latter with a climactic series that reaches its high point on "abominable," and then limps lamely to a stop in the final member. The pretentiousness of the sentence, with its chain of suspensions and its dying fall of an *esse videatur*, serves added notice, if any were needed, of the lingual scrofula from which the speaker is suffering.

The number of logical connectives that intrude into his speeches at certain points leads one to suspect a further perversion: that of logic. When Dame Purecraft appeals for justification to visit the Fair — "O brother *Busy!* your helpe heere to edifie, and raise vs vp in a scruple" (I.vi.39–40), she is demanding the solution of a case of conscience, in which the scruple itself forms the irritant, or moral obstacle, "the thing that troubleth the conscience," [16] according to the most celebrated practitioner of Puritan casuistry, William Perkins. And Busy's answer sounds suspiciously like a parody of the method used by casuists such as Perkins in unraveling moral dilemmas. *The Whole Treatise of the Cases of Conscience* explicates each problem by a question-and-answer formula. Every answer and every question may be further analyzed into other questions, according to the dichotomous scheme inherited from Ramus.[17] The discussion of the problem is preceded by a definition.

> I. Question
> *What is a Religious Fast?*
> *Ans.* It is a voluntary and extraordinary abstinence, taken vp for a religious end; what this end is, we shall see afterward.
> First, I call it *voluntarie*, because the time, and particular manner of Fasting, is not imposed, or determined, but left free to our owne li[b]ertie. Againe, I tearme it *extraordinary*, to distinguish it from ordinarie fasting; which stands in the practise of temperance and sobrietie; whereby the appetite is restrained, in the vse of meates and drinkes, that it doe not exceed moderation.[18]

To comply with Dame Purecraft's request, and find lawful grounds for visiting the Fair, Busy is obliged to talk his way out of the usual Puritan position, which viewed fairs as furnaces of Satan. Busy, like Perkins, commences with definition.

> Verily, for the disease of longing, it is a disease, a carnall disease, or appetite, incident to women: and as it is carnall, and incident, it is naturall, very naturall.   (I.vi.48–50)

The "definition" — it is breaking a butterfly on a wheel to say so — is of course a tissue of tautologies, beginning with the comically outrageous tautology "for the disease of longing, it is a disease," and proceeding to a bogus redefinition, "disease, or appetite," where the modifier "incident to women" uses the philosophical-sounding word "incident" to convey the impression that some sort of logical distinction is being drawn. The same absurdity prevails when Busy reaches the stickiest point in his survey of the subject, the sanction for eating roast pig:

Now Pigge, it is a meat, and a meat that is nourishing, and may be long'd for, and so consequently eaten; it may be eaten; very exceeding well eaten. (I.vi.50–53)

Without dwelling on the question of whether pig may be "long'd for" because it is a meat, and whether the fact that it is long'd for permits it to be indulged in, Busy climbs quickly over the hump of the argument and settles fast in a conclusion, repeating it twice and buttressing it the second time with three thunderously vacuous intensives. But it is unnecessary to follow the argument further to see that it is a parade of sophistries, a smog of meaningless accretive phrases masquerading as logical distinctions, perpetual nonsense-reworkings of what is nonsense to begin with. And that Jonson is poking fun at the panoply of logic, derived from Ramus, to be found in Puritan manuals of conduct, seems equally plain. Pascal, when he came to conduct the more polemical, more devastating exposé of Jesuit casuistry in the *Lettres provinciales*, invented a comic method of his own, but he based it on the same principle: comic deformation of logic as a means of suggesting hypocrisy.

Busy's language speaks — or rants — for itself so unmistakably that further comment on it is probably needless. One may notice, however, that into the play with the most densely realistic setting he had attempted, Jonson has deposited a character with one of the most preposterously unreal ways of speaking ever heard on any stage.[19] Inch for inch, Busy's language is as packed with eccentricity as Tucca's, but because it is so much more sharply confined to a single manner, it ends by sounding even more like that of a creature from outer space. Prose, it may also be noticed, was in this case an absolute necessity. The stupefying sing-song of the rhythm needed to be free of metrical interference in order to establish itself so totally. Busy ends by being perhaps the most complete linguistic impostor in Jonson. With the other knaves and gulls, one feels that their excrescences of diction and syntax have grown like funguses onto a language still partly their own. The vocal disguise distorts but does not obliterate the "true" voice. With Busy, one feels that every syllable is ersatz, maliciously manufactured out of alien matter to produce an impenetrable mask. The "conversion" of the finale hence results in an even more abject collapse into nonexistence than in the case of the earlier humors figures: a converted Busy is even more unimaginable than a reformed Bobadill or a chastened Crispinus. Like the hero of Max Beerbohm's *Happy Hypocrite*, Busy has worn his mask so long that when he comes to remove it, there can be nothing beneath but a replica of the mask, now the authentic face — or voice — itself.

4

If Rabbi Busy affects the eloquence of the pulpit and the logic of the casebook, Adam Overdo strives after the rhetoric of the forum. As justice of the peace, presiding over the dusty-footed court of piepowders at the Fair, Overdo nevertheless imagines himself to be the Compleat Magistrate, whose job is nothing less than the salvation of the commonwealth. In his mind's eye he sees himself as a member of an apocalyptic senate of the just and wise, surrounded by his "friends" Cicero, Persius, Ovid, Horace, and Epictetus, whose admonitions are forever spurring him to the fulfillment of his mission. And to vindicate his claim to the title of Cicero reincarnate, he has confected for himself a language bulging with the devices of classic oratory, a style composed of "exhortations" and "pretty gradations" to which he points with self-conscious pride.[20]

Unlike Busy, who practices his perfervid rhetoric in order to delude others, Overdo is autointoxicate. His fervor, as it springs from simplicity rather than cunning, imposes on no one but himself. And indeed, it is designed largely for purposes of self-gratification. Busy is unthinkable without an audience, but Overdo is his own best audience, as we learn when — locked in the stocks — he prefers grandly to apostrophize himself rather than commune with his neighbor. Of his three major speeches, two are elaborate soliloquies in which he debates matters of commonweal with himself. The effect of these is somewhat as though one were to bring Cicero himself on the stage soliloquizing in the style of the orations against Catiline, a style whose every gesture presupposes an auditory.

Overdo's third speech (II.vi.1–86) is a public performance of sorts, a philippic against bottle-ale and tobacco, delivered in the guise of mad Arthur of Bradbury to a dozen or so ragged onlookers, who divert themselves with his oddness like a crowd at Marble Arch listening to a preachment from a soapbox. To rise to the sublimity of his subject, Overdo marshals all of the techniques of persuasion enjoined by classical precedent. He starts with the "ethical proof" advised by Aristotle, in which the speaker wins a favorable hearing for himself by demonstrating his own virtue and disinterestedness: [21] "Stay, young man, and despise not the wisedome of these few hayres, that are growne gray in care of thee." "Despise not" is of course a rhetorically inverted way of saying "have great respect for"; the "few hayres" stand synecdochically for Overdo and his years. The claim that his hairs have grown gray in care of Edgeworth, whom he saw for the first time only a few moments before, is of course absurd, as at least one critic has pointed out,[22] but it is an absurdity in which Overdo himself thoroughly believes. Having devoted his life to the public good, he has grown gray in the service of the whole state, and hence — in his own eyes — of any particular member of it.

Launching rapidly into his main theme, he exhorts his hearers to avoid bottle-ale, "for, who knowes, when hee openeth the stopple, what may be in the bottle? hath not a Snaile, a Spider, yea, a Neuft bin found there?" Here the self-interruption of the "yea," the climactic order of snail, spider, and newt, oratorical mannerisms both advised and practiced by Cicero, derive their comic force from the contrast between the grandness of the manner and the triviality of the matter, as well as from the farcical nature of the reasoning. The injunction against ale is now extended to tobacco; Overdo, adhering to the classical custom of offering *confirmatio*, or learned testimony, in support of a position, cites "some late writers" as evidence of the venomous properties of the alligator, supposed to have poisoned the tobacco plant by urinating on it. The attack on tobacco leads to a minor climax, arranged in traditionally ladderlike fashion: "Hence it is, that the lungs of the Tabacconist are rotted, the Liuer spotted, the braine smoak'd like the back-side of the Pig-womans Booth, here, and the whole body within, blacke, as her Pan, you saw e'en now, without." [23] The gradation, with its interior ornaments — the rhyme on "rotted, spotted," the pointless antithesis between the body "within" and the pan "without" — provides a fair sample of the laboriously worked-up character of Overdo's oratory.

He turns next to another evil effect of tobacco: the decay of the nose. The establishment of this point requires a bit of *reprehensio*, or the setting aside of an objection, the objection in this case being the vulgar error that the nose decays as a consequence of venereal disease. It is tobacco that causes the phenomenon in question, exclaims Overdo, "when the poore innocent pox, hauing nothing to doe there, is miserably, and most vnconscionably slander'd." Again it is the speaker's ability to lash himself into a fine frenzy of indignation against tobacco while shedding pitying tears for "the poore innocent pox" that turns his misapplication of rhetorical formulas into parody.

At this point comes a new maneuver in the manner of Cicero. The orator now feigns to recollect himself, to shift to a more important aspect of his argument, which he has been neglecting so far. "But what speake I of the diseases of the body, children of the *Fayre?* . . . Harke, O, you sonnes and daughters of Smithfield! and heare what mallady it doth the minde." The idiom "what speake I" for "why speake I," though not anomalous in Elizabethan language, sounds, in the present context, suspiciously like an imitation of the Latin particle *quid*, and adds a further smack of Ciceronianism to what is already a travesty of Cicero. The heightened emotional temperature produced by a consideration of the destructive effects of tobacco on the mind leads to a new and more impassioned gradation: "Harke, O, you sonnes and daughters of Smithfield! and heare what mallady it doth the minde: It causeth swearing, it causeth swaggering, it causeth snuffling, and snarling, and now and then a hurt" — where the sudden abandonment of alliteration and homoeoteleuton, the sudden reduction of the lordly participles to a silly monosyllabic noun, causeth a bathos. At the culmination of his indictment, Overdo affects a piece of *enargia:* he takes his hearers into a sordid quarter of London where bottle-ale and tobacco are being imbibed as adjuncts to a quarreling lesson, shrinking the purses and befouling the suits of the novices. The peroration to all of this, which would doubtless have been magnificent, is cut short by the violent interference of Wasp. Overdo's only success has been to bring on a beating for himself and to afford the pickpockets of the Fair an opportunity to filch Cokes's purse.

And so, with variations, for Overdo's language throughout.

When he is not pompously imitating his "friend" Cicero in formal oratory, he is preening himself on other kinds of rhetorical finery. The same imitative pedantry that leads him to jam his speeches with apostrophes and gradations leads him to prefer certain stilted syntactic formations: the inversion of subject and verb so as to isolate and give prominence to some initial adverb or conjunction ("Thus must we doe, though, that wake for the publike good" [II.i.9–10], "Neuer shall I enough commend a worthy worshipfull man" [II.i.12–13]); the inversion of subject and object ("Two maine works I haue to prosecute" [V.ii.6–7], "This wee are subiect to, that liue in high place" [II.i.36]); and the like.

The impropriety, to repeat, lies not in the use of such-and-such a figure of rhetoric, but in the relentless, continuous use of all of them, in the misapplication of them in petty contexts, and finally in the way they shape Overdo's view of the world instead of being shaped by it. Like Morose, Overdo has acquired most of his knowledge of life from books, and this knowledge obstructs his understanding instead of enlarging it. Just as Morose attempts to translate courtly literature into a manual of gallantry, so Overdo tries to turn the rhetoric of antiquity into a code of justice and a mirror for magistrates. But, instead of being, like Morose, morbidly satiric, Overdo is simply quixotic. He only half understands his own classical sources, and many of his allusions harbor an irony against himself of which he remains unaware. When, exulting over his disguise as a fool, he announces, "faine would I meet the *Linceus* now, that Eagles eye, that peircing *Epidaurian* serpent (as my *Quint. Horace* cal's him) that could discouer a Iustice of Peace . . . vnder this couering" (II.i.4–7), he marvelously misses the real point that his Quint. Horace is making in the lines to which he refers. Horace is upbraiding men for the myopia they show toward their own faults compared to the Epidaurian sharpsightedness with which they spy out the failings of others.[24] The burden of the whole satire is that no one is exempt from folly, and that if men would scrutinize themselves more closely, they would learn charity toward the vices of others; further, that wisdom consists in weighing offenses and distributing censure according to reason, and not according to the brutal leveling principles of the Stoics, who regard all faults as equal. The satire, then, and above all the passage cited by Overdo, delivers the most patent rebuke to Overdo's pose as the stainless statesman, and to his tendency to lump together all of the petty delinquencies and minor breaches of conduct of the Fair as "enormities."

By ridiculing Overdo's intimacy with Latin authors and his half-baked Stoicism, Jonson shows a new recognition that learning is not enough to preserve a man from folly,[25] just as the fatuous endearments of the Littlewits teach us, more forcibly than elsewhere in Jonson, that stupidity can coexist with innocence. The aggressive declaration prefixed to *Every Man out of his Humour*, "if we faile, / We must impute it to this onely chance, / '*Arte* hath an enemy cal'd *Ignorance*'" (Ind. 217–219), has mellowed into a realization that art has other enemies, among them the learned themselves. Overdo, who quotes Horace and Persius, distrusts the poets and players as much as any ignorant citizen. The classical authors he has memorized cannot guide him through the mazes of rascality he has resolved to spy out at the Fair, nor can they — which comes to the same thing — enlighten him concerning his own foolishness.

Overdo's self-appointed role as agent of reform links him directly with Rabbi Busy. Though Busy and Overdo quarrel, they are allied in the one matter that is a touchstone for all else: their attitude toward the Fair. The Fair, for one the symbol of everything carnal summed up in the word "abomination," is for the other the symbol of everything disorderly summed up in the term "enormity." The bond between them, moreover, is not accidental, but reflects a real state of affairs, the alliance between the Puritan preachers and the city magistrates against playhouses and other forms of popular recreation.[26] Busy and Overdo recoil in virtuous horror, as their live counterparts might have recoiled, from the iniquities of bottle-ale, tobacco, and roast pig. Both come to the Fair to reclaim it, one by justice because it offends civic order, the other by prophesying, because it offends divine prescription. Both create enough commotion to wind up in the stocks as disturbers of the peace. In the stocks, each welcomes his punishment with a certain masochistic relish: one regards it as an affliction consequent on and emblematic of his sainthood; the other thinks of it as affording the opportunity for a display of Stoic indifference. Both, finally, rise in wrath against the crowning enormity, the ultimate abomination, of the puppet show, and both are at that moment jolted out of their affectations and converted, brought down to the level of the vulgar humanity they have pretended to judge.

The alliance between them, as one might expect, is strengthened by a linguistic kinship, and the linguistic kinship in turn can also be traced to a real state of affairs: to the fact that by this time preaching and public speaking had become simply two versions of the same rhetoric: "Moreouer, the whole craft of varienge the Oration by *Schemes* and *Tropes*, pertaineth indifferently to the Preacher and Orator, as Sainct *Augustine* . . . doth wittily confesse and learnedly proue." [27] Overdo and Busy share a surprisingly large number of verbal mannerisms.

Overdo's censorious epithets, though they are less ostentatiously logical than Busy's, have some of the same definitive flavor: "that frothy liquor, Ale," "that tawney weede, tabacco," "The creeping venome," "the perrillous plant." Like Busy, Overdo chooses the literary "thou" form of the second person singular pronoun, with the "-est" form of the verb to match, and the "-eth" inflection of the third person. Also, like Busy, Overdo is fond of imperatives, of negative particles placed after the verb, and of the conjunction "neither." One might compare "So . . . turne neyther to the right hand, not to the left . . . Look not toward them, harken not," with "Thirst not after that frothy liquor, Ale . . . thirst not after it, youth: thirst not after it. . . . Neither doe thou lust after that tawney weede, tabacco," where Overdo's reiterated "thirst not" and the scriptural-sounding "lust after" evoke Busy rather forcibly. Or, for the use of gradation, repetitions of "it," and final bathos, one might compare "it were not well, it were not fit, it were abominable, and not good" with "It causeth swearing, it causeth swaggering, it causeth snuffling, and snarling, and now and then a hurt."

Overdo's cry of protest at the moment of his beating from Wasp recalls still other traits of Busy's: "Hold thy hand, childe of wrath, and heyre of anger, make it not Childermasse day in thy fury, or the feast of the French *Bartholmew*, Parent of the Massacre" (II.vi.146–151). Though Busy would have scorned to utter the popish term "mass," he would have welcomed the chance to shed a tear for the martyrs of St. Bartholomew's Day, and he might have done so in very similar fashion: the flurry of genitive phrases, especially those containing the names of semipersonified sins ("childe of wrath," "heyre of anger"), is, as we have seen, one of his specialties. Overdo has his own penchant for genitive phrases: "the fruites of bottle-ale, and tabacco! the fome of the one, and the fumes of the other!" "children of the *Fayre*," "the very *wombe*, and *bedde* of enormitie" (II.ii.106).[28]

In addition, there occur a number of incidental verbal

parallels that may or may not be significant. Busy speaks of "a spice of Idolatry" and Overdo of "a spice of collaterall Iustice" (III.iii.2–3), Busy of the "peeping of *Popery* vpon the stals" and Overdo of the bad events which may "peepe out o' the taile of good purposes" (III.iii.13–14), Busy of the iniquity of "high *Places*" (I.vi.56), and Overdo (shortly after) of the cares of those "that liue in high place" (II.i.36).

Such stylistic and lexical correspondences may indicate no more than that self-righteous reformers who work themselves up into rhetorical passions end by sounding alike, whatever their motives. But even to say this much is to declare the kinship between the knaves whose false attitudes issue in vicious language (Busy) and the fools whose language betrays them into false attitudes (Overdo). The fool, practicing the same cant to deceive himself that the knave uses to dupe others, imposes between himself and the world a distorting screen through which nothing can be seen as it really is. The example of Overdo offers sufficient evidence that mimicry of the Great Books can be as perilous as mimicry of high society.

Finally, it should be added that both Busy and Overdo embody self-parody and self-penance on Jonson's part. In the early plays, those with a passion for setting others right are themselves right, and end by making their standards prevail. The judicial tribunal stands behind the custodians of virtue and scatters their enemies. But in *Bartholomew Fair* the custodians of virtue themselves are mocked, and the fools are vindicated. Busy, a projection of everything censorious and morally scathing in Jonson's own view of the world, would very likely, at an earlier date, have had the satisfaction of dissolving "this knot of spiders" (*CR* III.iv.88) and whipping vice until it bled — instead of which, he is pilloried as a hypocrite. In the figure of Overdo, *Bartholomew Fair* turns justice itself topsy-turvy. The learned man, the zealous public officer, appears as the bumbling magistrate victimized by his own learning and his misdirected crusading fervor. Overdo's whole pose as savior of the state converts to burlesque what Jonson had just finished dramatizing with the most awful solemnity in *Catiline*. *Catiline* offers the spectacle of the authentic Cicero — or what Jonson took to be the authentic Cicero — endlessly orating against malefactors, tirelessly parading his patriotism, ceaselessly being acclaimed by the Senate for his zeal, ferreting out a plot against the state devised by a villain whose absolute blackness is not allowed a single mitigating trait. For Jonson to parody the admired Cicero in the crackbrained Overdo, and the conspiracy of Catiline in the "enormities" of Bartholomew Fair, was to turn the tables on himself with a vengeance, to acknowledge the suspicion that Cicero was a canting prig and Catiline a preposterous bogey, to affirm once again the truthfulness of appearances, and so, in a sense, to heap ridicule on his own lifelong stance as watchdog of public morality.[29]

5

During the year prior to the writing of *Bartholomew Fair*, Jonson had traveled on the continent as tutor to the scapegrace son of Sir Walter Raleigh; and memories of the vexations and embarrassments of that mission are now compounded to produce a third self-projection and self-parody in the figure of Master Humphrey Wasp.[30] Wasp, unlike the rest of the dramatis personae, belongs to no clearly defined social or professional category. His one obligation, and his one ruling passion, is to guide his bird-witted pupil, Bartholomew Cokes, through the dangers of London.

Wasp speaks almost entirely in fierce little jabs of language, in irate questions and choleric exclamations and furious parentheses. He splices together his characteristically short phrases either by interminable rows of the same conjunction — usually "and" — or else by the omission of conjunctions, in either case hammering on the phrase itself with something of the obsessive fixity of Busy:

Sir, I do not know, and I will not know, and I scorne to know, and yet, (now I think on't) I will, and do know, as well as another. (I.iv.20–22)

I looke like a cutpurse? death! your Sister's a cutpurse! and your mother and father, and all your kinne were cutpurses! And here is a Rogue is the baud o' the cutpurses, whom I will beat to begin with. (II.vi.142–145)

But where Busy lingers over his phrases and prolongs his repetitions in order to cast his listeners into a trance, Wasp hops up and down on his phrases in order to jolt himself into a frenzy.[31] When he grows really excited, he can scarcely compose a connected sentence, but simply flings himself violently and repeatedly at the same phrase until he exhausts himself: "Why, see it, Sir, see it, doe see it! who hinders you? why doe you not goe see it? 'Slid see it" (I.v.88–89).

In order to keep the air forever astir with words, however useless, Wasp employs various devices of emphasis that fill in the silence when his thought, but not his outrage, has spent itself. He will, for example, affix a last sharp stab of an interrogative clause to the end of a statement, turning the statement into a heated demand. The stabbing coda may consist merely of subject and auxiliary verb repeated from the main statement ("you see no dust or cobwebs come out o' my mouth: doe you? you'ld ha' me gone, would you?" [I.iv.97–99]; "*Whetston* has set an edge vpon you, has hee?" [I.v.25–26]; "You are the *Patrico!* are you?" [II.vi.148–149]; "you'ld be sold too, would you?" [III.iv.110]) or of the question "doe you see?" appended as a thrust of fierce emphasis ("and turd i' your *French-hoods* teeth, too, to doe you seruice, doe you see?" [I.v.16–17]; "Blesse 'hem with all my heart, with all my heart, do you see!" [II.vi.106–107]) or of the belligerent challenge "how then?" ("Why, say I haue a humour not to be ciuill; how then?" [I.iv.60–61]; "and they were all the braue words in a Countrey, how then?" [II.vi.29–30]). Or the last lash of the tail may be declarative or imperative: "I am for no anon's, I assure you" (I.iv.11–12), "it's labour in vaine, you know" (I.iv.6–7), "she has as little wit, as her husband, it seemes" (I.iv.103), "say, *Numps* is a witch, with all my heart, doe, say so" (II.vi.33–34).[32]

In addition, Jonson has provided Wasp with the most extensive repertory of oaths, expletives, and interjections of any character in the play: "Good Lord," "forsooth," "S'blood," "heart," "Cry you mercy," "Gods so," "Why the meazills," "What, the mischiefe," "Hoyday," "i'faith," "S'pretious," "Mary gip," "S'lid," "By this light," "pray God," and others, and variations on them, as well as such lexical and phrasal addictions as "with all my heart," "turd i' your teeth," "too," "now," and "so." If there is any one dominant characteristic to which all these linguistic details refer, it is the absurd disproportion between sheer buzzing and solid meaning in all of Wasp's speeches.

Like Overdo and Busy, Wasp may be said to represent the moral authority of the earlier plays subverted, though in his case the authority is merely tutorial. The satiric commentator of an earlier period, who remained scornfully aloof, passing judgment on the procession of fools, has become, in this instance, the frenzied busybody whose passionate exposures of folly in others serves only to expose it the more damningly in himself. Wasp's relatively private relation to the Fair does not abate the intensity of his dislike for it, which approaches that of Busy and Overdo, and coincides with theirs at several points. Like them, he is an enemy of license, of pleasure, of anything smacking of carnal weakness. He expresses fury at his pupil's habit of picking up "vile tunes" (I.iv.77). He denounces the London signs and the vogue of tobacco with a vehemence worthy of a puritan or reforming magistrate, and labels as "*heathen*" (I.iv.112) the frivolities that fascinate Cokes. The sight of his ward enjoying himself drives him to fury, immune as he is to the seductions of the festival season. Fittingly, then, he becomes, with Busy and Overdo, the third disturber of the peace to be placed in the stocks, and the third disruptive element to be shaken to his senses by a confrontation with his own folly.

Unlike his companions in zeal, however, Wasp takes no pains to mimic a learned or a modish language, or even to talk correctly. His speech, in fact, is distinguished by heedlessness rather than pickedness. Linguistic corruption is suggested by the incessant tautologizing, the thudding repetitions, the farcing of every statement with mouthfuls of senseless expletives. And these traits, in turn, point to an ailment more venial, but more incurable, than the posturing of the other two. We cannot, in Wasp's case, assign any motive for his endless agitation other than mere perversity. He bickers stridently throughout the first act with Littlewit, without any provocation, and with Mrs. Overdo, rudely claiming a precedency over her in the management of Cokes which she has no wish to dispute. He embarks on futile wrangles with Cokes over such trivialities as whether Cokes shall or shall not examine the marriage license. Having so commenced, he so continues, quarreling passionately for the rest of the day with all who cross his path, and, characteristically, with himself not least. Finally, after a long pilgrimage of self-imposed vexation, he reaches his earthly paradise in the drunken game of vapors before Ursula's tent. Here, where the rest contradict each other lazily for sport, Wasp contradicts more than ever from pure truculence, and having out-vapored the whole crew of noisy roarers, is carried off to the stocks as an offense to the peace.

This apparently meaningless perversity may be elucidated with reference to the key concept of "vapors." Although the word belongs almost exclusively to the vocabulary of the horse-courser, Master Jordan Knockhem, its implications extend over the entire action of the play. In the most limited sense, vapors is simply a game played by several of the characters in Act IV, a kind of drunken mock quarrel explained marginally by Jonson: *"Here they continue their game of* vapours, *which is* non sense. *Euery man to oppose the last man that spoke: whethe[r] it concern'd him, or no"* (marginal to IV.iv.27–38). The game, then, which codifies contradictoriness into a formal rule, supplies us with a paradigm for Wasp's usual behavior, and to a lesser extent, for the behavior of all who visit or inhabit the Fair.

The more general meaning of the term — "disposition, conceit, fancy, whim" [33] — associates it closely with the older Jonsonian word "humor," for which, in this play, it becomes a substitute.[34] The two were already linked in the popular psychology of the period: the humors, or body fluids, engendered certain vapors, or fumes, which passed through the blood and acted directly on the brain. Strictly speaking, their effects would be identical. In Jonson, however, the shift in terms involves a shift in meaning. "Humor" referred primarily to a physiological unbalance. Secondarily, and more significantly for Jonsonian drama, it connoted affectation; its commonest symptom was mimicry, a ridiculous straining to become what one was not, often compounded with an affected attempt to differ from others. As a primarily self-induced malady, it was amenable to purgation through ridicule.

Or so, at least, ran the prescription. But in fact, the secondary kind of humor, the affectation, was unlikely to occur without the first, the metabolic imbalance, and the combination left little hope for pharmacy. Crites, in *Cynthia's Revels*, is praised for the perfection of his temper, the concord of elements and humors within him, which implies that his enemies, the oafs and dolts, suffer from varieties of discord, from being "phantastikely melancholy" or "slowly phlegmaticke" or "lightly sanguine" or "rashly cholericke" (*CR* II.iii.126–127) — in short, from maladies beyond the reach of medicine. And as we have already noticed in discussing *Poetaster*, both the grammar of discontinuity and the purely symbolic punishments meted out to offending characters forbid our believing in the reform as anything but a theatrical convenience. The determinism thus lurking beneath the doctrine of humors now erupts in the concept of vapors. The vapors represent a strain of perversity inseparable from flesh and blood, a deep-seated folly that may be acknowledged and to some extent neutralized, but never cured. Unlike the humors, which tend to make men affect singularity and withdraw from each other, the vapors tend to make them intrude on each other, to meddle, and quarrel. We see this plainly in the behavior of Wasp. We see it also in the behavior of Quarlous, who, like Wasp a survival of the satiric expositor, competes with Wasp for the distinction of being the most pugnacious character in a play rampant with pugnacity. Both share a lively awareness of the folly that courses through the Fair, and both end by being engulfed in its current themselves.

To carry the distinction between humors and vapors into the linguistic sphere, one may suggest, somewhat diagrammatically, that if the cardinal sin of the humors characters is mimicry, that of the vapors characters is solecism. In one case, speech is hyperconscious, mannered, and finicky; in the other, slovenly, boneless, and sometimes so unconscious as to approach free association. But if the sins of mimicry are the distempers of language, because unnatural, the sins of solecism are its peccant humors, or — not to mix vocabularies — its peccant vapors. Busy and Overdo, plainly enough, belong to an older Jonsonian race. By cultivating the mortal sin of affectation, they succeed in transforming themselves into "careful fools," who take pains to be so, or "beyond" fools. The rest — Littlewit, Quarlous, Wasp, Cokes, and the people of the Fair — remain natural fools, or fools positive.

For Swift, who uses the term in a sense roughly analogous to Jonson's, vapors are responsible for most of the mad, absurd, and hostile actions of mankind. Every species of madness, according to the digression on the subject in *A Tale of a Tub*, "proceeds from a redundancy of vapours." But so, also, do other violent human activities not usually regarded as mad: ". . . if the moderns mean by madness, only a disturbance or transposition of the brain, by force of certain vapours issuing up from the lower faculties, then has this madness been the parent of all those mighty revolutions that have happened in empire, in philosophy, and in religion." [35] *Bartholomew Fair*, like *A Tale of a Tub*, reduces all human activity to the gross level of an organic disturbance. Whether it is the fatuousness of a Cokes or the out-and-out lunacy of a Troubleall, our behavior comes down to a series of reflexes stimulated in the "lower faculties."

6

Cokes, "unquestionably the most finished picture of a simpleton that the mimetic art ever produced," [36] epitomizes silly humanity itself, as Jonson views it in the *Discoveries*.

What petty things they are, wee wonder at? like children, that esteeme every trifle; and preferre a *Fairing* before their Fathers:

what difference is betweene us, and them? but that we are dearer
Fooles, Cockscombes, at a higher rate? They are pleas'd with
Cockleshels, Whistles, Hobby-horses, and such like: wee with
Statues, marble Pillars, Pictures, guilded Roofes, where under-
neath is Lath, and Lyme; perhaps Lome.   (*Disc.* 1437–44)

All the world's a Fair, as a critic has observed of this paraphrase from Seneca,[37] and all the people in it merely Cokeses.
Cokes is linked with the Fair in various ways. It is, as he
understands, "his" Fair, the world for which he was created.
In name and character he is the human counterpart of the
gingerbread images sold by Joan Trash, as well as of the
hobbyhorses vended by Lantern Leatherhead, and of the puppets. Like Master Stephen in *Every Man in his Humour*, he is
"a drumme; for euery one may play vpon him," or "a childes
whistle," that anyone may pipe on. He is the ideal gull in a
world of cony-catchers, the eternal credulous spectator in a
universe of marvels. Only playthings attract him, the little
mimic images of reality of which the Fair contains an inexhaustible supply.

Earlier Jonsonian specimens of the type to which Cokes
belongs — the numbskull young heir up from the country —
all display the same itch to strut about in fine clothes and fine
language, and all begin by finding some impostor to copy.
Cokes is different. Instead of affecting connoisseurship in poesy
or tobacco, or yearning for the company of his social betters,
he throws himself with infantine abandon into the joys of
Smithfield. And instead of aping the polite parlance of courtly
circles, or brandishing his intellectual credentials in the form
of playhouse scraps or bits of plagiarized sonnets, he speaks a
kind of baby talk. His vocabulary of enthusiasm is restricted
to a half-dozen or so favorite epithets, "delicate," "fine,"
"pretty," "brave," that serve for all occasions of wonder.
From time to time he brings out a big word ("aedified" [III.

v.141]; "contumacious" [I.v.105]) with the self-consciousness of the child that knows it is being precocious. He is addicted to meaningless pleonasms like "else" and "and all" ("my Sister is heere, and all" [I.v.3]; "feele else" [III.v.179]), and to the kind of tautological explanations one associates with infants first learning how to think: "hee is my brother in Law, hee marryed my sister" (IV.ii.93). One hears the lisp of the nursery in his particular kinds of archaism, solecism, and illiterate colloquialism: "Nay, doe not looke angerly, *Numpes*" (I.v. 2–3), "nay, neuer fidge vp and downe, *Numpes*, and vexe it selfe" (I.v.62–63), "I had bin better ha' gone to mum chance for you, I wusse" (IV.ii.75), and in his quotations from popular ballads.

Finally, his method of making a transition from one idea to another is to make no transition at all. As the sight of Goody Trash's gingerbread makes him forget the hobbyhorse bargain he is cheapening with Lantern Leatherhead, so the emergence of one thought in his head drives out the old one as one nail drives out another. He appears in IV.ii lamenting the loss of his purse and unable to find his way out of the Fair, and then, at the first sound of Nightingale's tune, abandons himself to the delights of whistling.

COKES. By this light, I cannot finde my ginger-bread-Wife, nor my Hobby-horse-man in all the *Fayre*, now; to ha' my money againe. And I do not know the way out on't, to go home for more, doe you heare, friend, you that whistle; what tune is that, you whistle?
NIGHTINGALE. A new tune, I am practising, Sir.
COK. Dost thou know where I dwell, I pray thee? nay, on with thy tune, I ha' no such hast, for an answer: I'le practise with thee.
(IV.ii.23–31)

Punctuation in cold print has rarely exceeded in expressiveness the comma Jonson (or his printer) places between "And

I do not know the way out on't, to go home for more," and "doe you heare, friend, you that whistle; what tune is that, you whistle," to indicate the short circuit between one idea and another in Cokes's head. The absence of verbal posturing, the childlike unselfconsciousness of Cokes's behavior, his passion for ballads, cut-out pictures, gingerbread images, toys, and puppets, imply a kind of primal folly that — unlike the more virulent strain based on affectation — is incapable of hurting others and almost incapable of being hurt itself. Cokes carries his innocence like a magic cloak through all the perils of the Fair. When his frivolities defeat the wrath of Busy, the scorn of Wasp, and the zeal of Overdo, we realize with a shock that Jonson is pronouncing a kind of blessing on the idiots of the world, on the gulls and naïfs, and their state of being perpetually deceived. If the world itself is a deceit, and if none can hope to escape its corruption, there is much to be said for the state of oblivion common to infants and simpletons.

Mistress Grace, Cokes's destined bride, and the nominal heroine of the play as Winwife is its nominal hero, suffers badly from Jonson's inability to make "straight" characters interesting. Doubtless, when Jonson created her, he thought he was paying a handsome compliment to her sex. She possesses good sense, judgment, and sobriety, qualities he rarely admitted in women. The trouble is that these are no longer the qualities that the play itself is primarily recommending, and they clash rather disastrously with the dominant spirit of warmth and animal appetite. The play views the excesses of the season unsentimentally, but indulgently, as a product of irredeemable human weakness, and one chief office of the Fair is to lure or coerce back into the human fold the numerous kill-joys who threaten it. Like Wasp, Busy, and Overdo, Grace is a kill-joy. She shrinks, almost visibly, from the organic, irrational warmth that pervades the carnival, and the mere sound of her voice casts a chill over it. "If you both loue mee, as you pretend, your owne reason will tell you, but one can enioy me" (IV.iii.7–8); "I am so secure of mine owne manners, as I suspect not yours" (III.v.298–299); "Truely, I haue no such fancy to the *Fayre;* nor ambition to see it; there's none goes thither of any quality or fashion" (I.v.130–132). That Jonson permitted the last of these remarks, with its prate of "quality" and "fashion," to creep into the dialogue of a character otherwise labeled "admirable," is perhaps sufficient indication of how little, at this moment, he really cared for reason and sobriety. The play itself moves steadily toward greater expansiveness and inclusiveness. The repressive trio of reformers succumb at last to the merry world they have tried to defy, but Grace, who has merely disengaged herself, continues disengaged to the end, poised, judicious, and slightly inhuman.

But the one false note loses itself rapidly in the swirl of strange voices that rise from the stage. Jonson has bestowed on the raffish denizens of the Fair an armory of styles even more licentious and picturesque than those of its visitors. Ursula, the pig-woman, broods over her fiery tent like a great earth-mother, roasting pigs and coining scurrilous epithets with indifferent mastery. She has a sheaf of belittling appellations for her tapster Mooncalf alone: "you false faucet you" (II.ii.48), "you vnlucky vermine" (II.ii.75), "you thinne leane Polcat you" (II.v.59), "thou errant *Incubee*" (II.ii.84), "Changeling" (II.ii.66), "*Stote*" (II.ii.70), "Weasell" (II.v. 64), "Rogue" (II.ii.97), "Rascall" (II.ii.49). Even less fastidious are the insults hurled at Winwife and Quarlous: "you Rogue, you hedge bird, you Pimpe, you pannier-mans bastard" (II.v.120–121), "you dogs-head, you *Trendle tayle*" (II.v.123), "snotty nose" (II.v.135), "rotten, roguy Cheaters" (II.v.104). Knockhem becomes, almost in endearment, "hors-leach" (II.iii.13) and "Baboun" (II.v.164), and Mistress Alice, in anger, "foule ramping Iade" (IV.v.72) and "tripe of *Turne-bull*" (IV.v.76).

Ursula thus anatomizes friend and foe alike in physical terms, and equates them with fish, flesh, and fowl. In her abusive similitudes, thin whores become "long lac'd *Congers*[s]" (II.v.87) or "leane playhouse poultry" (II.v.106), Quarlous' putative dam a "whelp" (II.v.125). The carnality of her speech reflects the grossness of both her trade and person. As the atmosphere of *The Silent Woman* was tacitly dominated by the epicene figure of the titular heroine, both less than a man and less than a woman, so that of *Bartholomew Fair* is noisily ruled by the androgynous person of the pig-wife, very much of a woman and something of a man to boot. Her occupations of *"Punke, Pinnace* and *Bawd"* (II.ii.72–73), her maternal empire of pigs and prostitutes, the fatness that makes her "the very *wombe*, and *bedde* of enormitie" (II.ii.106), her fear of melting away "to the first woman, a ribbe againe" (II.ii.50–51), establish her archetypal femininity, while the fact that she smokes a pipe, drinks ale, swears horribly, and quarrels fiercely endows her with some of the attributes of masculinity as well. She presides over the Fair like the life force, imperturbably fleshly, her tent a disreputable monument to the four elements of life and the three enemies of man. If she streams vile epithets and lewd solecisms as freely as she streams sweat, it is merely the primordial disorder of life finding its linguistic vent in disorder of language.

Her partner in rascality, Jordan Knockhem, carries on a similar double trade in flesh, horse-flesh by day and punk-flesh by night, and his incessant horse talk does almost more than Ursula's insults to obliterate the distinction between men and animals. He views Ursula herself as a "shee-Beare" (II.iii.1) and a whale, and almost everyone else as hippic: a

"*Galloway* Nag" (IV.iv.4), a "delicate darke chestnut" (IV. v.21), a "stone-puritane, with a sorrell head" (III.ii.120–121), "a couple of Stallions" (II.v.171). And when he is not finding equine metaphors for his acquaintances, he is busy sizing them up as possible candidates, or potential customers, for his stable of whores.

Of the language of the Fair people in general, it is perhaps enough to say that Jonson's reportorial realism has never been more exact or wide-ranging, and that he has never exercised it with less malice. The ear is assaulted unceasingly by linguistic anomalies, by every form of corrupt vocabulary, syntax, and diction, by dialect deformations and drunken brayings. But, as we have already observed, this linguistic muddle no longer carries very much moral stigma, because it is no longer correlated with the really capital vice of mimicry. The debased language of the Smithfieldians represents a kind of linguistic original sin, from which only a few coldly reasonable individuals — Mistress Grace and Winwife — are exempt, and the exemption from verbal folly in their case coincides significantly with an absence of vitality. Since there is no sacrament that will wash away this sin, these vapors, since education will probably only produce affectation, Jonson is content to cry "Duc-dame," place himself in the center of the circle, and let it go at that.

7

The most striking thing, perhaps, about all of the language of this play, as about so much of its action, is its insistent physicality. We know far more than usual in Jonson about the physical appearances of the characters — their actual bodies, not merely their fashionable clothes or nervous mannerisms. Ursula, one is scarcely allowed to forget, is hugely fat and forever sweating. Mooncalf is lean, Goody Trash "a little crooked" (II.ii.24) in her body, Wasp small, Mrs. Little-wit "little" (I.iv.26), and Cokes tall and gangling. We have not this kind of information for a single one of the characters in *The Silent Woman*. Furthermore, the language of the play is permeated with the imagery of the human body, and this refers not merely to arms and legs but to internal organs — kidneys, lungs, heart, brain, and blood. The sense of organic process is everywhere. Ursula not merely bulks great in her fleshly monumentality, she drips, melts, and sweats before our eyes, a visible symbol of the corruptibility of the flesh. The result of this emphasis on physiology, on dissolution, is to strip the human organism of transcendental qualities.

The point is strikingly made by a series of tropes that re-duce first the brain and then the soul itself to the level of crass physicality. Wasp imagines the interior of Cokes's head as a sort of idiot wasteland, "hung with cockle-shels, pebbles, fine wheat-strawes, and here and there a chicken's feather, and a cob-web" (I.v.95–97). The primary sense is one of aridity, but the void implies a physical space that might well be filled by something more substantial. When Winwife pro-poses to visit the Fair, forecasting "excellent creeping sport," Quarlous concurs: "A man that has but a spoone-full of braine, would think so" (I.v.142–143), thus bringing the mind directly into the realm of the palpable, something to be meas-ured by a spoon. Wasp's later outcry of despair at his way-ward pupil carries the idea a step further: "Would I had beene set i' the ground, all but the head on me, and had my braines bowl'd at, or thresh'd out, when first I vnderwent this plague of a charge" (III.iv.50–52). Here the brain has be-come an object of sport, a bowling pin, or a vegetable to be harvested from the soil, something palpable, perhaps edible, and grotesquely degraded from its philosophical status as the seat of reason. The final debasement, however, occurs when

Edgeworth, commenting scornfully on Cokes's imbecility, degrades the soul itself to the level of matter. "Talke of him to haue a soule? 'heart, if hee haue any more then a thing giuen him in stead of salt, onely to keepe him from stinking, I'le be hang'd afore my time, presently" (IV.ii.54–56). With this view of the soul as a kind of preservative in the blood, placed there to keep the body from putrefaction, the reduction of the spirit to the flesh is complete. Humankind becomes as strictly a composite of flesh and blood as pig or horse.

If the higher faculties are degraded to the level of physicality, the body itself is persistently viewed in its grossest aspects; even inorganic matter seems to take on some of the decaying character of flesh. The ubiquitous word "belly" focuses our attention on the center of appetite, the stomach, as well as on the center of fertility, the womb, and merges with the remarkable number of references to fat things, soft things, and greasy things in the language. Many of these references, understandably, cluster about Ursula. Overdo speaks of her as "oyly as the Kings constables Lampe" (II.ii. 118–119), Knockhem as a whale, Quarlous as "some walking Sow of tallow," "excellent geere . . . to anoynt wheeles and axell trees with" (II.v.78–82), as a "quagmire," a "Bogge" (II.v.90–91), and "a whole *Shire* of butter" (II.v.100). Mooncalf mentions her "greasie kerchiefe" (II.iii.38); Winwife is revolted by her language, "greasier then her Pigs" (II.v.133–134); and Littlewit patronizingly identifies her as "the poore greasie soule" (III.vi.129–130). Appropriately, when she scalds her leg, Goody Trash is dispatched for cream and salad oil, and Knockhem promises to dose her as he would an ailing horse, "with the white of an egge, a little honey, and hogs grease" (II.v.186–187). With the oozing and sweating, the dripping and melting that go on before our eyes and in the language, one might compare the icebound imagery of *Epi-*

cene, where the rare mention of a thaw suggests only the cracking of a frozen river.

Expressive in a related way of the omnipresent carnality is the persistent appearance of food and drink in the figurative language, as well as, of course, in the action. Winwife compares Mrs. Littlewit to a garden with "a *Strawbery*-breath, *Chery*-lips, *Apricot*-cheekes, and a soft veluet head, like a *Melicotton*" (I.ii.15–16). In contrast to Truewit's "delicate garden" of femininity in *Epicene* (I.i.105), a pruned and ordered plot of ground blossoming only under careful husbandry, here all of the blossoming plants have fructified: the garden is virtually an orchard. Busy, we learn, quarreled with a grocer over currants; he is described before his first entrance in a posture of gluttony; and there is evident fitness in his having been, prior to his conversion, a baker who sold cakes for folk festivals. The Puritan family as a whole hankers after roast pig. Cokes, for his part, is a "Rauener after fruite" (I.v.117). And Leatherhead's disenchanting recital of the ingredients in Goody Trash's gingerbread — "stale bread, rotten egges, musty ginger, and dead honey" (II.ii.9–10) — does not alter the fact that the ingredients add up to something edible, and not to a fucus, a magic elixir, or the philosophers' stone.

The word "fruit" forms a juncture between the eating and the procreative images of the play. In contrast to *The Silent Woman*, where all is barrenness and impotence, *Bartholomew Fair* teems with suggestions of fecundity. These are externalized in Mrs. Littlewit's pregnancy, which sets the plot in motion. Unlike the young heroes of *Epicene*, who occupy their time thwarting the marriages of others, Quarlous and Winwife spend the day successfully promoting their own. Winwife's prediction that "These flies cannot, this hot season, but engender vs excellent creeping sport" (I.v.140–141) compresses into a single image the notion that nature breeds more recklessly during the dog days, and that fools will spawn their folly more promiscuously in the same season. When Winwife and Quarlous choose their words to enter in the madman's book, they speak of "conceiving" and "creating" those words (IV.iii.56–57), lending a carnal tinge to the operations of the mind. The madman himself, running through the Fair crying his quasi-scriptural injunction, "Quit yee, and multiply yee" (IV.i.112–113), supplies his own demented sanction to the procreative orgy implied by the place and season.[38]

The accent, throughout, is thus on the gratification of the senses, on physical release, and this release achieves its final expression in the uninhibited debauch of the puppet play. The drinking of sack, the eating of herring and bacon in the puppet alehouse, form a link with the perpetual gluttonizing of the Fair. Wasp's excremental abuse reappears in the even nastier abuse of the puppets and their master. And the whoring and pimping that run like a leitmotif through the day's activities at the Fair reach their unsavory climax in the puppet tavern when Cupid, appearing in his own person, assumes the twin roles of tapster and pander played earlier at Ursula's tent by Captain Whit.

The fact that the puppets are not, after all, human, but mere wooden automatons, accentuates on the one hand the subhuman character of so much of what passes for human behavior at the Fair. It suggests the view of life — all vileness and irrationality — held by the Fair-going public. The sinfulness that relates Ursula to "the first woman, a ribbe," and Adam Overdo to his eponymous first ancestor is reduced to its most mechanistic and most contemptible. On the other hand, the fact that the puppets cannot decompose, that they are heartless little dummies exempt from the evils of the flesh, lends a certain pathos to flesh and blood itself.

There is no particular surprise in Jonson's use of the puppets to represent live people in their Bergsonian aspect. His attitude toward the puppets, however, is unexpectedly indulgent, as his attitude toward their critics is severe. If the moralists and justicers of early Jonsonian comedy have at last become butts and dupes instead of heroes, and if the rogues and fools are now vindicated, to execute this subversive justice the puppet play supplants the high tribunal as an instrument of correction. Behind Asper looms the figure of Queen Elizabeth, behind Crites the court of Cynthia, behind Horace the throne of Augustus; but behind Cokes, Littlewit, and the underworld of Smithfield stands the imbecile puppet show, which concentrates in itself all of the folly of the world, as the other court concentrated all of the wisdom. The royal tribunal of the comical satires separated the sheep from the goats, the wise from the foolish. The puppet show obliterates the distinction, confounding the wise so as to prove them fools, and dismissing the fools with a birching.

The vapors, it may be remembered, though they issue in quarrels, at the same time form a compelling reminder of the kinship between men. The prominence in *Bartholomew Fair* of figurative language involving the family has already been remarked by an astute critic: the image of Wasp as dry nurse to Cokes, Goody Trash with her "ginger-bread-progeny" (II.ii.4), Overdo's frustrated fatherhood reflected in his solicitude for Edgeworth, and Ursula's tendency to become "a kind of universal mother," mirror the dramatic fact that "in this play, for the first time since *Every Man in His Humour*, family relationships are depicted on the stage." [39] Other images exhibit people in gregarious groups larger than the family, in herds, flocks, and tribes. Such language stresses the communal impulses of the species, the forces that bind it together, rather than the aberrations that splinter it into disconnected atoms.

In contrast to the misanthropic withdrawal of a Morose, or the calculated seclusion of a Volpone, or the self-absorbed egomania of the characters of *Every Man Out*, the Fair draws its visitors and inhabitants together into the fold of a shared humanity and involves them inextricably with one another.

For this disorderly gregariousness, the vapors may be held responsible. But even in their stricter sense of quarrelsomeness the vapors tyrannize over the action. From the wrangling between Wasp and his acquaintances in Act I we pass to the nearly uninterrupted series of brawls and squabbles that punctuate the day's events at the Fair. Almost every episode culminates in a scrimmage. The Justice discovers that he cannot maintain his Olympian aloofness from the general tumult, and even the fastidious Winwife finds himself twice drawn into quarrels. Three times the constables appear to halt a quarrel and to carry the troublemakers off to the stocks, until at length they in their turn succumb to the ubiquitous vapors and fall to fighting with the lunatic Troubleall.

A preliminary climax to all of this vaporing comes in the appalling game played before Ursula's tent in Act IV, but the real climax is the puppet play. The puppet show is an absolute orgy of quarrels, a saturnale of vapors, which raises to a hysterical pitch the vulgar bickerings of the day. The puppets berate each other out of sheer perversity. No reason is offered for their compulsive trading of insults, nor any intimation that they might act otherwise. As miniature men, created and activated in the image of live men, they simply do what is natural: they quarrel. In their grotesque travesty of humankind, they prove the breath of the spirit to be nothing but wind. The inspiration that animates them, like the inspiration that animates Busy, is pure flatulence.

Through their association with Cokes, the puppets reflect another feature of the Fair and of the world it symbolizes:

human littleness. Cokes, we have already seen, is held spell-bound by the marvels of this world, and above all by the little mimic doubles of reality that the Fair procreates as it pro-creates so much else. As Ursula presides over her roast pigs and is the mother of these, so Goody Trash reigns maternally over her gingerbread images, while Lantern Leatherhead plays sire both to the hobbyhorses and the puppets. The toys them-selves come in families: Cokes buys "sixe horses . . . And the three Iewes trumps; and halfe a dozen o' Birds . . . and foure Halberts — and . . . that fine painted great Lady, and her three women for state" (III.iv.76–82), and a set of violins, "euery one a size lesse then another" (III.iv.91–92). The world shrinks to a Lilliputian array of dolls and baubles in which children play at being grown up.

The microcosmic images come to a natural climax in the puppet play. The puppets are linked with the dolls and hobby-horses not only etymologically (*pupa, poupée*) and through the joint enterprise of Lantern Leatherhead, but because Cokes names them after his toys. "I am in loue with the *Actors* already, and I'll be allyed to them presently. . . . *Hero* shall be my fayring: But, which of my fayrings? (Le'me see) i'faith, my *fiddle!* and *Leander* my *fiddle-sticke:* Then *Damon,* my *drum;* and *Pythias,* my *Pipe,* and the ghost of *Dionysius,* my *hobby-horse*" (V.iii.131–137). Having thus formally "allied" himself to the puppets, he confirms the alliance during the course of the motion by acting out with them their own diminutive passions.

The puppet play itself, written in the jog-trot couplets of the old interludes (like the jig in *Volpone*), shrinks litera-ture as well as life into the tiny compass of a peep show, and decomposes it into the grossness of its baser elements. For this technique of belittlement, Jonson had sufficient precedent. In burlesquing the most famous mythological poem of the previous generation, he was merely completing a process begun by his Latin masters, the satirists of the silver age. Juvenal had commenced his satires with a sweeping refusal to write on the old, outworn mythological themes, and Persius had disrespectfully protested that he had never washed his lips in the horsey spring; both had promised their readers to stick to transcriptions of daily life.[40] Martial, in a celebrated passage forever in Jonson's mind, had spurned poetic traffic with Oedipus and Thyestes, Endymion and Hylas, in favor of the kind of realism to which the reader can respond by crying "Meum est." [41] The glut of mythological poems that poured from English presses in the 1590's had aroused a somewhat similar revulsion in Jonson's own generation. And one characteristic rejoinder was to combine realism with travesty. One need only cite Nashe's earlier parody of the Hero and Leander myth,[42] or Dekker's offhand vulgarization of the Orpheus story,[43] or, for that matter, the scathing debasement of the Troy legend in *Troilus and Cressida*, to see the puppet show as part of a familiar process which placed heroic story under the disillusioning lens of satire and found it to be as squalid and carbuncular as anything in quotidian life.[44]

The puppet show takes the two great idyls of Hero and Leander and Damon and Pythias — each almost an archetypal myth for earlier Elizabethans — and domesticates them rudely into the London scene. Leander becomes a dyer's son, Hero a Bankside tart, and Damon and Pythias a pair of alehouse roarers. The two great themes of Renaissance literature, love and friendship, are thus debased, along with everything else in the play, to the level of vapors. The noble love of Hero and Leander becomes a smutty tavern anecdote. The even nobler tale of Damon and Pythias becomes an obscene tavern brawl, and both stories reach a simultaneous climax in the battle of the puppets, where the vapors go wholly out of control.

Jonson's attitude toward the puppet show is complex. Puppets, along with "the concupisence of *Iigges* and *Dances*" (*BF* Ind. 131–132), ordinarily aroused his aversion. "A man cannot imagine that thing so foolish, or rude, but will find, and enioy an Admirer; at least, a Reader, or *Spectator*. The Puppets are seene now in despight of the Players" (*Disc.* 608–611). Even within *Bartholomew Fair* itself, the silent, disapproving presences of Grace and Winwife remain to remind us that Jonson kept a corner of his mind aloof from such foolishness. But on the other hand, as the Fair is the microcosm, so the puppet show becomes the microtheater. By enlisting our sympathies on behalf of Lantern Leatherhead and his troupe and against the reformers, Jonson adds a new element to the familiar rebuttals of poets against their Puritan attackers. The Puritans had leveled much of their fire against the vicious moral atmosphere of the playhouses, and when they discussed the dramatic fare itself, they tended to dwell on the more specifically popular kinds of entertainment: morris dancing, jigging, clowning, and the like, lumping together "baudie Stage-playes and enterludes" with "May-games, Church-ales, feasts, and wakeesses . . . pyping, dauncing, dicing, carding, bowling, tennisse playing . . . Beare-bayting, cock-fighting, hawking, hunting . . . foot-ball playing, and such other deuilish pastimes." [45] The poets, for their part, not only failed to defend these ruder entertainments, they disclaimed any intention of defending them, often adding their own execrations to those of the Puritans before going on to exalt epic and tragedy. Lodge tells Gosson that "if you had wisely wayed the abuse of poetry, if you had reprehended the foolish fantasies of our Poets *nomine non re* which they bring forth on stage, my self wold haue liked of you and allowed your labor." And he proceeds to cap Gosson's rebuke of such abuses with his own, and to clamor for their suppression on his own behalf:

I abhore those poets that sauor of ribaldry: I will with the zealous admit the expullcion of such enormities: poetry is dispraised not for the folly that is in it, but for the abuse whiche manye ill Wryters couller by it. Beleeue mee the magestrats may take aduise (as I knowe wisely can) to roote out those odde rymes which runnes in euery rascales mouth, sauoring of rybaldry. Those foolishe ballets that are admitted make poets good and godly practises to be refused.[46]

Sidney, similarly, rehearsing the charge of immorality brought against the stage, laments the low state of "the Comick, whom naughtie Play-makers and Stage-keepers haue iustly made odious," before going on to censure the abuse of tragedy, always adulterated by "scurrility, vnwoorthy of any chast eares, or some extreame shew of doltishnes." [47] And even Jonson's fellow dramatist, Thomas Heywood, apologizing not merely for plays but for players, strictly withholds his endorsement from the "lasciuious shewes, scurrelous ieasts, or scandalous inuectiues" [48] that disfigure the stage.

Now it is quite likely that Jonson, *in propria persona*, would have concurred with these strictures, with those of Sidney and Heywood at least, if not those of Lodge. Like them, he tends in his critical writings to defend the Idea of a Theater rather than the living theater itself. Like them, he grows indignant over the prostitution of the drama to spectacle and scurrility. But *Bartholomew Fair*, more radical than its author, meets the opposition head-on. It grounds itself on the premise that if the ministry and the civic authorities are clamoring for the suppression of the theater, then the theater must be, if not defended, at least tolerated, even in its vilest and rowdiest manifestations, even where the appeal is exclusively to the senses and not at all to the understanding. The crude jollities of Fair and carnival, as well as the pompous pageantries of the stage, belong under the trusteeship of the festival spirit, and satisfy a legitimate craving for joy. There is no attempt to whitewash the Fair; corruption oozes from every seam of it, and the little theater of the motion proves to be more than a match for its real-life counterparts as a gathering ground of whores and pimps and rascals. As for the puppet show itself, it is a monstrous travesty of the drama, not only scurrilous, but disjointed, chaotic, and full of imbecile repetition.[49] Yet the puppet show epitomizes the Fair, which in turn epitomizes the world, a world inhabited by the descendants of Adam. If one is to legislate against folly, where does the legislation stop? And who is so disinfected of flesh and blood as to qualify as a legislator? The old game of *tu quoque* leads this time to its most drastic conclusion, in which the morons and numbskulls, without ceasing to incur their maker's ridicule, triumph over the reformers and justicers. Littlewit's puppet play, with Lantern Leatherhead as its impresario and Bartholomew Cokes as its most impassioned partisan, becomes the agent of reform for the reformers. As in Shakespeare's "saturnalian" comedy, pleasure, rather than learning or wisdom, has become the touchstone. The exhilarating finale of *Bartholomew Fair* rebaptizes the repressive spirits in a communal joy.

Wasp is the first to be converted. Discovering that Cokes has learned of his session in the stocks, he resigns his tutorial office with sententious formality: "Do's he know that? nay, then the date of my *Authority* is out; I must thinke no longer to raigne, my gouernment is at an end. He that will correct another, must want fault in himselfe" (V.iv.97–100). And with this recognition that he is, like the rest of the world, "an Asse," and "a kinne to the *Cokeses*," Wasp is ready to join with Cokes in applauding the puppets, to become a participant in pleasure instead of an enemy of it, to share with his fellows instead of perpetually setting his hand against theirs.

Busy's reformation, much more sudden, has been viewed by some as a flaw.[50] But its abruptness accords well with the arbitrary veerings of the vapors, the "mechanical operations of the spirit." The same winds that have puffed through him to inspire a fanatic (though hypocritical) denial of life may shift suddenly to inspire a renewed acceptance of it. In his dispute with the puppet Dionysius (whose name enjoys incidental propriety in that as god of the theater and lord of the revels he symbolizes everything hated by Puritanism) Busy repeats some of the arguments his pamphleteering forebears had already urged against the stage, its alleged descent from Satan,[51] and the wickedness of its players, "an *abomination:* for the Male, among you, putteth on the apparell of the *Female*, and the *Female* of the *Male*" (V.v.99–100). To the latter accusation the puppet replies by pulling up its garment and revealing its sexlessness. Without wishing to grow solemn over such a detail, one may suggest that Jonson is hereby intimating the essential innocence of the theater, an innocence based on its quality of make-believe and on its character as licensed release. To deny the legitimacy of such release is to deny one's own impulses, and to become, all the more blindly and self-deludedly, a puppet. Only, it would appear, by acknowledging his kinship with the puppets can a man begin to transcend his own grossness, vaporousness, and automatism. The moment of fullest recognition thus precedes the conversion. "*Nay*," declares the puppet Dionysius, "*I'le proue, against ere a* Rabbin *of 'hem all, that my standing is as lawfull as his; that I speak by inspiration, as well as he; that I haue as little to doe with learning as he; and doe scorne her helps as much as he*" (V.v.109–112). With this, the identification be-

tween Busy and the puppets is complete. Thoroughly confuted by the "demonstration," Busy abdicates as reformer and
subsides into the more wholesome role of spectator.

It remains only for this lesson to be learned by Justice
Overdo, who interrupts the motion a second time, to throw
off his disguise and expose the enormities he has been collect-
ing all day. With the worst and least expected enormity prov-
ing to be his own wife, in a state of drunken coma, seated
amidst the most disreputable members of the audience, Overdo
is stricken into a stiffness as wooden as that of the puppets.
The further disclosures proffered by Quarlous teach him that
his fervor has only embroiled him in the enormities he has
been pursuing, that with his disguises and his deep policy he
has only hoodwinked himself. Quarlous draws the moral
squarely: "remember you are but *Adam*, Flesh, and blood!
you haue your frailty, forget your other name of *Ouerdoo*,
and inuite vs all to supper" (V.vi.96–98). It is left to the
archetypal puppet, Cokes, to pronounce the final words of the
play, which carry the human comedy indefinitely forward
into the future: ". . . and bring the *Actors* along, wee'll ha'
the rest o' the *Play* at home" (V.vi.114–115).

One might suggest, finally, that with this play, in which the
reformers are reformed by the fools, Jonson confesses his own
frailty and his own flesh and blood. Though he continues to
satirize popular taste, he now — momentarily at least — identifies his own interests with it. Having, like Busy, failed to
affect public morality, having like Wasp failed to educate
fools, and having, like Adam Overdo, failed to maintain his
Stoic neutrality amid the pressures and passions of life, he resigns himself to the status of a fool among fools. The falling-
out among thieves, in *The Alchemist*, ended in a total rupture.
In *Bartholomew Fair*, the hucksters and sharpsters of the Fair
quarrel among themselves, but close ranks solidly when con-

fronted by attacks on their existence from the outside. Jonson, in similar fashion, having waged the war of the theaters at the turn of the century, and having spent fifteen years denouncing the usual fare of the public playhouses, now closes ranks with them to present a united front against the enemies of all the theaters, the Puritan preachers and the city fathers, whose hostility, unappeased by such appeals to flesh and blood, was shortly to kill both Fair and Theater at once.

❧ VI ❧

Painting, Carpentry, and Prose

AFTER *Bartholomew Fair*, Jonson unexpectedly renounces prose in the theater. Except for the intermean of gossips in *The Staple of News*, the induction and chorus of *The Magnetic Lady*, and a tiny patch of courtroom language in *The New Inn*, verse reigns undisputed in the last comedies. Why Jonson abandoned a technique he had done so much to develop remains mysterious, especially in view of his continuing use of the London setting and other realistic elements. The final plays, indeed, compose a kind of anthology of contemporary economic abuses; [1] the hard economic facts of life play an increasingly important role in the lives of the characters. Moreover, though linguistic satire momentarily disappears from *The Devil is an Ass*, it makes a spectacular comeback in *The Staple of News*, where a whole series of special vocabularies is pilloried as "canting." The moral, in fact, has never been so explicit or so comprehensive. "All the whole world are *Canters*" (IV.i.56), we are informed by an auctorial spokesman, himself named Penniboy Canter: the perversion of language no longer knows any limits or exceptions; all who are human practice it, and gobbledygook covers the earth. The Staple office, it is true, shares some of the illusory quality of Subtle's workshop, but whether by design or accident, the motives of those who run it and those who frequent it are kept on a far more humanly plausible scale. The flamboyant mystification and the prodigious credulity are equally missing. To account for the return to verse, therefore, one must speak, instead, of the symptoms of regression in the last plays: the devil scenes of *The Devil is an Ass*, the morality-allegory of Lady Pecunia in *The Staple of News*, the unabashed romance plots of *The New Inn* and *The Magnetic Lady*. This resumption of old-fashioned themes, which Jonson had banished from his stage early in his career, testifies either to a decline in his experimental energy or to a more aggressive wooing of his dwindling audience; probably it is to both painful phenomena that one must ascribe the discarding of prose and the return to the more conventional medium of blank verse.

At the same time, however, Jonson's career as masque-maker to the court was still in midstream. The prose that he henceforth withheld from the public stage he lavished with unflagging vigor and brilliance upon the more fugitive genre of the masque, carrying into the masque many of the preoccupations that had engrossed him for so long in comedy.

The radical differences between the masque [2] and the regular theater may be reduced to two. One is the far greater importance in the masque of music, dance, and stage spectacle. These ancillary delights of the public stage become paramount in the court banqueting hall. The text becomes a scenario, to be fulfilled by the arts of choreography and stage design, or a libretto, in which at key moments the supremacy passes to the melodic line or the harmony of the instrumental ensemble. One anomaly in the history of the masque is that its full flowering as a spectacular entertainment coincides with its decline as a literary form. Considered as verbal structures, the best masques occur during the Jacobean period, when Italian stagecraft was still a not quite familiar toy, and spoken language still held its pre-eminence over the singing voice. If there is a moment of ascendancy for music, it is in 1617, when *Lovers made Men* was sung throughout "*(after the Italian manner)* Stylo Recitativo" (26–27) to a score by Nicholas Lanier, but this experiment seems not to have been repeated. The Caroline masques, on the other hand, more and more triumphant as feats of stage engineering, deteriorate as literature into twaddle. Whether this progress is properly to be regarded as a fulfillment or a degeneration depends, perhaps, on one's point of view, but if one thinks of the masque as ideally a composite of music, poetry, and the arts of the dance and stage architecture, with poetry occupying the central position, then certainly the peak achievements occur during the early years, and most of them are Jonson's.

The war between poetry and spectacle, it may be added, would seem to be strikingly epitomized in the quarrel between Jonson and Inigo Jones: between the learned poet, striving to convert the perishable diversion into a lasting monument, and the wizard-architect, impatient of all restraint on the building of his cloud-capped towers, and indifferent to their fate. And this rivalry, in turn, might be said to mirror a conflict within Jonson himself: between the platonizing effort to read sensible things as symbols of a higher reality, on the one hand, and the more pragmatic, more theatrical attachment to things of sense for their own sake, on the other. Oddly, if the things of sense earned his final allegiance in the public playhouse, it was the world of "soul" and emblem to which he remained devoted in the royal banqueting hall. As enthusiasm grew, in court and public, for pure spectacle, Jonson's pleasure in it seemed to wane. The printed versions of his early masques supply abundant accounts of décor and costume; those of the later masques print only the bare text. And yet, paradoxically, the things of sense that he so sternly worked to subordinate, in so far as they presented themselves under the aspect of spectacle, he allowed to creep back in, as we shall see, through the more verbal channel of the comic prose antimasque.

The other signal feature of the masque is rooted in its function as a court festival: the intimate bond between players and audience, and the crucial role of the king. The masquers, or chief dancers, belong mostly to the nobility, sometimes to the royal family itself; hence no social barrier divides stage from spectators. The play, in fact, is designed to lead up to the climactic moment at which players and onlookers actually mingle: the masquers descend from their platform and "take out" the members of the audience to dance, the dramatic spectacle thus forming a kind of mimetic prelude to the main business of the evening, the revels. Heightening the solemnity of the event is the physical presence of the king, enthroned opposite the stage, acting as host for the occasion and providing a focus for the atmosphere of symbolism in which it takes place. One of the playwright's problems, hence, is to find a dramatic formula that will allow the right gestures to be made, naturally but emphatically, to the king.

The gestures to the sovereign, of course, often take the form of hyperbolic compliment, which we may understand better if we quote Northrop Frye on the place of the masque among other dramatic genres.

The further comedy moves from irony, and the more it rejoices in the free movement of its happy society, the more readily it takes to music and dancing. As music and scenery increase in importance, the ideal comedy crosses the boundary line of spectacular drama and becomes the masque. . . . [The masque] thus differs from comedy in its more intimate attitude to the audience: there is more insistence on the connection between the audience and the community on the stage. . . . The ideal masque is in fact a myth-play like the *auto*, to which it is related much as comedy is to tragedy. It is designed to emphasize, not the ideals to be achieved by discipline or faith, but ideals which are desired or considered to be already possessed.[3]

The masque, that is, represents a society not so much aspiring after as joyfully contemplating its own well-being, the possession of the blessings it considers itself to have achieved. The compliments to the king, so often dismissed as ignoble flattery, are one expression of this self-congratulation on the part of the community. To eulogize the king is to congratulate the society, of which the king is figurehead, for the communal virtues symbolized in him. To the extent that the actuality falls short of the ideal, the masque may be taken as a kind of mimetic magic on a sophisticated level, the attempt to secure social health and tranquillity for the realm by miming it in front of its chief figure. The frequency of prayer as a rhetorical mode in the masques is hence not accidental. E. K. Chambers regards the masks themselves, of the dancers, as vestiges of the animal exuviae worn in folk rituals in order to ensure good luck.[4]

In Jonson's masques, particularly, as critics have noticed, there is the further element of counsel.[5] The masque becomes a mirror for magistrates in which the king sees himself transfigured by the virtues he ought to possess, the justice he ought to exercise, the magnanimity that should ennoble the realm. It becomes a mirror for subjects as well. The "magnificence" of the event combines with the climactic recognition of the king's visible presence to infuse a sense of "wonder" into participants and spectators; the "wonder," in turn, creates a frame of mind uniquely favorable to the absorption of all the virtues appropriate to them as loyal subjects.[6] Similarly, the celebration of a noble wedding involves the whole community in a feast of Hymen and a prayer for fertility, in which the actual personalities of the bride and groom, whether an attractive couple like the Princess Elizabeth and the Elector

Palatine or an unsavory pair like the Earl of Somerset and
Lady Frances Howard, count for far less than their symbolic
function.

According to the premises of the masque, then, the king
embodies all the wisdom, justice, and mercy — real and potential — in the kingdom; the nuptial pair symbolizes the
youth and perpetuation of the society; the masquers and the
spectators form a phalanx of loving and loyal vassals. These
assumptions go deeper than mere etiquette, but they are reflected in the etiquette of the masque: nothing may be said to
the sovereign that does not follow from them. This for the
main masque itself. The antimasque, an abbreviated symbol
of misrule, permits itself greater liberties, especially in the
prose interludes that concern us here. In the antimasque, a
certain amount of disrespect is not only tolerable but desirable.
It must come, however, only from certain kinds of characters:
from clowns whose ignorance makes them comic and touch-
ing, or from wicked children of darkness whose destiny it is
to be driven from the stage and supplanted by ministers of
light.

Besides the king, the court sits as witness to the masque, and
may be made the group recipient of rhetorical appeals; the
ladies, especially, tend to be singled out for compliment or
playful admonition. The privileged bourgeois who throng the
outer edges of the banqueting hall may in their turn be fitted
into the rhetorical scheme, though more tangentially. Finally,
there are the players themselves, the noble lords and ladies who
dance as masquers, headed perhaps by the queen or prince, and
— in the more extended speaking parts — the professional
actors hired for the occasion. These too tend increasingly to be
recognized in their dual capacity within the action. The circle
of recognition is thus complete. There is no moment at which
the dramatic situation cannot look beyond itself or at itself,

out to the society of which it is the purified image, back to itself as to the image in process of formation.

The circumstances of production impose further limitations on the masquewright. He must allow for transformation scenes. He must contrive to lead up to the main activity of the evening, the revels. He must restrict the number of speaking characters to a half dozen or fewer. He must provide songs and integrate them into the plot.

If we glance back toward more rudimentary forms of pageantry, we can distinguish two basic rhetorical structures: the speech and the debate. The speech plays an important part in pageants like that of Elizabeth's coronation, where richly clad children, stationed at triumphal arches along the route, broke out into eulogy at her approach — eulogy, however, not unmixed with edification: one of the speaker's main jobs was to explain the iconography of the site, the mottoes, emblems, and imprese inscribed on the arch, the detailed symbolism of garment and gesture, the riddles wrought into sculpted flora and fauna. The debate comes into prominence at court, in the "barriers" or "tourney" festival, where competing knights, wearing symbolic devices, utter challenging speeches to each other before entering the lists. Country entertainments like those offered to Elizabeth on her progresses employ both the panegyric and the *conflictus*, which may be made more dramatic by being predicated on the fiction of her absence, or her incognito. The climax comes when the speakers "recognize" the queen, and the recognition in turn produces that "wonder" that magically reveals the truth, resolves discords, and irradiates everyone present with a sacramental sense of the wholeness of the realm. The Jacobean masque characteristically combines both eulogy and debate. The eulogist becomes a presenter, whose duty it is to introduce the debaters, explicate the symbolism of their costumes, arbitrate their differences, and mediate between them and the spectators, whether by way of apology or reprimand.

This highly schematic account ignores, of course, all of the particular variations that lend the masques their interest. Jonson, especially, as Herford and Simpson observe, "is so free from the vices of system and the grooves of habit that his technique is hard to grasp" (II, 334). Nevertheless, the debate, with its attendant presenter, provides the basic pattern for a surprisingly large number of masques. Even the antimasque merely affords a more radically theatrical way of dramatizing an antagonism whose essentials can usually be reduced to the terms of a formal dispute.

I

Looking at *The Entertainment at Highgate*, a May Day pageant performed for the new monarchs at a country house in 1604, we find that the presenter, Mercury, speaks prose, but that his language, far from being comic or realistic, has the austere dignity of Jonson's most formal writing. If there is comedy here, it is in the drunken couplets of Pan, which strike the note of impudent misrule later channeled into the antimasque. Mercury speaks in a style full of Latinate constructions and intricacies of syntax. Greeting the sovereigns, he refuses to identify himself because, as he claims, the devices he wears decipher him sufficiently.

To tell you, who I am, and weare all these notable, and speaking ensignes about me, were to challenge you of most impossible ignorance, and accuse my selfe of as palpable glorie: It is inough that you know me here, and come with the licence of my father Iove, who is the bountie of heauen, to giue you early welcome to the bower of my mother Maia, no lesse the goodnesse of earth.

(52–59)

The antithetic turns here ("the licence of my father Iove . . .

247

the bower of my mother MAIA") appear, as so often in Jonson, embedded in a refractory syntax that dissembles the exactness of the oppositions, and keeps the articulated parallels moving forward in a fluid mass without permitting them to separate out into cleanly defined subsections. If the procedure reminds us of the prose in *Every Man out of his Humour* and *Cynthia's Revels*, the reason is plain enough: Jonson has not yet ceased to experiment with the more florid kinds of baroque syntax as a dramatic language. Here, however, as in, let us say, Mercury's portrait of Crites, the floridity suggests spaciousness and composure, not, as in the speeches of Amorphus, self-satisfied magniloquence.

But Jonson is aiming at other effects. Having identified the mythic site on which he stands as the Arcadian hill, and the figures seated about it as certain goddesses, Mercury describes the nymphs and dryads at play amid the greenery. Suddenly he interrupts himself to announce that the revels have ceased at the approach of the royal couple.

But, see! vpon your approch their pleasures are instantly remitted. The birds are hush'd, ZEPHYRE is still, the MORNE forbeares her office, FLORA is dumbe, and herselfe amazed, to behold two such maruailes, that doe more adorne place, then shee can time.

(82–87)

The succession of dense periods, knotted with internal antitheses, yields to a series of short, hesitant, widely spaced clauses that wonderfully convey the sense of hushed expectancy produced by the king's arrival.

The afternoon's entertainment centers about Pan, whom Mercury presents with due apology for his own fault in begetting him, and for his notorious rudeness. Again the approach of the monarchs is accompanied by an affecting change of pace in the language; the thickly woven tissue of relative clauses clears like a mist, leaving only brief startled fragments of clauses, heavily punctuated by interstitial silences, during which, presumably, the sounds of the earth are heard. Jonson has plainly chosen to make the country setting, the spring festival, and the symbolism of rebirth implicit in the arrival of a new monarch the basis for one of his infrequent essays at "poetic," or delicate, prose. The gravity and sweetness of Mercury's speeches reflect the idyllic spirit of May Day, the hopefulness with which the kingdom greets its new rulers, while the rowdier implications of the season find a congenial harbor in the scapegrace Pan and his doggerel couplets.

Within a few years the fate of prose in the masque was settled in another way, by the development of a new convention. According to Jonson's own account, the antimasque began, or rather crystallized, when the queen commanded him "to think on some *Daunce*, or shew, that might praecede hers, and haue the place of a foyle, or false-*Masque*" (*Queens* 12–13). Jonson, as usual, gave more than full measure. He addressed himself at once to the problem of preserving thematic consistency between the two halves of the expanded entertainment, of making the preliminary diversion not merely "a spectacle of strangenesse," atmospherically in contrast to the main dance, but also linked to it symbolically, "sorting with the current, and whole fall of the Deuise" (20–22). For the "foyle" to the *Masque of Queens* he devised a dance of witches, in which twelve hags personifying Malice, Slander, Credulity, and the like, under their leader Ate, mutter wicked charms to poison the fame of the good and bring about a return to chaos. Suddenly their incantations fail, the witches flee back to darkness, their sinister grotto is transformed into a radiant temple, and Fame herself descends in triumph, flanked by twelve celebrated heroines of history and myth.

The antimasque thus articulates dramatically the dualism already implicit in the masque form.[7] In *The Haddington*

Masque, a wedding festival of the previous year, Jonson had preceded the main dance of lords and ladies — a dignified and commodious sacrament betokening matrimony — with "*a subtle* capriccious Daunce" (171) of boy cupids, "*most antickly attyr'd*" (159), expressive of the more wayward and sportive aspects of love. And the year before that, in another nuptial ceremony, *Hymenaei*, he had blocked out a kind of archetypal masque plot in the revolt of the Humors and Affections against Reason. The four "vntemp'red *Humors*" and the four "wild *affections*" (121–122), emerging from "*a* Microcosme, *or* Globe, (*figuring Man*)," rush in with drawn swords to "*a kind of contentious Musique*" (109–110) to disrupt the wedding solemnities being conducted by Hymen. But while Hymen helplessly utters prayers for aid, Reason — "*a venerable* personage," seated "*in the top of the* Globe (*as in the braine, or highest part of* Man)" (129–130) — descends to restore discipline among her unruly followers, who then retire "*amazed to the sides of the stage, while* HYMEN *began to ranke the* Persons, *and order the* Ceremonies" (158–159). The rebellion thus aborted, and Reason having explained the mysteries of the nuptial rite, Juno appears in splendor in the clouds, the true spiritual mistress of the occasion. Her descent is followed by the joyful main dance, significantly conducted by "ORDER, *the seruant of* REASON" (272).

Hymenaei thus dramatizes the pattern of the microcosmic war in which the rebellious lower faculties attempt to subvert the regency of the higher. Reason, working through priests like Order, performs her traditional office as mediator between the sentient world and the intellectual world, preserving the sanctity of the wedding rites and so keeping the link intact. Jonson's favorite emblem of the broken and perfect circles pervades the action. Above the globe of man stands Jupiter "*brandishing his thunder*" (225–226) in the circular whirling of the sphere of fire. The perfection of the celestial spheres is mirrored in the earthly perfection of the "*faire* orbe, *or* circle" composed by the dancers in their final measure, with Reason "*standing in the midst*" (400–401), while the descent of Juno, symbolizing Union, welds higher and lower spheres together in a universal harmony.[8]

Abstractions from this pattern form the basis for many of the best of the subsequent masques. In each case the anti-masquers, whether malignant powers invoking chaos, or unruly spirits hovering about the fringes of an ordered society, or merely the wanton impulses within the society, momentarily at large, embody the disruptive pressure of "vntemp'red *Humors*" and "wild *affections*," while the apotheosis celebrates the reinstatement of one or another virtue attendant on Reason, and the repairing of the broken links between earth and heaven. In each case the antimasque itself, "*odde*," "*ridiculous*," "capriccious" (*Haddington* 171–173), "strange," "phantastique," "praeposterous" (*Queens* 344–350), to use some of Jonson's own words for it, is appropriately crowned by the full, spacious ritual of the main masque, where the dance becomes a visible symbol of concord restored. To the degree that the antimasque distorts or parodies the theme of the masque, it functions, as E. K. Chambers has pointed out, like the subplot of an Elizabethan play.[9] As in Shakespeare's "ideal comedies,"[10] whose affinities with the masque are close, the subplot of the antimasque decrees that the good society enshrined at the end shall not triumph without at least a token protest from the forces of disorder.

2

But Jonson's bent was toward the realistic and critical rather than the mythic and festive, and it was perhaps inevitable that after some years of chasing shadows in the phantasmagoric underworld of the antimasque, he should begin to hanker after the fleshpots of realism.[11] Perhaps by way of reaction, then, *Love Restored*, played at court on Twelfth Night of 1612, sweeps us without warning back into the clear, dry air of prose comedy. Instead of the customary "discovery" of a pastoral or mythological scene, peopled by nymphs or goddesses, there bustles breathless onto the stage a character named Masquerado, who proves to be merely one of the actors speaking in his own person, though in costume, apologizing to the king and court in Jonson's liveliest prose for the unlikelihood of their seeing any masque at all that night. Something has gone amiss backstage, and the preparations for the masque have come to a halt.

In troth, Ladies, I pittie you all. You are here in expectation of a deuice to night, and I am afraid you can doe little else but expect it. Though I dare not shew my face, I can speake truth, vnder a vizard. Good faith, and't please your Maiestie, Your Masquers are all at a stand; I cannot thinke your Maiestie wil see any shew to night, at least worth your patience. (1–9)

The direct appeal to the spectators, which forms a constant feature of the masque at its best, here takes on some of the comic impertinence of Roman comedy. Where the usual presenter maintains a deferential formality toward the audience, Masquerado teases it in a manner both jocose and slangy. Furthermore, the subject of his remarks, here as throughout the prologue, is nothing less than the theory and practice of the masque itself. Jonson had already, in some of the prefaces to the published quartos, begun to articulate a critical view of the genre. With *Love Restored* he begins to carry his theorizing before the audience, as he had for comedy, plentifully mingling formal precept with practical comment on the craft of masquemaking.

But *Love Restored* contains other surprises. Jonson has not merely interpolated prose comedy into the antimasque: he has in fact suppressed the antimasque entirely. No antic ballet precedes the unveiling of the masquers, nothing but the spirited comic dialogue between Masquerado, Plutus, and Robin Goodfellow. Before Masquerado has finished cataloguing the confusions behind the scenes, Plutus, disguised as Cupid, bursts from the tiring house to interrupt the proceedings: "I tell thee, I will haue no more masquing; I will not buy a false, and fleeting delight so deare: The merry madnesse of one hower shall not cost me the repentance of an age" (34–36). As it happens, Jonson's previous masque, *Love Freed from Ignorance and Folly*, had aroused disapproval in certain quarters because of its costliness. Jonson, never one to shrink from polemic, now turns Plutus into a puritanical spokesman for the party of "economy," and endows him with a language recognizably drawn from life. The churlish intruder of the antimasque, the witch, goblin, or satyr of earlier entertainments, has finally taken on the pocks and pimples of realistic caricature; the allegorical vice has incarnated itself in the Jonsonian fool. Once again Jonson is crusading against visible, social forms of folly, this time the officious purse-pinching of those who would hoard but not spend, who would restrict the court in its necessary function of "magnificence." When we hear the series of portentous epithets flung by Plutus at Masquerado — "fether'd vanitie" (22), "common corruption" (25), "impertinent folly" (23), "vizarded impudence" (28) — we recognize the kind of "wresting, and writhing" of speech that spells moral confusion. We recognize, more specifically, the same quirk of personification that is scribbled all over the dialogue of Ananias and Busy, the latter a creature still unborn. Similarly with Plutus' outraged allusion to the "vanities" of the "high places" (146–147). Jonson has at one stroke reintroduced into the fragile world of the masque not merely realism, but satire, and linguistic satire at that, his preferred weapon against fools.

But before the debate between Plutus and Masquerado can get far, a third party blunders onto the stage, in search of a place among the spectators. Obliged to explain his presence, the new arrival identifies himself as

the honest plaine countery spirit, and harmelesse: ROBBIN goodfellow, hee that sweepes the harth, and the house cleane, riddles for the countery maides, and does all their other drudgerie, while they are at hot-cockles: one, that ha's discours'd with your court spirits, e're now; but was faine to night to run a thousand hazards to arriue at this place; neuer poore goblin was so put to his shifts, to get in, to see nothing. (56–63)

It is scarcely necessary to quote from the "characters" prefixed to *Every Man out of his Humour*, or the thumbnail sketches of the gulls in *Cynthia's Revels*, or from Clerimont on Sir Amorous or Quarlous on Busy, to recognize Robin's self-portrait as a new variant on the familiar Jonsonian *caractère*. All the hallmarks appear: the summary introduction, the selective details that describe Robin's rustic chores, the shift from the pronoun "hee" to the impersonal "one" (almost as if a third person were in question), and then the elaborated final detail that acts as a cadence to the period and brings the narrative up to date. The only important difference is that Robin is anatomizing himself rather than someone else, and that he makes himself sound amiably, rather than affectedly, foolish.

A moment later and our ears have picked up another familiar Jonsonian device: the satiric catalogue. Robin's account of the obstacles he has surmounted in order to penetrate the banqueting hall turns into a condensed parade of realistic vignettes, each type drawn from the purlieus of the court and the tiring house: an "inginer," an old tire-woman, a feather-maker of Blackfriars, a wire man, a citizen's fine wife. The resemblance to formal satire is emphasized by the fact that these characters remain purely verbal constructions; they do not, as one might have expected, appear to dance an anti-masque, but appear only in Robin's narration.

After some three-cornered dispute, Robin finally exposes Plutus as a counterfeit Cupid, as the god of money who has stolen Love's ensigns, and who rules the world in that bor-rowed shape while Love lives captive in a frozen zone of the North. But unfortunately, as his denunciation progresses, Robin's tone grows steadily more solemn. The vivid collo-quialism of his style, with its "mary's" and "slights" and "would fains" scattered about like pins, changes into the formal eloquence of the magician-presenter:

Come, follow me. Ile bring you where you shall find Love, and by the vertue of this Maiestie, who proiecteth so powerfull beames of light and heat through this Hemispheare, thaw his icie fetters, and scatter the darknesse that obscures him. Then, in despight of this insolent and barbarous *Mammon*, your sports may proceed, and the solemnities of the night be complete, without depending on so earthie an idoll. (193–200)

Whatever may be the virtues of this stern prose, they are not those appropriate to the feckless bumpkin who has suffered so many embarrassing mishaps in his effort to get into the hall. We are faced with an erosion of decorum such as Jonson would never have permitted himself in the theater. And we discover, as we look at other masques, that this same point of transition between antimasque and masque proper poses a cardinal threat to the unity of the entertainment as a whole. Too often, as this point is neared, the boisterous interloper of the prologue fades into the colorless expositor; his racy vernac-ular congeals into a hieratic formality. If, on the other hand, a new character is brought in to effect the transition, decorum may be preserved, but the shift in presenters tends to emphasize the bifurcate nature of the entertainment and create a discontinuity between its two halves. And, one must add, the inherent difficulty is aggravated by the use of comic prose in the induction. To exorcise witches by the triumphal descent of Fame with her minions, to supplant wanton cupids by solemn votaries of the goddess of Love, to chase shaggy satyrs from the palace of Oberon, requires skilful maneuvering, no doubt, but does not transplant the audience from one plane of artistic reality to another. But to pass from realistic gabble among mechanic types to a purely symbolic epiphany in a purely symbolic landscape imposes obstacles of accommodation such as even Jonson only succeeded once or twice in surmounting.

In *Love Restored*, he has bound the two halves together by using Plutus in a double role: first as a sniping critic of court luxury, a meddlesome disparager of the diversions represented by Robin, and then as the great god Mammon, usurper of the title of Love and false ruler of the world. Cupid, in his speech of self-assertion, charges Robin, "honest spirit," with the job of chasing hence the sour tyrant, thus further strengthening the continuity between prologue and masque proper. But Plutus makes a somewhat equivocal symbol for Jonson's purposes, since in fact the masque cannot proceed without him, without the expenditure, that is, and hence the prior accumulation, of large sums of money. To banish Plutus indeed would be to outlaw the whole institution of masquing, together with all the other forms of pageantry that enriched court life. The opposition between Plutus and Robin Goodfellow on the one hand (roughly, thrift vs. mirth) and of Plutus and Cupid on the other (love vs. money) tends to overlook the hard economic realities behind both mirth and masquing. Chapman's

Middle Temple Masque of the following year, which imitates *Love Restored* in numerous ways (and is, on the whole, much inferior to it) improves on it in one significant particular. Chapman borrows the figure of Plutus from Jonson, but makes him the patron rather than the foe of masques; in the course of the action his proverbial blindness, dullness, and deformity are purged so that he may take command as a benign and munificent master of ceremonies over the whole occasion. Perhaps, for Jonson, the problem of Plutus was less an artistic than an ethical one: the lingering distrust of prodigality that kept him from approving a costly bauble like the masque even when, on rational grounds, he had persuaded himself of its value. A decade later, in *The Staple of News*, we find the ambivalence still alive: into the mouth of Penniboy Senior, the most disagreeable miser among his entire dramatis personae, Jonson places the same fervent invective against waste and luxury, against the "pleasures" and "fashions" and "pomp" of courts (III.iv.45–64), that he had already incorporated into the *Discoveries* (1387–1414) as a comment of his own.

But whatever the reason for the slight haze of uncertainty that lies behind its clear surface, *Love Restored* remains a brilliant experiment and a landmark in the history of the genre. Once Jonson had discovered — or rather rediscovered [12] — comic prose for court entertainments, other poets came scurrying along the same path. Somewhat oddly, though they often imitated Jonsonian motifs — such as the difficulty of access to the banqueting hall during a performance [13] — they tended not to copy his specific stylistic devices. Jonson's strategies of the *caractère* and the satiric procession found few imitators. Only the so-called *Mountebank's Masque* attributed to Marston makes the verbal portrait into a significant structural element. Other writers rely on costume, dance, and stage décor to amplify the dialogue (if any) of their antic personages.

The indications in Campion's *Lord's Masque* (1612–13) are typical:

> *At the sound of a strange musicke twelue Franticks enter, six men and six women, all presented in sundry habits and humours: there was the Louer, the Selfe-Louer, the melancholicke-man full of feare, the Schoole-man ouer-come with phantasie, the ouer-watched Vsurer, with others that made an absolute medly of madnesse . . .*[14]

Just the sort of procession for which Jonson would have enlisted the services of a presenter for raillery and explication. And almost equally rare, among his followers, are echoes of Jonson's own endless mulling of the problems of the genre itself.

For Jonson himself, on the other hand, *Love Restored* sets a host of precedents. Henceforth the antimasque concerns itself almost compulsively with the rules of the genre and the hazards of actual performance caused by the bewildering number of things that could go wrong backstage. At times, Jonson seems to be using the antimasque to vent a suppressed impatience with the whole elaborate, costly, frivolous operation. He manages at the same time, as one might expect, to express his contempt for the uninstructed taste of the auditory, its quenchless appetite for spectacle, and its indifference to solid poetic values.

The same restrictions of form and protocol, however, that made the masque an irritating medium also forbade its being attacked directly, and Jonson tends to keep the criticism oblique — as in *Love Restored* itself, no doubt, where (perhaps unconsciously) through the figure of Plutus he insinuates his own dislike of these gilded trifles. Often the complaints, if complaints they are, come filtered through the personae of clowns, whose ignorance of etiquette allows them a wider margin for disrespect; even here, though, the salty tirades are liberally sweetened with clownish compliments to the king and court. This is the case in *The Irish Masque*, *For the Honour of Wales*, *Christmas his Masque*, and others. But in any case it is plain that whatever the restrictions imposed by the form, the use of comic prose has liberated a certain area of Jonson's artistic personality that up to this moment has found no outlet.

One almost inevitable consequence of the resumption of prose proves to be a revitalization of character. In the earlier masques, as in formal allegory, character remains severely abstract; the dramatis personae embody aspects of personality rather than whole individuals. Literary elaboration takes the form of a deeper and deeper plumbing of the iconographic possibilities of the theme. But comic prose, with its freedom of syntax and diction, its range of informal rhetorical effects, and its habit of amassing concrete particulars, produces a realistic breakthrough, after which the Jonsonian gallery of eccentrics reconstitutes itself almost automatically.

But realism, introduced into a genre essentially hostile to it, a genre designed as a myth-play, puts a dangerous strain on the unity of the form. As the realistic material loses its allegorical bearings, the strain becomes greater. It becomes more and more difficult to collapse the graphic creatures of the antimasque into the abstract personae of the main masque; it becomes more difficult to reconcile the local habitation of the prologue with the Arcadian skyscape of the triumph. And the difficulty only redoubles when realism is compounded with satire. Satire, with its eye fastened on the squalider surfaces of life, its ear cocked for the scratch in the voice, is not likely to be of much help in bringing to birth a vision of the Golden Age restored. The more foolish the addleheads who caper about in the prologue, the more patently we recognize in them the oafs around the corner, the more arbitrary and *voulu* is likely to seem the triumph of Reason in the main masque.

That Jonson instinctively felt this we can infer from the fact that the satire in the masques never burns with the degree of fierceness that sometimes scorches us in the comedies. Plutus, in *Love Restored*, may be, on the symbolic level, the baleful spirit to be exposed and cast out, but on the more realistic plane of the induction, Plutus the niggardly Puritan is handled with infinite gentleness compared to his dramatic kinsmen Busy and Ananias. As for Christmas and Venus, the bowl-bearer of *Pleasure Reconciled to Virtue*, the Irish footmen or the Welsh bumpkins or the louts in the masque of Gypsies, their numerous solecisms seem recorded in a spirit of affectionate amusement; there is no hint that they are affected, or that they ought to speak any better than they do, or that their unkempt speech springs from anything more reprehensible than simplicity. From time to time, in Mercury's parody of alchemical cant, or in Plutus' complacent personifications, we hear a trace of the kind of linguistic abuse that once engrossed Jonson. But of sustained ridicule, backed up by moral censure, there is virtually none, perhaps because Jonson had to some extent mellowed by this time, perhaps also because affected language for him had always primarily meant the parroting of court jargon by those anxious to rise socially, and he could hardly ridicule imitation of court language before those who actually spoke it, without seeming to be deriding the language itself. The emphasis shifts, then, as it does in *Bartholomew Fair*, from contemptuous burlesque to good-natured chaffing, from stern objurgation to avuncular indulgence, coupled as always, one should add, with an entirely amoral delight in the varied forms and shapes of language in the world.

3

In *Love Restored* Jonson had brought together a classical deity and a local folk spirit to debate a contemporary issue. In *Mercury Vindicated from the Alchemists at Court* he improvises a brilliant mock myth that allows him to move simultaneously on several thematic levels — to satirize alchemy, expound a theory of art, repudiate the doctrine of the decay of nature, and register his approval of the king's foreign policy by associating it with his creative potency — without once blurring the outlines of the fable.

James's policy of peace has left Vulcan and his "smoakie familie" unemployed, since there is no more demand for armor. To fill up the time normally spent in forging weapons, they have turned to alchemy, to the laboratory synthesis of deformed creatures that they dare to place in rivalry with the true creatures of Nature. The fire of Vulcan's forge competes presumptuously against the life-giving heat of the sun, who is misled by the cold winter into thinking that Nature has lost her power. But Nature is only waiting to be acknowledged again as the true source of life, and Mercury, whom the alchemists have forcibly conscripted into their service, is only biding his time until he can return to Olympus. Just beneath the burlesque of alchemy [15] that forms the manifest content of the masque runs an impassioned Jonsonian metaphor whereby the alchemists, trying to palm off their synthetic creatures against the true coin minted by Nature, stand for charlatan artists who engender monsters instead of copying the truth.

The conception is worked out in a vivid prose induction that consists largely of a monologue by Mercury. After a song from the Cyclops, who tends the forge and explains that the fire will replace the sun because the latter has grown cold, Mercury bolts from the furnace and runs about the stage pursued by Vulcan. When he recovers breath, he appeals to the audience for help against his captors:

Now the place and goodnesse of it protect me. One tender-hearted creature, or other, saue *Mercury*, and free him. Ne're an olde Gentle-woman i' the house, that has a wrinckle about her, to hide mee in? I could run into a Seruing-womans pocket now; her gloue, any little hole. Some mercifull vardingale among so many, be bounteous, and vndertake me. (30–36)

Jonson had already, in *Love Freed from Ignorance and Folly*, shown the captive Cupid pleading for aid from the ladies against his cruel jailer, the Sphinx. In *The Haddington Masque*, he had imagined Venus instructing her nymphs to search for Cupid in the ladies' eyes, "Or in their bosomes, 'twixt their swelling brests: / (The *wag* affects to make him-selfe such nests)" (75–76), just as in a much earlier court entertainment, Tasso's *Aminta*, Venus had offered rewards to the spectators for information concerning Cupid's where-abouts.[16] But in each of these cases the deity had addressed herself (or himself) to the lords and ladies *en bloc*, to a solid legion of valor and beauty. Mercury not only enlists the ladies in his defense against Vulcan, he particularizes them, and by descending a few degrees in the social scale, he converts them into comic characters themselves. The old gentlewoman with the extra wrinkle, the serving-woman with a free pocket, the merciful farthingale, become participants in a comic action. The mock myth of the alchemists reaches out from the stage to encompass the watchers in the most explicit and imagina-tive way.

Mercury proceeds to give an account of himself. His self-portrait is brilliantly designed to exhibit his volatility by in-dicating the multiple uses to which the alchemists put him in their workshop, the gamut of names they confer on him, the varied indignities to which they subject him, and the changing appearances he presents after they have experimented on him.

I am their Crude, and their Sublimate; their Praecipitate, and their vnctuous; their male and their female; sometimes their *Hermaphrodite;* what they list to stile me. It is I, that am corroded, and exalted, and sublim'd, and reduc'd, and fetch'd ouer, and filtred, and wash'd, and wip'd; what betweene their salts and their sulphures; their oyles, and their tartars, their brines and their vinegers, you might take me out now a sous'd *Mercury,* now a salted *Mercury,* now a smoak'd and dri'd *Mercury,* now a pouldred and pickl'd *Mercury.*   (51–60)

But in the same moment that he is demonstrating his own protean versatility, Mercury is busily reducing the jargon of the alchemists to gibberish. The language grows progressively more stratified into figures of repetition, until we are left with the series of "now's," "Mercury's," and adjectives, whizzing by like telephone poles from a train, so fast that no individual pole can arrest the eye but only the pattern set up by the motion. The highly mannered burlesque comes to a climax in a series of asyndetic clauses, which, like the philosopher's circle of which they speak, rotate through all of the discomforts inflicted on the speaker.

. . . neuer Herring, Oyster, or Coucumer past so many vexations: my whole life with 'hem hath bene an exercise of torture; one, two, three, foure and fiue times an houre ha' they made mee dance the *Philosophicall* circle, like an Ape through a hoope, or a dogge in a wheele. I am their turne-spit indeed: They eate or smell no rost-meate but in my name. I am their bill of credit still, that passes for their victuals and house-roome.   (60–68)

This time it is the spirited evolution of figurative language, the wheeling mutations of herring, oyster, and cucumber into ape, dog, turn-spit, and bill of credit — fish and flesh, animal, vegetable, and mineral — that translate the mercuriality of the speaker into verbal action.

After a recital of the claims of the alchemists to cure disease, revive youth, melt down cracked maidenheads, and the like, Mercury sees his jailers approaching again, and this time pleads directly to the king: "The *Genius* of the place defend me! You that are both the *Sol* and *Iupiter* of this spheare, *Mercury* inuokes your maiesty against the sooty Tribe here; for in your fauour onely, I growe recouer'd and warme" (106–109). Since he has so far pleaded in vain to the audience as a whole, Mercury now entreats aid from the central member of it, in all of his multiple capacities. As monarch, James is automatically associated with Jupiter the king of the gods, and in Jonson's masque symbolism he often appears as a Neo-platonized Sol, the source of truth and beauty, partner of Nature in the work of creation.[17] Here he signifies in addition the Jupiter and Sol of the alchemists, the precious metals, tin and gold, prized for themselves and as instruments with which to work more profound transformations. In such a context, the linking of the sun, with its procreant warmth, and gold, with its restorative magic, evokes the king's own sacred potency, his sovereign touch, whereby he can transmute sickness into health and evil into good. The climax of the masque will vindicate this authentic power against the fraudulent claims of the "philosophers."

At this point a troupe of *"threedbare* Alchymists" (110–111) dances the first antimasque in a pantomime effort to recapture Mercury, who defends himself with his caduceus. When he speaks to the king again, it is with more assurance.

Sir, would you beleeue, it should be come to that height of impudence, in mankind, that such a nest of fire-wormes, as these are (because their Patron *Mulciber* heretofore has made stooles stirre, and statues dance, a dog of brasse to barke, and . . . a woman to speake, should therefore with their heats cal'd *Balnei, cineris*, or horse-doung, professe to outworke the *Sunne* in vertue, and contend to the great act of generation, nay, almost creation?

(126–134)

Since the king is already identified with Sol, Mercury's question explicitly makes him into the mighty antagonist of Vulcan, whose subterranean activities now assume the aspect of a threat to the order of the kingdom. Mercury goes on to specify some of the monstrous births that have issued from Vulcan's workshop, and the description rapidly evolves into a series of grotesque vignettes in which each creature is identified by the nonsense ingredients that have gone into his composition. But Jonson wisely does not allow this verbal procession to continue too long. Instead, he completes it choreographically by introducing a second antimasque, this one of *"imperfect creatures, with helmes of lymbeckes* [alembics] *on their heads."*

Finally, having basked in the king's countenance long enough to regain his strength, Mercury takes the initiative and orders Vulcan and his stunted children back to darkness:

Vanish with thy insolence, thou and thy Impostors, and all mention of you melt, before the Maiesty of this light, whose *Mercury* henceforth I professe to be, and neuer again the *Philosophers*. Vanish, I say, that all who haue but their senses, may see and iudge the difference betweene thy ridiculous monsters, and his absolute features. (189–195)

The "absolute features" of the monarch, then, become the touchstone by which Vulcan's monsters are judged and found wanting, the "light" in which they are finally recognized as impostors, even, it should be noted, by those who have "but their senses." Ocular confrontation between deformity and excellence must now convince those unable to perceive the truth in any other way. Mercury's language, also, has shifted into the severe ceremoniousness of the omniscient presenter, this time, however, in strict congruence with the dramatic situation. Having earlier adopted the cant of the alchemists in order to ridicule it and explain his own plight, Mercury has now been freed by the presence of the king, and can reassume the style proper to him as a god.

The transformation scene that follows, if it does not quite live up to the brilliance of its overture, forms a perfect thematic sequel. Nature is discovered in her bower surrounded by her "sons," the masquers, who are also, fittingly, the vassals of the king, her partner Sol. The precious influence of the sun having once more replaced the forge of Vulcan as the source of life, Nature emerges from her temporary eclipse to resume the great work of creation. When she bids her masquers dance, the celestial concord threatened by the alchemists is restored and the reign of truth reaffirmed against the impostures of the laboratory.

4

Frye has observed that "the further comedy moves from irony, the less social power is allowed to the humors. In the masque, where the ideal society is still more in the ascendant, the humors become degraded into the uncouth figures of the Jonsonian antimasque." [18] Jonson's masques, it will be evident by this time, move in the opposite direction, toward irony instead of away from it, toward a less and less convincing image of the ideal society in the ascendant. He starts with the "pure" antimasque of grotesques, the witches in *The Masque of Queens*, abstract embodiments of sinister forces. He moves then to the antimasques of *Love Restored* and *Mercury Vindicated*, where figures like Plutus and Vulcan, conceived realistically up to a point, nevertheless retain their symbolic function as emissaries of darkness. In the third stage, he abandons the symbolic scaffolding for the antimasquers entirely: the city humors of *The Masque of Augurs* or *News from the New World* represent little but their own oddity. No triumph or vindication is possible, because the antimasquers represent nothing to be triumphed over; a meaningful transition from prologue to apotheosis becomes almost out of the question.

Oddly enough, Jonson himself recognized the growing irrelevancy of the comic prologue. *Neptune's Triumph*, in prose and blank verse, contains a Cook and a Poet who discuss the matter. The Poet, who is also the author of the masque in which he appears, declines to write in an antimasque, regarding them as unworthy of presentation, "Being things so *heterogene*, to all deuise, / Meere *By-workes*, and at best *Outlandish* nothings" (222–223). But what was making the antimasque "*heterogene*" and "*Out-landish*" was precisely Jonson's failure, at this moment, to lash it firmly to the fable of the whole masque, to make it sort "with the current, and whole fall of the Deuise," as he had done in former years.

In *The Masque of Augurs* a crew of London mechanics, headed by a brewer's clerk, invade the court buttery hatch in order to offer the court a show of their own devising. Intercepted by the groom of the revels, they fall with him into the customary chatter about the propriety of such entertainments. John Urson, a bearward, sings a ballad about bears while his bears lumber about him to make the antimasque. A so-called "rare Artist" in the group, a Dutchman by the name of Vangoose, is displeased by the tameness of this interlude, and proposes to erect an optical machine that will create the illusion of monarchs and battles, or, since someone happens to mention pilgrims, a dance of pilgrims. When the groom protests the irrelevancy of the suggestion — "what has all this to doe with our Maske?" Vangoose replies, "*O Sir, all de better, vor an Antick-maske, de more absurd it be, and vrom de purpose, it be ever all de better. If it goe from de Nature of de ting, it is de more Art: for deare is Art, and deare is Nature; yow sall see. Hochos-pochos, Paucos Palabros.*" Whereupon he flourishes his wand, and the "*straying, and deform'd Pil-*

grims" dance in (265–274). It is hardly necessary to point out that Jonson is once again waxing scornful over the taste for the fantastic that had given birth to the antimasque in the first place. But to air one's artistic problems publicly is not necessarily to solve them. To grow indignant over the irrelevance of the antimasque, during the antimasque, is not a magic talisman that will ensure its relevance. The imbecilities of Vangoose do little but call our attention to the desultory satire of the prologue as a whole, and to the lame transition by which the pilgrims, having been brought on stage in the first place through the idlest of whims, suddenly become symbols of *"brave error"* (254) and the *"erring mazes of mankinde"* (318), just long enough to create the illusion of a juncture, and then are dropped into limbo. The ritual of augury that completes the action remains wholly divorced from the proceedings of the induction. It is perhaps not without significance that in *The Masque of Augurs*, for the first time, the name of Inigo Jones appears on the title page as co-inventor.

It is, however, largely in the "triumph" masque, the type so far discussed, that comic prose threatens the integrity of the form. In more intimate entertainments, where no deity needs to burst forth in a cloud machine or sweep out in a baroque chariot — or, to put it another way, where there is no occasion to enlist the services of Inigo Jones — the problem of the mixture of levels hardly poses itself. In *The Irish Masque*, for example, four Irish footmen come stumbling before the king to explain that their costumes have been lost in a storm at sea, and that they cannot put on the splendid show they have planned. They convey this intelligence only with much jostling and prompting and interrupting of each other in Elizabethan stage Irish, and conclude by breaking into an awkward caper *"to the bag-pipe, and other rude musique"* (136), which serves as antimasque. Their masters, four Irish gentlemen, then perform a graver measure *"to a solemne musique of harpes"* (141). But when their masters have danced, the footmen elbow each other back to the center of the stage and resume their clownish chatter, until finally evicted by *"a ciuill gentleman of the nation"* (143). The civil gentleman recites a verse eulogy, introduces a bard who sings two ballads, and the little masque is over. Obviously, by dispensing with a transformation scene, the masque may also dispense with the severely dualistic structure that the transformation scene imposes. The antimasquers need not be banished during the main ceremony; they need only be subordinated, after which, with no incongruity of tone, they may revive the spirit of the antimasque. In the present case, as it also happens, the use of the civil gentleman as presenter turns the pivot between sportive and solemn very adroitly, without losing the Irish motif, and without creating any problems of decorum.

Similarly, *Christmas his Masque*, a burlesque of the old-fashioned mummers' play, can accomplish its realistic foolery without any discord of tone, since the homespun merriment of Captain Christmas and the distracted prattle of Goodwife Venus lead only to the parade of Christmas' "boys" and the singing of popular ballads. Here, as in *The Irish Masque*, there is no attempt to allegorize; the freshness of Jonson's comic invention is not obliged to compete with or be worked into a mythological design. And in country *divertissements* like *Pan's Anniversary* or *The Masque of Gypsies*, where stage machinery must have been almost nonexistent and elaborate transformation scenes out of the question, Jonson can make the masque and antimasque virtually coextensive, mingling them and overlapping them at pleasure, so as to disguise the dualism inherent in the genre. Which leads one to suspect that it was not so much the infusion of prose comedy as the tyrannous clamor for more and more stage metamorphoses, more and more "entries," or antimasques, that wrecked the masque as a unified art form — if it ever was that — and turned it into extravaganza.[19]

The real collapse follows Jonson. Though he may not have fully recognized the risk in cutting the antimasque loose from its allegorical moorings, he reacted with almost morbid alertness to the threat posed by the experimental stagecraft of Inigo Jones, and the taste for aimless display fostered by the queen, Henrietta Maria, as a result of her acquaintance with French *ballets de cour*. The feud between Jones and Jonson was a professional even more than a temperamental clash; it grew out of conflicting views on the nature of the masque. Jonson regarded music, dance, and stage design as the mortal vesture of an organism whose soul was poetry. The very mutability of the whole redoubled the poet's obligation to ensure what survival he could for it through the power of his fable and his language. Otherwise the "glorie of all these *solemnities*" would perish "like a blaze" (*Hym.* 4–5). It goes without saying that the introduction of comic prose in no way dispensed the artist from his obligations: it merely posed new challenges and exacted new solutions. Whatever the materials, the watchword was unity, and the ideal the seamless garment.

Jones, on the other hand, seems to have held not so much a theory of the masque as a theory of architecture.[20] The proscenium designs for the two masques he composed in conjunction with Aurelian Townshend invoke Renaissance and earlier tradition in enrolling architecture under the liberal rather than the mechanic arts, deriving its inspiration from heaven, and requiring the fullest knowledge for its practice.[21] The corollary of this exaltation of architecture was the claim that the architect, like the poet, was an inventor, and from this it apparently followed, for Jones, that the architect, not the poet, should be the prime mover and ordering spirit of the masque. In fact, however, in Jones's hands the text of the

masque became little more than a pretext, a malleable arma-
ture on which to drape Italian scenic effects and sumptuous
costumes.

This more frivolous view seems also to have been the com-
moner one. Bacon cuttingly dismisses masques as "toyes." [22]
Campion, with courtly self-deprecation, disclaims any ambition in his masques higher than that of pleasing the ladies "with
smooth and gentle verse"; [23] the masque is a sugarplum to melt
in a lady's mouth, as *Euphues and his England* was a *bibelot*
to lie unread in a lady's lap. With even more strenuous self-
effacement, Samuel Daniel falls to genuflecting before the
arts of carpentry and painting, belittling his own contribution.
Since masques are merely "Pun[c]tillos of Dreames," exactness of composition and curious erudition are wasted on them
(the snipe at Jonson is obvious); since their only life consists
of "shew," the "arte and inuention of the Architect" is of sole
importance; that of the poet is "the least part and of least
note." [24] Altogether, the common attitude might be summed
up in Antonin Artaud's more truculent injunction to the contemporary theater: "En finir avec les chefs-d'oeuvre!" [25] Characteristically, only George Chapman joins Jonson in the effort
to confer some literary dignity on the form, to recognize it
as a distinct genre with laws of its own.[26]

Time and taste were on the side of Jones. Under the pressure of that Gresham's Law of the theater whereby the more
spectacular drives out the less spectacular — and stimulates
anew the appetite it is designed to appease — the require-
ments of "show" had come to domineer over the integrity of
the fable. The long, wearing rivalry for control over court
masquing ends in 1625 with the ascent of Charles I and Henrietta Maria to the throne. From this moment the authority
passes decisively into Jones's hands, and from this moment
dates the obsession with spectacular stagecraft that marks the
Caroline masque. In the hands of Jonson's successors, the

masque deteriorated into just the kind of episodic variety show that would have warmed the heart of Vangoose. Shirley's *Triumph of Peace*, with its gallimaufry of antimasques, and Carew's *Coelum Britannicum*, with its endless series of pomps and "discoveries" — to mention two of the best post-Jonsonian entertainments — illustrate what could happen when a strong hand like Jonson's was lacking to combat the thirst for spectacle and to coerce the diversified ingredients into some kind of order. As for the stuff-and-nonsense of Davenant's *Salmacida Spolia*, with its twenty antimasques, or Aurelian Townshend's *Tempe Restored*, with its *"Indians adoring their Pagode,"* and its apes with *"An Asse like a Pedante, teaching them Prick-song,"* [27] or the tumblers, buffeters, satyrs, pygmies, gladiators, and mimics that cover the stage in *Albion's Triumph*, they are all best summed up, perhaps, in the stage direction for the latter: "Such kind of pastimes as Victorious Emperors were wont to present as spectacles to the People, are heere produced for Anti-Maskes vpon the stage": [28] in other words, circuses.

Excessive realism is not the vice of the later Caroline masques. Outcroppings of comic prose in fact grow scarcer in the final years. What characterizes the entertainments of Townshend and, especially, Davenant, is dullness, and the erasure of poetic values in favor of scenic. Whatever pinnacles the masque may have reached as a visual spectacle, by the time civil war overtook the court it had virtually ceased to exist as a literary genre. Jonson's withering sarcasm, "Painting and Carpentry are the Soule of Masque," had become an accomplished fact, and his bitter reflections on its gaudy emptiness its fitting epitaph:

> O Showes! Showes! Mighty Showes!
> The Eloquence of Masques! What need of prose
> Or Verse, or Sense t'express Immortall you?   (VIII, 403)

⚜ VII ⚜

Jonson and the Language of Prose Comedy

Tʜᴇ triumph of prose as the language of comedy, and its convergence with realism, seem by hindsight an almost inevitable outcome of the history of the genre, perhaps the final issue of Aristotle's identification of comic style and comic characters as "low." Aristotle himself thought that with regard to tragic style, "nature herself" had discovered the appropriate meter, "as the iambic is of all meters most like ordinary speech. This is proved by the fact that iambic lines occur most frequently in ordinary conversation, whereas hexameters occur but rarely." [1]

But even closer to "ordinary speech" is nonmetrical language. If comedy portrays men as no better than they are, or worse, it must make them talk no better than they do, or worse, or give the illusion of doing so. The language must engage them in the trivia of daily existence, and suggest the heedlessness as well as the passion with which that existence is carried on. "Le commun peuple," says Larivey in 1579, defending his own use of prose in comedy, "le commun peuple, qui est le principal personnage de la scène, ne s'estudie tant à agencer ses paroles qu'à publier son affection, qu'il a plutost dicte que pensée." [2] "Plutost dicte que pensée": ordinary people, the personages of comedy, speak their feelings

273

directly, without thought, without planning. Prose rhythm, being uncommitted to any a priori metrical pattern, permits the rhythms of live speech to be traced more intimately, and it accommodates with less strain the masses of petty detail, the tautologies and slovenly usages, with which daily speech is loaded. From the lowness of Aristophanes, Plautus, and Terence, where realism manifests itself chiefly in smut or a vocabulary enlarged to admit quantities of nonpoetic words, we jump a long gap in time to the beginnings of prose comedy in Italy, thence to language relatively flat and colorless in Ariosto, expressively pungent in the best of Machiavelli and Aretino, and unabashedly regional and dialectic with Ruzzante. In England, after Lyly's sallies into fantasy and the crude neorealism of the popular playwrights, we find the major dramatists — Shakespeare and Jonson — fusing their different rhetorics with the demotic babel of the market place in such a way as to preserve both the expressive range of the former and the virile immediacy of the latter.

The most obvious trait of Jonson's style, its realism, thus brings to a climax a process toward which comedy had been moving for generations, perhaps since its origins. Jonson, strenuously seeking to copy "nature," displays an increasing preoccupation with lifelike speech, a growing suspicion of "literary" sounding language, except where this becomes an object of satire, and a closer and closer attachment to the kind of familiar subject matter for which everyday language is appropriate. And this, as we have seen already, without sacrificing the techniques of inflation that end by turning "realistic" talk into a transfigured babble.

In his programmatic effort to evolve a vital comic speech out of the raw materials of heard conversation, Jonson hence forms one of the pillars of the comic tradition. Comedy has always sought, and profited from, idiomatic language as a

delight in itself. Our language may be low, we think to ourselves, but at least we can say certain things — chiefly scoun-
drelly things — never dreamed of by the poets, and say them
with such rightness and picturesqueness that they become a
sort of poetry in themselves. The craving for a dramatic
speech with sap and savor in it is as perennial as any other
desire with which audiences have wedged themselves, century after century, into box, pit, or gallery. Synge's manifesto
merely pleads for the resumption of such speech after the
long winter of its nineteenth-century eclipse. Realistic prose,
of which Synge's folk poetry is a subspecies, depends on the
high charge of expressiveness latent in ordinary language,
which in turn depends on the complex of local mores shared
by the spectators. Good "realistic" dialogue releases the expressive voltage, finds definitive form for that aspect of our
sensibility — wherever one locates it — commonly denoted
as "low." Hence the prominent role played by flyting in
comedy. Ursula's greasy invective appeals precisely to our
wish to hear vulgar abuse wielded with the kind of mastery
that raises it to the level of an art form. Cokes's imbecilities,
similarly, satisfy a craving for a language so hopelessly im-
becilic that it seems to issue from the original simpleton of
the universe, as well as from the village booby.

The more intimately it reflects the specific culture and
speech of its audience, however, the less well realistic comedy
survives translation in time and space. *Bartholomew Fair* has
endured the centuries less well than *Volpone*; one can scarcely
imagine it at all on a stage outside the English-speaking
world. An extremer kind of linguistic realism, dialect comedy,
exploits the audience's sense of self-identity by speaking to it
in its own tongue, and capitalizing on the expressive potency
locked up in that tongue and in no other. Ruzzante, ignoring
his humanist education, writes in his native Padovan not to

lampoon it, but to unlock its expressive possibilities, to create a gamut of types who can scarcely be said to exist at all divorced from their peculiar patois. Goldoni, when he writes in Venetian, can draw closer to his special audience than in Italian, and so create a nearly hermetic world of mutual understanders, from which outsiders are barred. In both cases, as in much dialect comedy, we have a special brand of coterie drama, where the coterie is linguistic rather than social; some of the pleasure felt by a Neapolitan audience at the theater of Scarpetta and Eduardo de Filippo, or of an audience at the Yiddish theater, springs from the close bond between stage and pit created by a language from which outsiders are barred.

But realistic comedy tends to be social, and social comedy tends to be critical. Comedy, if it aims at laughter, must make its spectators laugh *at* something, and the pleased recognition produced by the sound of vulgarity can quickly transform itself into a more patronizing pleasure at the sound of imperfect vulgarity, or of vulgarity striving after elegance. When Goldoni brings a Venetian pantaloon into his Italian plays, or when an Elizabethan playwright drops country bumpkins or stage Irishmen onto the scene, the insider of dialect comedy becomes the outsider, his speech not so much an object of affectionate amusement as of derision. Or when Ruzzante, in *La moschetta*, makes the protagonist prettify her rustic language with city locutions, he reinforces the prejudices of the community against deviations from its linguistic norm. The dialect of Captain Whit or Puppy in *Bartholomew Fair*, or of the Irish ambassadors or Welsh footmen in the masques devoted to them, or, on the modern American stage, of a Southern belle or a Broadway floozie, may not be — usually is not — funny in itself, but it may suggest the automaton, trapped in his quaint linguistic compulsions, struggling to make himself sound human. Or the medley of dialects may afford a more simple pleasure, that of the queer, pied forms into which language is constantly transforming itself, the endless capacity for the tongue to trip and err and create new linguistic shapes. In Goldoni's *Impresario delle Smirne*, when the three prima donnas, Florentine, Venetian, and Bolognese respectively, put a truce to their feuding by blowing each other a conciliatory kiss, the mere juxtaposition of three variant forms, "un bacio," "un baso," "un bas," [3] the certainty of each that she is speaking the one true language, composes a rich linguistic document in itself.

The moment, hence, that we move any distance into the sphere of critical comedy, the language begins to draw attention not merely to its own agility and gusto, but to its own absurdity. Telltale quirks of diction, tag ends of phrase, bits and pieces of expletive associated with recognizable social attitudes, begin to spring to the surface, and as these multiply, we find ourselves in the world that is peculiarly Jonson's, that of linguistic satire. Even the most clinical realism can never be more than an approximation whereby an author claims a certain degree of plausibility for his material; even the most dispassionate realist is already distilling the language of the tribe into a brew more potent than its normal self. But even this soberer realism so rapidly transforms itself into linguistic satire that we need a special term for the latter, for the hallucinatory jabberwocky that results when a few empirically observed traits are puffed to such monstrous proportions as to produce a kind of gargoyle speech. If we label it "mock realism," we can insinuate the fact that it both mimics real speech and also distorts and derides it.

Like most borderlines, that between plain realism and "mock" realism is difficult to fix, but we can distinguish between the lifelike fretting of the carriers at Gadshill on the one hand and the distorted muddle of Dame Quickly's speech

on the other, between the hard-bitten naturalism of Bellafront in *The Honest Whore*, Part I (II.i), and the surrealistic
flamboyance of Simon Eyre, between the old-maid querulous-
ness of Goody Trash and the maddened buzzing of Wasp.
In the first cases, the author refrains from exceeding the effects of ordinary speech, even if he chooses to copy ordinary
speech in its more picturesque moments. In the second, the
technique involves purposeful exaggeration; the object is to
make us grin, or laugh outright, and, in Jonson's case, to make
us judge and condemn.

In most playwrights, when we find linguistic satire, we also
find a firm backwall of linguistic normalcy. In Shakespeare,
for example, we know where we are: Hamlet not only holds
a mirror up to the curled and combed parlance of Osric, his
own speech provides a standard against which to measure that
of the other. Similarly, in Restoration comedy, with its strong
social orientation, the language of the hero and his friends is
to be emulated, that of the fops and eccentrics to be shunned.
But Jonson, like Swift, whets his irony not only against de-
viants from the norm, but against the norm itself. He tends
to present a world wholly composed of fops and eccentrics,
or else, as in the early plays, a world where a few characters
deliberately made more perfect than life speak a blank verse
that symbolizes their more than human — and hence unreach-
able — perfection. *Epicene* implies a certain preference for
Truewit's way of talking, but the language of the professional
japester, with its tirades and sermons, is too deeply lodged
in a context of farce, and too hedged about with indecisions,
to be regarded as more than a hesitant sketch. *Bartholomew
Fair* offers a choice only among impossible alternatives: the
posturing ventriloquism of Busy and Overdo, the gutter
speech of Ursula, the mushy inanities of Cokes or Littlewit,
the dialect of the yokels, the frigidly unreal reasonableness of

Mistress Grace. The "pure and neat . . . yet plaine and customary" language elsewhere recommended by Jonson (*Disc.* 1870–71), like other positive standards, evidently resists embodiment on the Jonsonian stage. It remains an ideal unrealized in concrete terms, and perhaps even ultimately unrealizable. Language being the man-made phenomenon it is, a thing of flux with boundaries as shifting and impalpable as those of morality, and speakers being cursed by birth with humors or vapors, all speech, we finally feel, in the Jonsonian theater, tingles with latent if not explicit absurdity. If men can be divided into fools and knaves, and then lumped together into the still more comprehensive category of fools, then all language reduces itself to the expression of one or another variety of folly.

But such comprehensiveness involves its penalties as well as its strengths, as we may judge by recalling Jonson's failures with Maximilian and Grace Wellborn. In these cases Jonson was trying to *suppress* the undercurrent of absurdity, and could not. The language seemed to go on leading a life of its own, outside the conscious control of its maker. Something in Jonson insists on probing until it has exposed a layer of folly in everyone, in everything. Perhaps his vision was too absolutely comic to give him the widest scope even in comedy. Jonsonian drama takes as a major premise the total moral expressiveness of language, and activates the premise so as to create a short circuit between language and folly. But there are times when words sink in importance, or when they do, after all, say what we feel and mean, or when they fail us altogether. An art that cannot reckon with this elementary reality, even when it wants to, has plainly blocked itself off from one source of insight, and perhaps constricted the fullness of its own.

I

By a parallel process that may be more than coincidence, prose and linguistic satire flourish and collapse together in Elizabethan drama. The flowering time lasts roughly from 1595 to 1614, or from Armado and Holofernes to Adam Overdo and Zeal-of-the-Land Busy. The practitioners include most of the chief playwrights active at the time. Nashe, tentatively, Shakespeare, and Chapman form a first wave; Jonson is the towering central figure, who annexes the field of mock realism as his own province; Dekker, Marston, and Beaumont (in *The Knight of the Burning Pestle*) compose a closely overlapping third wave. Middleton, in the same years, ignores linguistic satire and cultivates his own vein of plainer realism. With the decline of prose after about 1614 — a mysterious phenomenon for which no immediate explanation offers itself — linguistic satire also withers away. Middleton returns to verse, and the chief worthies of comedy of the following generation, Massinger, Fletcher, and Shirley, eschew prose almost altogether.

Like so much in Elizabethan dramatic technique, the styles of realism and mock realism form part of a common vocabulary, into which original contributions are so swiftly assimilated that they can rarely be detected with confidence. King has pointed out the series of ricochets by which Jonson's Juniper is imitated to produce Dekker's Simon Eyre, who in turn re-emerges metamorphosed into Jonson's Tucca, who then becomes the direct model for the Tucca of *Satiromastix*; and to this same group King adds the Host in *The Merry Wives of Windsor* and Sir Gozlin in *Westward Ho*, and still others for resemblances of occasional detail.[4] One might remark further bits of imitation, such as the episode in *Patient Grissill* copied from Fastidious Brisk's dueling narrative, where Dekker not only borrows the central motif intact, but manages to invest it in a style at times indistinguishable from Jonson's; or — less obviously — the brothel scene in *The Honest Whore*, where Bellafront's bullying of her servant Roger seems to have served as pattern and to have provided verbal details for the similar relation between Ursula and her tapster Mooncalf in *Bartholomew Fair*. The chameleon habits of most Elizabethan playwrights, the steady cross-pollenization of techniques that goes on among them, forbids our expecting the kind of stylistic uniqueness that we are accustomed to, and prize, today. One would be unlikely to confound a passage of Henry James with one from Shaw or Hardy, but Elizabethan style, in the theater particularly, tends toward anonymity. Only the whole configuration of stylistic traits can be regarded as unique, and even then only in the case of authors like Jonson, whose artistic personality was emphatic enough to wrest a style of its own from the common materials.

However, if the stylistic devices themselves compose a sort of lingua franca on which all writers drew freely, their function varies decisively from one playwright to the next. In Dekker, for instance, the verbal motley borrowed from Juniper to fit Simon Eyre — and then replundered, with further patchwork, by Jonson to make a pied mantle for Tucca — does not produce linguistic satire at all. The effusion of bizarre endearments, sesquipedalian words, and truncated phrases that in Jonson signify Juniper's irresponsibility and Tucca's moral incoherence, in Dekker are meant to endear us to the speaker, to display his generosity, whimsical merriment, and madcap geniality, his lordly unconcern for petty economy, and his wholesome indifference to social distinctions. Eyre is a "character," a lovable eccentric with a heart of gold. The booming voice, the loud laugh, even the off-beat vocabulary, notify us that their possessor is just plain folks at all times, whether bullyragging his apprentices or jollying the king. In Jonson the clutter of verbal gimcrackery defines a corresponding moral confusion. In Dekker it is an emblem of democracy: even a cobbler can use these elephantine words; even ol' Sim Eyre can talk about Assyrians and Cappadochians, and only snobs and pedants will quibble over their meaning, or piddle over their relevance. Far from serving as an oblique criticism of the speaker, in ways strictly controlled by the author, Eyre's verbal high jinks, in fact, serve to conceal the less savory recesses of his disposition that Dekker is unwilling to bring to light. The instant we peer behind the facade of heartiness, we discover "Shylock masquerading as Falstaff"; [5] beneath the gaudy camouflage lurks the clock-watching overseer, the driver of hard bargains, the niggard with his pints of ale. The style, in short, is a red herring, designed to secure an illegitimate sympathy for the character by throwing us off the track of his acquisitiveness.

An even more puzzling use of somewhat the same set of mannerisms occurs in *The Dutch Courtesan*. Cocledemoy, according to Marston *"a knavishly witty City companion"* (II, 70),[6] is a cozening rascal, merry as a grig, who spends his time — for little apparent reason — swindling silver plate out of a vintner named Mulligrub. His tumultuous style, at times even wilder than that of Eyre or Tucca, is evidently intended to indicate the gusto with which he goes about his knavery, the joy he takes in his own rascally virtuosity. "Conscience does not repine," he confides (II, 106), as he prepares to filch a goblet. Without warning, then, having brought Mulligrub to the foot of the gallows, he suddenly restores all he has stolen, and declares himself to be "honest *Cocledemoy*" who has been playing pranks "for *Emphises* of wit" (II, 136). Truewit, in short, has been masquerading as Autolycus. We are left with a merrie conceited jester posing as a rogue, with a fun-loving japester who consorts with a broken-down bawd named Mary Faugh and makes her his accomplice in roguery. What meaning, if any, can be assigned to his language, with its feverish heartiness, its spate of obscene *double-entendres*, its crazy splatter of gutter words and classical allusions? The attempt to pin borrowed linguistic feathers on a character conceived with no consistent purpose ends in artistic confusion. One is obliged to conclude that the idiom Jonson worked out as a symbol of moral incoherence has become a piece of incoherence pure and simple, a furious raving or perpetual motion of words signifying nothing.

Satiric comment, on the other hand, of the kind Jonson placed in the mouths of Carlo Buffone and Macilente, becomes for Marston a mere convenience that allows him to indulge in his favorite sport of railing. Jonson's railers effect a scorching indictment of folly, but they are far more than mere auctorial surrogates placed on the scene with a patent to fulminate: they have their place in a larger design. As the spirits of envy and detraction respectively, they suffer from their own imbalance of humors, from their own distempered view of the world, and so, having spitefully presided over the dishumoring and purgation of so many others, they fall victim to the same process themselves. But the satiric speech of Malevole, in *The Malcontent*, amounts to little more than a club, placed in the hands of the author's chosen spokesman, with which to batter the world. Malevole's language lashes society unmercifully, but it forms no criticism of the speaker himself; rather, it creates the kind of unacknowledged short circuit that Katherine Anne Porter, in another context, once described as "criminal collusion between author and character." [7] One might add that Malevole's prose — like that of Cocledemoy, for that matter, and other Marstonian characters — has little consistent texture, but wobbles uncertainly between a piebald manner remini-

scent of Carlo Buffone and a clearheaded logicality suggestive of Shakespeare. But, in any case, it is less the details themselves of style that matter than the playwright's power to convert them into meaningful symbols. Marston, by borrowing
the idiom of Tucca for *The Dutch Courtesan*, does not really
imitate Jonson: he imitates Tucca. The masterly linguistic
structure by which Jonson probes Tucca's moral chaos becomes, in Marston's hands, a self-indulgent thrashing-about in
language equal to Tucca's.

Shakespeare alone, in fact, who virtually invented linguistic
satire on the English stage, wields it with a trenchancy and a
sophistication equal to Jonson's. In Shakespeare, however, it
forms a subsidiary pattern rather than a central comic axis,
often appearing only in the subplot, as in the Lancastrian histories or *Measure for Measure*, or being confined to marginal
characters — Osric, the nurse in *Romeo and Juliet*, the clown
in *Antony*. Or it may appear as a passing episode in a more
encyclopedic history of folly, as in the case of Sir Andrew
Aguecheek, who for one moment collects precious words as
zealously as any Jonsonian gull, and then forgets to use them,
which the Jonsonian gull would not. Morever, with a few
exceptions, Shakespeare's butts are not total fools. Holofernes
breaks out of his pedantry to deliver a moving rebuke to the
nobles who have scoffed at his play; Cleopatra's clown speaks
metaphysical conundrums wrapped up in rustic solecisms;
and Pandarus proves an affectionate uncle as well as a simpering go-between. The language of Polonius, to take a different
kind of instance, is tinged with rather than steeped in mock
realism. It stays closer to its realistic bearings, or at least to a
center of good sense to which it can return, and generally
Shakespeare does not aim at linguistic satire on the barbaric,
gargantuan scale that Jonson does. Rather, he plays with it as
with a leitmotif, allowing it now to rise to the surface, now to

undergo rich elaboration, now to ebb, now to fade away. And this use reflects Shakespeare's conception of character itself as something mingled and complex, in which good and evil, folly and wisdom, intermingle so tightly that often they cannot be disentangled at all. Needless to say, it is this view that governs the conception of most of the tragic heroes, and in certain of them — Richard II, Othello, occasionally Antony — we find a wantonness or exhibitionism of language that recalls the only-half-controlled play-acting of some of Jonson's verse characters like Volpone and Subtle. Linguistic satire, in Shakespeare, forms a complicating element, an enriching ingredient, almost, one might say, a component of psychological realism, rather than, as in Jonson's case, a defiance of it.

2

The comic dramatists of the twenties and thirties, to repeat, give up linguistic satire and revert to blank verse. But with the reopening of the theaters in 1660, Jonsonian comic modes renew themselves. The comedy of manners inherits from the Jonsonian stage both the crowded gallery of "humors" that Dryden loved and a prose strongly tinged with mock realism. Even where the impulse seems realistic, as in "easy, graceful" Etherege, a streak of willful heightening in the language infects it with a touch of caricature. Are "Foggy *Nan* the Orange Woman, and swearing *Tom* the Shoomaker" (I.i.22–23) [8] realistic or mock-realistic creations? And Dorimant himself? Each speaks with the stamp of his trade or class, using words and phrasal rhythms clearly based on live language, yet the idiom is so highly flavored that it borders on the grotesque. Particularly when compared to French prose of the same period, Restoration comic style seems mottled with density and speckled with particularity. French prose tends to respect what W. K. Wimsatt has called the "substantive level," [9] avoiding extreme concreteness on the one hand and extreme abstraction on the other, and is perhaps, by this token, more deserving of the epithet "classical." [10] Which of the two is more "real," a more authentic transcription of actual talk, is a question impossible to answer — among other things, it raises the equally impossible question of what, precisely, constitutes "actual talk" — but English style at least tends more toward self-conscious virtuosity, toward wrought surfaces and high coloring, than French. Even in its tamer moments, it gives off a certain *haut gout*, as of ripe cheese, that would have been judged offensive in France, and was later to be found malodorous in England by William Archer.[11] When Wycherley transposes *Le misanthrope* into *The Plain-Dealer*, he not only adds a good many melodramatic twists to the intrigue, sanctioned by the precedent of English dramaturgy, he also writes throughout in the gamey style sanctioned by English linguistic tradition. The politely scathing raillery of Célimène and her suitors suffers a corrosive sea-change into the savage backbiting of Olivia and the toadlike spatter of Novel. Into a few scenes of the subplot Wycherley packs as much legal jargon as Racine does into the whole of *Les plaideurs*, the latter having nevertheless felt obliged to defend himself in advance for his "quelques mots barbares" and against the charge of having fatigued the ears of his listeners with "trop de chicane." [12] Wycherley's language is everywhere pocked and pitted with violent terms, words of abuse, pounding repetitions, special vocabularies. In such a context of heavy emphasis and linguistic chiaroscuro, Molière's *raisonneur*, with his discreet insistence on moderation, would have appeared merely insipid, and Wycherley accordingly replaces him with the unattractive Freeman, pursuing the fortune of the widow Blackacre without regard to her defects of person.

On the other hand, with the absorption of so much linguistic high voltage into the language, mock realism itself tends to lose its precise moral focus. The ship-ahoy lingo of Manly's sailors is given so much gratuitous emphasis that it ought to have some significance; but apart from suggesting that they are bluff, sturdy fellows, unacquainted with landlubberly hypocrisy, their salt-water similes amount to little more than identifying labels. Like Marston, in this instance at least, Wycherley seems chiefly concerned to prevent the language from lapsing into a calm, and he does so by agitating the surface of it wherever he can. Similarly, an early post-Restoration comedy, Wilson's *The Cheats*, copies *The Alchemist* in using pseudoscientific mumbo jumbo to stand for quackery, but by the time we reach Congreve's *Love for Love* (1697), old Foresight's obsession with astrology comes to little more than oddity for oddity's sake, entertaining in its silliness but containing no particular moral implication other than that old men dote and grow singular in their tastes. Foresight's weakness for astrological abracadabra reveals his credulity, of course, and his shortsightedness, and these affect his behavior, but one feels that Congreve is engaged primarily in spoofing an occult vocabulary, not in using it to probe the moral nature of its user.

Again, Benjamin's sailor slang, like its equivalent in *The Plain-Dealer*, merely identifies the milieu in which the speaker has lived. Far from implying pitiable mimicry or verbal strutting, the seafaring jargon reflects positive qualities: the inability of the plain-spoken seaman to use fine speech, a certain unworldliness, the good nature of the diamond in the rough, the bluntness of one who has mastered a dangerous trade. Here, as in *The Plain-Dealer*, one suspects that the jolly Jack Tar, with his bluff heartiness and his naive translation of shore phenomena into shipboard terms, is being sentimentalized.

Oddly enough, it was Congreve himself who complained of the deadly ease with which such characters could be manufactured: "One may almost give a Receipt for the Composition of such a Character: For the Poet has nothing to do, but to collect a few proper Phrases and terms of Art, and to make the Person apply them by ridiculous Metaphors in his Conversation, with Characters of different Natures." [13]

With the legal jargon of *The Plain-Dealer*, we are in somewhat more Jonsonian territory. A connection exists, though it is not made explicit, between the widow Blackacre's fondness for litigation and her bedazzlement with the arcane parlance of chancery. Corruption of style and corruption of manners coincide with something like Jonsonian exactness. However, as with the humors that crowd the pages of Shadwell's *Sullen Lovers*, the author does not engage them in an action that will expose them *to themselves*. In *The Sullen Lovers*, Ninny and Woodcock lose Emilia, and Sir Positive At-all finds himself married to a wrecked courtesan posing as a lady, but they are not forced to recognize the fact that their own folly has undone them and made them laughingstocks. Huffe is never obliged to confront his own cowardice, nor do the two principals, Stanford and Emilia, ever arrive at any recognition — even retrospective — of the absurdity of their own misanthropic biliousness. Of the five chief fools in *Bury Fair*, only two — Lady Fantast and Mistress Fantast — are really unmasked; they storm out, however, rather more with the rage of the tragic villainess than with the crestfallen mien of the chastened fool. In the cases of Trim and Oldwit, a steady enfeeblement of decorum relieves the author of the need to inflict on them the consequences of their own folly: the former, pointlessly made valiant, takes the lead in exposing the cowardice of a French barber disguised as a count — unfairly, because the barber has been bribed and cajoled into his masquerade in order to make sport for others; the latter, having been correctly defined as "an arrant ass" in the opening scene, ends as the sensible, benevolent father in the final one. And in *The Squire of Alsatia*, where Shadwell lays on the White-friars' cant with a trowel, the sentimental nature of the plot turns the Alsatian cheaters into villains of melodrama, foiled in their dark schemes by the noble brother of their victim, and finally hauled off to jail by the constables. Satire here has dropped over the deep edge into homily.

On the whole it was left to Swift to make the point that might have been made earlier about all of the shop talk and trade talk that clutters the pages of Restoration comedy. Gulliver's extracts from his log, for example, at the outset of the second voyage, turn the language of navigation into something so impenetrable as to wring from us the acknowledgment that such discourse, instead of aiding communication, thwarts it, since it links men only on the level that concerns them as narrow specialists, and not on the level of their humanity. Beyond this, of course, probably lies the more drastic implication that such discourse serves no purpose other than to mystify. Jonson, no doubt, would have made the point less sweepingly. In a culture in which a man might still with modesty claim all knowledge for his province, Jonson would probably not have condemned the special parlance, as an evil in itself, but only the weaklings who affect it in order to disguise their own emptiness. But it is only a short step from deriding the practitioners of such a vocabulary to deriding the vocabulary itself, and Swift merely completes the process begun by Jonson.

Except in Shadwell, satire of social types like the foppish heir and the country blockhead tends to do without much linguistic machinery. The pseudo-French dandy is a favorite target of derision, but in most cases he is distinguished linguistically by little more than a few French phrases. With the court itself now taking the lead in "easy" and "pliant" conversation, if we can trust Dryden,[14] the laborious mimicry of a Fastidious Brisk or an Amorphus no longer has anything very precise to mimic. The aimless, empty-headed chatter of Sir Amorous La Fool becomes a more usual prototype. In *The Relapse*, one discovers the Jonsonian situation in reverse: Lord Foppington's linguistic folly is vestigial rather than acquired. The fun comes from hearing the periwig-pated, pomander-scented dandy still using provincial expletives in an upcountry accent, from the incongruity between the modish wardrobe and the hayseed speech. But again, the precise correlation between Lord Foppington's speech habits and the rest of his behavior eludes definition. Since a fop must needs be ridiculous, Vanbrugh takes pains to make him ridiculous on all counts, without, apparently, worrying about the relation of one kind of ridiculousness to another.

Finally, with the collapse of comedy into sentimentality, linguistic satire becomes untenable, except in an occasional marginal figure. Characters who exist to wring tears from the audience cannot be made grotesque; characters who are presumed to be basically good cannot be subject to prolonged ridicule; characters whose destiny it is to be converted or perfected by noble sentiments cannot be pressed into the mask of compulsive marionettes, or provided with a language whose very premise is the ineradicable folly that underlies it. Comic speech, in *The Conscious Lovers*, turns into an insufferable parade of noble protestations, where even the flirtatious servants speak of the "generous passion" in their hearts, and even the weakly drawn fools deliver sage maxims concerning the opacity of professional jargon. Comic prose of the Jonsonian kind, whether relatively realistic or mock realistic, now passes into the novel, producing the woolgathering of Parson Adams, the olfactory fixations of Humphry Clinker, or the sententiousness of Mary Bennet.

3

Two linguistic modes frequent in prose comedy seem uncharacteristic of Jonson. One is the kind of style that may be called "neutral," or better, "transparent," a style that at its best delights with its fluidity and musicality, but does so at the expense of realism and sharpness of characterization. The specific gravity of most English comic prose being high, and Renaissance prose tending also toward density, this style occurs more usually on the Continent, and appears infrequently before the seventeenth century. However, one might cite Ariosto and Larivey as early, somewhat academic practitioners of it; both are concerned rather with maintaining comic pace than with niceties of decorum, and neither goes very deep into linguistic realism. Shakespeare, who commands all styles, also commands this one. The first scene in *The Winter's Tale* might be described as a choric dialogue between Camillo and Archidamus: the tone is highly ceremonial, the syntax compact and supple, but nothing is done linguistically to differentiate the two speakers, and realism of the sort that names kitchen utensils and articles of dress is absent. Shakespeare is here interested not in exploiting the possibilities of the language for graphic description, but in initiating a certain rhythm, a mysterious loftiness of manner, in which graphic realism has no place. Jonson, as we have noticed, attempted something similar in the figure of Maximilian in *The Case is Altered*, but without much success, and, again without much success, in the coldly judicial discourses of Mistress Grace in *Bartholomew Fair*.

The best examples of this choric style come in the eighteenth century, with Goldoni and Marivaux, and perhaps also,

somewhat earlier, with Molière. Molière, with his unshakable
sense of decorum, his keen ear for linguistic silliness, his celebrated crusades against pedantry and preciosity, seems to be
a very close counterpart to Jonson. But he does not, like Jonson, make himself a formal connoisseur of verbal foppery, or
elaborate it into an entire comic vision. He keeps the temperature of his dialogue at a lower point, allowing it to boil over
into outright nonsense only at crucial moments. *L'avare*
scandalized the court because Molière had had the audacity
to write a full-length, five-act play in prose, but in fact Molière's prose displays much the same neutral clarity as his verse.
Once we get beyond a slight harshness of phrase, "sans dot,"
and a habit of flying into rages, Harpagon talks much like the
rest of his family. Once we leave behind the litany of drugs
and appliances, and the stock endearments reserved for his
wife, the same is true of Argan. In *Le malade imaginaire*, as in *Le
bourgeois gentilhomme*, linguistic satire is concentrated in the
ridicule of professional cant: in the former, the medical patter
of Monsieur Fleurant and the schoolboy rhetoric of the booby
Thomas Diafoirus; in the latter, the technical languages of the
music master, the dancing master, the fencing master, and the
professor of philosophy, which form a hubbub of competing
jargons that succeed in reducing the various sciences to nonsense.

In both cases, the point is Jonsonian: Monsieur Jourdain
and Argan are hypnotized, and victimized, by the glitter of
professional parlance. But Molière only sparingly translates
their infatuation into linguistic terms. They speak like members of their class, to be sure, and Monsieur Jourdain ad-
vertises his intellectual pretensions with a few fine words, but
primarily both are characterized not by lexical peculiarities or
mimicked phrases but simply by their sentiments. An occasional telltale lapse such as the confusion between "drôlerie"

and "divertissement" with which Monsieur Jourdain makes his entrance, or the jumble he produces in trying to extend a "courtly" greeting to Dorimène, serves to imply a whole world of linguistic derangement that Molière prefers, for the most part, to leave only half-exploited.

Molière's apparent heedlessness in this regard, however, points to a limitation in Jonson. Jonson could scarcely conceive, and certainly could not execute, a dramatic portrait except in terms of total articulateness. Such a moment as that in *Le bourgeois gentilhomme* when Nicole, seeing Monsieur Jourdain decked out for the first time in his courtly plumage, breaks down in helpless, uncontrollable laughter, would have been outside his compass. The apparently similar case in *Every Man out of his Humour* — Sogliardo succumbing to the giggles while trying to describe Puntarvolo's quaint courtship — is the exception that proves the rule. Sogliardo is a mere blockhead. His collapse into inarticulateness forms a judgment not of Puntarvolo but of himself. In Molière, it is the other way around. Nicole's peasant grossness of tongue in no way dulls her tart good sense, nor is it meant to imply grossness of perception. To do the scene in the *Bourgeois gentilhomme*, Jonson would have had to provide Monsieur Jourdain with a battery of courtly terms to match his new clothes, and he would have had to make Nicole a critic, commenting on her master's folly. The isomorphism of language and character would have had to bear all the weight of the moral indictment. But linguistic and moral stature do not absolutely and forever coincide. Just as wisdom may on occasion express itself in hoots of laughter, so there are forms of vice that defy exact linguistic translation, or to which total linguistic expression is unnecessary: Harpagon searching La Flèche's breeches for stolen gold. For Jonson, what cannot be said scarcely exists. Volpone's way of expressing avarice is to *praise* his gold. Molière, who makes no absolute equation between the moral and verbal dimensions, hence moves within a larger, more humane frame of reference than Jonson.

In Marivaux and Goldoni, the verbal surface becomes even smoother than in Molière: linguistic satire recedes to the fringes of the action. Servants talk like servants, counts like counts, boors like boors, to be sure, and when they reverse roles they can betray themselves by an improper phrase, but the individual idioms are not highly inflected, nor do they in themselves make their speakers ridiculous. The satiric component is slighter in these authors, and the component of pure fun and sentiment larger. The "blocking characters," when they appear at all, no longer stand with the massive immobility or move with the threatening intensity of their seventeenth-century ancestors. In *Le bourru bienfaisant*, as the title tells us, the blocking character is only a lovable curmudgeon. The shift, in fact, in Goldoni and Marivaux, and a critical one it is, is from blocking from without to blocking from within. The young heroes and heroines are impeded by their own false pride, or needless jealousy, or their imperfect understanding of others, so that the action consists of an inner evolution whereby they find freedom and happiness for themselves. The twists and turns of the plotting, the disguises and misunderstandings, provide a context within which the process of self-discovery and change may take place. With the emphasis thus decisively shifting from exterior to internal forces, to psychological change, language acquires a kind of transparency through which the operations of the heart may be tracked. The surface is rarely allowed to engross one's attention and distract from the play of psychic forces. The musicality of Goldoni's dialogue or of *marivaudage* provides a continuous rhythm in which the characters move and alter, but rarely an object offered for inspection on its own account.

A relation would seem to exist, therefore, between Jonson's conception of character as closed and fixed, and the exhaustive linguistic scrutiny to which he subjects his dramatis personae. The moment psychological realism comes into play, with its premise of growth, the language sheds its high eccentricity, its contorted peculiarity, and becomes a pliant instrument for registering change. E. M. Forster's familiar and exasperating distinction between "two dimensional" and "three dimensional" characters [15] is relevant here. It is always the "two dimensional" characters, those incapable of growth — the Thwackums and Squares, the Miss Bateses and Alfred Jingles — who pipe away in a strange mock realistic falsetto, and always the more "organic" figures, the Elizabeth Bennets and David Copperfields, who speak in a relatively neutral, flexible, and transparent style.

Playwrights and novelists alike, in fact, for over two centuries, have understood that the surest way to arouse laughter — even when the main theme is serious — is to surround the chief figures with supernumeraries whose weird little speech fixations rapidly take on the rigid automatism of Bergson's jack-in-the-box. It is understood from the beginning that such characters will remain unchanged, no matter what evolution occurs among the protagonists. When a writer like Eugene O'Neill sets out to write a purely "ironic" comedy — *The Iceman Cometh* — which presents all its characters paralyzed in the grip of their various delusions, almost the first requisite, and certainly the most powerful expressive device, is to provide each with a characteristic speech from which he cannot deviate from curtain to curtain. The seeming change wrought by the intervention of an obsessed charlatan is then predictably illusory from the outset. Not unexpectedly, this particular applecart has been upset only by Bernard Shaw, in *Pygmalion*. With Eliza Doolittle, character changes *because* language changes. The great scene in the third act shows her at a moment of awkward transition, with her accent purified but her Cockney vocabulary and attitudes still dominant; by the final curtain, her emancipation from dialect has resulted in her emancipation from tribal mores. But by making character transformation a function of linguistic transformation, Shaw merely reasserts the traditional link between "fully revealed, end-stopped" characters and linguistic satire. The tenacity of the tradition itself suggests that when comedy deals with such characters, each with his fixed language, it is pursuing one of its most central themes, and not merely dabbling with "caricature." And if this is so, Jonson, who crowded as many such characters as he could onto the same stage, and pitted their jargons shrilly against each other, was exploring one of the basic "comic truths" with a fullness that no other dramatist before or since has even remotely approached.

More typical of English comedy than the "choric" style, and almost equally alien to Jonsonian drama, is the use of pointed, witty, or epigrammatic speech. Jonson can be witty and pointed when he chooses, but usually he would rather poke fun at witlessness and pointlessness. Despite the proverbial bent of Senecan style toward aphorism, Jonson designed his own particular version of it to offer maximum scope for effects of discomposure, less for effects of masterful composure. The logical syntax of Lyly makes a more congenial medium for persiflage, and the wit combats that start with Lyly, and continue with Shakespeare through Congreve and Wilde to Shaw and Noel Coward, leave Jonson somewhat to one side. The "comeback" is not a Jonsonian specialty. Truewit's cavalier tone, his urbane interest in mistresses and social trifling, contribute much to the manner of his Restoration descendants, but the latter have a way of licking their lips over a good antithesis that would have spelled affectation in Jonson. Jonson is not interested in creating the sharpshooters of language who score a bull's-eye with every retort, but rather the would-be marksmen, forever overshooting the mark or falling pitiably short of it, or the magniloquent rhetoricians bewitched by their own eloquence.

To put it another way, Jonson used prose not to allow his dramatis personae to display their intellectual prowess but to make them reveal their moral defects. The knaves must invest themselves in a self-intoxicated exaltation that can collapse at a touch into the mechanistic twitch, the fools in a verbal coat of many colors that is itself little more than a patchwork of mechanistic twitches. In either case, in the precise moment when the character imagines himself to be imposing his own delusions on the world, the nature of his language is constantly betraying him. Jonson anticipates the importance attached by Freud to trifling verbal gestures as an index of psychic disturbance, and also the textual "close reading" to which recent criticism has accustomed us, where every grain, every atom of discourse, is weighed for its expressive substance. In the plays of Samuel Beckett and Eugène Ionesco we discover a partial analogy to Jonson's ways with language, since these writers too are fascinated by the kind of talk that at first sounds normal, and then on closer range proves to be a series of mechanistic twitches that express the emptiness and desperation of the speakers' lives. And it is perhaps not mere coincidence that these authors show a further resemblance to Jonson: in the renunciation of causality as a dramatic principle, with a corresponding exploitation of surfaces, of the momentary configuration, as a reality sufficient unto itself.

Jonson's prose — one must say it sooner or later — is a monumental achievement, monumental in the way it gives definitive shape to one aspect of the language of a generation, and makes that language not merely an adjunct of comedy,

but comedy itself. Jonson, it is true, rarely achieves the re-
laxed sureness of Shakespeare's best prose. His style remains
tense and high strung almost to the last. But within his range
he achieved a remarkable array of triumphs. He went from
one experiment to the next, grappling with each artistic problem as though his salvation depended on it, and has been re-
warded by a posterity which remembered — until recently
at least — only that he slighted Shakespeare's erudition while
he exalted him above Aeschylus.

There are reasons, certainly, why Jonson ceased over a century ago to be a popular author. The negative aspects of his
artistic temperament — a certain coldness, coupled with an
intense egoism, a sexual philistinism, and a rarely absent sense
of hard work — such traits are scarcely designed to delight
the reader, especially the casual reader, whose grandfather
wept over the death of little Nell, worshiped Wordsworthian
nature, considered romantic love the highest human experience,
and regarded spontaneity as the central artistic virtue. Jonson
does not, as the past century would say, "soar"; he does not
display the human spirit grasping after infinities, as Marlowe
does, nor gaze with a shudder into the abyss, as Webster
does; nor is he, on the other hand, *gemütlich* and matey like
Dekker, or graceful, witty, and accommodating like his Restoration followers. He lacks "tenderness," "magic," and the
like. Sometimes it seems as though his own device of the
negative catalogue has been turned against him; he is pelted
with a barrage of the things he is not.

Such insistent nay-saying was perhaps an inevitable reaction against an artist who erased positive standards from the
surface of his art to the extent Jonson did. But if his artistic
techniques are negative, they can be defined positively. If linguistic realism is a valuable artistic technique, no playwright
before Jonson copied live speech more tellingly, and few

since have more powerfully worked it into a design that transcends mere realism. If linguistic satire is a perennial feature of European comedy, no dramatist has perceived its relevance to life more acutely, or plumbed its possibilities more exhaustively, or elevated it into such a major comic insight. None, certainly, is more responsible for making it one of the hallmarks of English dramatic literature. (One wonders, incidentally, to what extent Jonson is responsible for one of the most familiar images of themselves that the English have been presenting to each other and the rest of the world for over two centuries — that of crotchetiness, of rampant eccentricity akin to that of mad dogs.) If self-deluding rhetoric ranks as one of the permanent distempers of *homo loquens*, no playwright has explored more grandly the triumphs of autointoxication and the bleak depths of disillusion to which it can lead. If mimicry is a vice ineradicable from the species, no one has more shrewdly perceived its ubiquitousness or presented it more variously in action. Further, if style consists in absolute control, in shaping every phrase with regard to its function in a vital whole, in ruthlessly suppressing digressiveness and self-indulgence, few artists at any time have more tightly curbed their natural power and forced it to obey their larger designs.

And all of this, of course, within the bounds of the comic theater, and without grudging the comic artist's first job — to make his audience laugh. If the present discussion has often seemed solemn compared to its subject, the reason is simply that as soon as the autumn judgments of critics sit in conclave to define *Quid sit comoedia*, the precious essence, whatever it is, that provokes laughter from spectators evaporates. But the fault is not Jonson's, whose plays roused laughter in the theater for two centuries. They might do so again, given a fair chance.

Notes

Notes

Chapter I. Antecedents

1. With due apology, I shirk at the outset any formal discussion of the difference between prose and verse. The distinction, like that between night and day, is plain to all, but the borderline is impossible to fix; wrangles over the respective "essences" of the two techniques have led nowhere. It is a relief to find one of the distinguished poetic practitioners of this century refusing to join the dispute: "I know that the difference between poetry and prose is a topic for school debating societies, but I am not aware that the debating societies have arrived at a solution. . . . There are doubtless many empirical generalisations which one may draw from a study of existing poetry and prose, but after much reflection I conclude that the only absolute distinction to be drawn is that poetry is written in verse, and prose is written in prose; or, in other words, that there is prose rhythm and verse rhythm. And any other essential difference is still to seek" (T. S. Eliot, "The Borderline of Prose," *The New Statesman*, IX [May 19, 1917], 158). A triple distinction between prose ("the rhythm of continuity"), metrical rhythm, and "lyric" rhythm is elaborated by Northrop Frye (*Anatomy of Criticism* [Princeton, 1957], pp. 263–268 and *passim*), in what seems to me the most valuable contribution to the problem so far.

2. First pointed out and documented by John W. Cunliffe in his edition of *Supposes and Jocasta*, Belles Lettres Series (Boston, 1906), to which all citations of *Supposes* will refer. See also C. T. Prouty, *George Gascoigne* (New York, 1942), pp. 160–161ff.

3. Ludovico Ariosto, *Le commedie*, ed. Michele Catalano, 2 vols. (Bologna, 1933). Numbers in parentheses will refer to volume and page for the prose text, and act, scene, and line for the verse text.

4. See R. Warwick Bond, ed., *The Complete Works of John Lyly*, 3 vols. (Oxford, 1902), II, 473–485; and Winifred Smith, "Italian and Elizabethan Comedy," *Modern Philology*, V (1907–08), 555–567.

5. Attempts to account for Lyly's use of prose in his plays have tended to fall back on the prejudice mentioned in the opening sen-

tence of this study — that prose is the "natural" medium for comedy. According to John Dover Wilson (*John Lyly* [Cambridge, 1905], p. 97), "Lyly, with the instinct of a born conversationalist, realised that prose was the only possible dress for comedy that should seek to represent contemporary life" — which contains the additional false premise that Lyly was seeking to represent contemporary life. According to George Peirce Baker, Lyly "had the good sense to see the superiority of prose to verse as the expression of comedy" (Charles Mills Gayley, ed., *Representative English Comedies*, 4 vols. [New York, 1903–36], I, 273). The most sensible conjecture is also the simplest, that of Clarence Griffin Child (*John Lyly and Euphuism* [Erlangen and Leipzig, 1894], p. 85) that Lyly wanted to capitalize on the popularity of his prose style. In addition, there is the matter of "cumulative Italian example" (Winifred Smith, "Italian and Elizabethan Comedy," p. 558).

6. Citations from Lyly will be to Bond's edition, volume and page, except in the case of the plays, where act, scene, and line numbers are supplied instead.

7. See my article, "The Prose Style of John Lyly," *ELH*, XXIII (1956), 14–35.

8. For a much more extreme, and (to me) mistaken view of Lyly's use of antithesis, see Morris William Croll and Harry Clemons, eds., *Euphues: The Anatomy of Wit; Euphues and His England* (London, 1916), p. xvii.

9. On calculated sophistry in *Euphues*, see Walter N. King, "John Lyly and Elizabethan Rhetoric," *Studies in Philology*, LII (1955), 149–161.

10. Certain of these recur so obsessively as to become an identifying trait of authorship. H. Dugdale Sykes (*The Authorship of 'The Taming of A Shrew', 'The Famous Victories of Henry V', and the Additions to Marlowe's 'Faustus'* [London, 1920]) proposes a theory of common authorship (that of Samuel Rowley) for these plays, based on the recurrence of details like the oath "Swownes."

11. The text cited is *The Famous Victories of Henry the Fifth*, ed. John S. Farmer, Tudor Facsimile Texts (Oxford, 1913).

12. See George Philip Krapp, *The Rise of English Literary Prose* (New York, 1915), p. 457. For other test passages like those in *The Famous Victories*, see many of the prose speeches of *The Taming of A Shrew*, ed. F. S. Boas, Shakespeare Library (New York, 1908), originally printed as doggerel verse, and some of the verse passages in Peele's *Edward I*, ed. W. W. Greg, Malone Society Reprints (Oxford, 1911), e.g., lines 166–187 and 462–586, with their counterparts printed as

prose by A. H. Bullen in Peele's *Works*, 2 vols. (London, 1888), I, 92–93, 105–109.

13. Thomas Deloney, *Works*, ed. Francis Oscar Mann (Oxford, 1912), pp. 3–4.

14. *Anatomy of Criticism*, p. 228.

15. *The Countesse of Pembroke's Arcadia*, ed. Albert Feuillerat (Cambridge, 1912), pp. 237–239 — a passage, incidentally, that Jonson must have forgotten when he complained that "Sidney did not keep a Decorum jn making every one speak as well as himself" (*Conversations*, 17–19).

16. Attribution is discussed by J. Churton Collins, ed., *The Plays and Poems of Robert Greene*, 2 vols. (Oxford, 1905), I, 140–141. Citations will be to *A Looking-Glass for London and England*, ed. W. W. Greg, Malone Society Reprints (Oxford, 1932), with conjectural readings from Collins supplied in brackets.

17. See Hardin Craig, "Shakespeare and Formal Logic," in *Studies in English Philology, A Miscellany in Honor of Frederick Klaeber*, ed. Kemp Malone and Martin B. Ruud (Minneapolis, 1929), pp. 380–396; Sister Miriam Joseph, *Shakespeare's Use of the Arts of Language* (New York, 1947), *passim;* and, for specimens of formal logic in the Elizabethan drama at large, Allan H. Gilbert, "Logic in the Elizabethan Drama," *Studies in Philology*, XXXII (1935), 527–545.

18. One approaches the subject with more than usual diffidence because of the beating it has taken at the hands of other critics. Setting aside the various attempts to discover a principle governing the shifts between verse and prose, for which (most of them absurd) see the critical bibliography in Milton Crane, *Shakespeare's Prose* (Chicago, 1951), pp. 214–216, one finds mainly a highly charged impressionism combined with a spurious classificationism, as in J. Churton Collins, "Shakespeare as a Prose Writer," *Studies in Shakespeare* (New York, 1904), or Henry W. Wells, "The Continuity of Shaksperian Prose," *Shakespeare Association Bulletin*, XV (July 1940), 175–183. For an up-to-date bibliography see M. C. Bradbrook, "Fifty Years of the Criticism of Shakespeare's Style: A Retrospect," *Shakespeare Survey*, VII (1954), 1–11. Miss Bradbrook's suspicion (p. 4) that the study of Euphuism and related traditional topics has by now exhausted its usefulness is perhaps a wholesome caution; nevertheless only Bond, it seems to me, has fully grasped the importance of Euphuism in Shakespeare, and his documentation remains to be interpreted.

19. Quotations will be from the Folio facsimile edited by Sir Sidney Lee (Oxford, 1902). Each extract is followed by the page number in Lee, then by the corresponding act, scene, and line number in the

edition of George Lyman Kittredge (New York, 1936). The following abbreviations are used:

IHIV: Henry the Fourth, Part One	*Troil.: Troilus and Cressida*
IIHIV: Henry the Fourth, Part Two	*MW: The Merry Wives of Windsor*
HV: Henry the Fifth	*Ham.: Hamlet*
Much Ado: Much Ado about Nothing	*Oth.: Othello*
	Lear: King Lear
Merch.: The Merchant of Venice	*Tim.: Timon of Athens*
TN: Twelfth Night	*Cor.: Coriolanus*
AYL: As You Like it	*Ant.: Antony and Cleopatra*
Alls W: All's Well that Ends Well	*Cymb.: Cymbeline*
MM: Measure for Measure	*WT: The Winter's Tale*
	Temp.: The Tempest

20. E. A. Abbott, *A Shakespearian Grammar*, 3d ed. (London, 1897), pp. 101–102, cites a few appearances of the conjunction "for," but without giving any inkling of its frequency. Abbott, interested primarily in irregularities, i.e., in points of difference between Elizabethan and modern grammar, also ignores causal connectives such as "hence" and "therefore" whose usage remains unchanged in the modern language. Wilhelm Franz's exhaustive and imposing *Die Sprache Shakespeares*, 4th ed. of *Shakespeare Grammatik* (Halle, 1939), tabulates many of the logical devices, the correlatives, etc., discussed below, especially in pp. 427–473 ("Die Konjunktion"), but, again, chiefly in order to define the limits of Shakespearean grammar, the range of its possibilities, without concerning himself with whether such-and-such a syntactic scheme occurs once or a hundred times in Shakespeare.

21. W. K. Wimsatt, Jr., *The Prose Style of Samuel Johnson* (New Haven, 1941), p. 12.

22. With the following observation of Kenneth Muir I naturally find myself in hearty accord: "Shakespeare was in no danger of becoming too colloquial in his dialogue. Even his apparently colloquial prose is a good deal further from actual Elizabethan speech than the dialogue of Middleton or Jonson; and when in his verse he uses language of extraordinary simplicity the powerful effect is obtained largely by contrast with the more complex language used elsewhere" ("Shakespeare and Rhetoric," *Shakespeare Jahrbuch*, XC [1954], 60).

23. *Johnson on Shakespeare*, ed. Walter Raleigh (London, 1908), p. 42 — speaking, evidently, of Shakespeare's prose and verse alike.

24. Surprisingly, something like the same point was made by Ralph Waldo Emerson, in "Shakespeare; or The Poet," *Complete Works*, ed. Edward Waldo Emerson, 12 vols. (Boston, 1903), IV, 214:

"Though the speeches in the plays, and single lines, have a beauty which tempts the ear to pause on them for their euphuism, yet the sentence is so loaded with meaning and so linked with its foregoers and followers, that the logician is satisfied."

Chapter II. Prose as Prose

1. Benjamin Lee Whorf, *Language, Thought, and Reality*, ed. John B. Carroll (New York, 1956), pp. 137, 147. For a stimulating, if inconclusive, discussion of the Whorf hypothesis see *Language in Culture*, ed. Harry Hoijer (Chicago, 1954).

2. *Meaning in the Visual Arts* (New York, 1955), pp. 329–330.

3. E.g., *Linguistique générale et linguistique française*, 2d ed. (Berne, 1944), esp. pp. 339–370, "Formes générales de l'expression," and *Le langage et la vie*, 3d ed. (Paris, 1952), pp. 53–57 and *passim*.

4. "Some Changes in the Prose Style of the Seventeenth Century," unpubl. diss. (Cambridge, 1938), p. 109. See also F. W. Bateson, *English Poetry and the English Language* (Oxford, 1934), a more speculative and impressionistic essay on the relations between linguistic change and literature, with special reference to poetry.

5. Especially " 'Attic Prose' in the Seventeenth Century," *Studies in Philology*, XVIII (1921), 79–128; "Attic Prose: Lipsius, Montaigne, Bacon," in *Schelling Anniversary Papers* (New York, 1923), pp. 117–150; "Muret and the History of 'Attic' Prose," *Publications of the Modern Language Association*, XXXIX (1924), 254–309; "The Baroque Style in Prose," in *Studies in English Philology*, ed. Malone and Ruud, pp. 427–456.

6. Especially George Williamson, *The Senecan Amble* (London, 1951).

7. On convention, see Harry Levin, "Notes on Convention," in *Perspectives of Criticism*, Harvard Studies in Comparative Literature, No. 20 (Cambridge, Mass., 1950), pp. 55–83.

8. René Wellek, "The Concept of Baroque in Literary Scholarship," *Journal of Aesthetics and Art Criticism*, V (1946), 96.

9. *Linguistics and Literary History* (Princeton, 1948), Ch. i.

10. For prose, see especially the chapters on *Don Quixote* and Diderot.

11. *The Handling of Words* (London, 1923).

12. *Mimesis*, trans. Willard R. Trask (Princeton, 1953).

13. *Situations I* (Paris, 1947), esp. "La temporalité chez Faulkner," p. 70–81; "M. Jean Giraudoux et la philosophie d'Aristote," pp. 82–98; and "Explication de *l'étranger*," pp. 99–121.

14. "Observations on the Style of Ernest Hemingway," *Kenyon Review*, XIII (1951), 581–609.

15. *Style in French Prose* (Oxford, 1953).

16. The struggles to convert this concept from art history into a meaningful term for literary history have not been entirely happy. The further attempt to differentiate, as the art historians do, between "baroque" and "mannerist" in literature has only compounded confusion and darkened counsel. René Wellek's caveat against the promiscuous use of "baroque" ("The Concept of Baroque in Literary Scholarship," pp. 77–109) has not prevented the appearance of more speculation concerning the baroque *Zeitgeist*, more freewheeling analogies between the arts, more attempts to define "baroque" in narrowly stylistic terms, as well as a generous quota of rebukes from the cautious. The present study will use the term "baroque" because Croll used it, because there is no satisfactory substitute, and because — for all its uncertainties — it still seems a useful way of suggesting stylistic procedures that may, in the last analysis, transcend the bounds of a single art and relate to a whole cultural conformation.

17. Of course the Shakespearean passage is not really Ciceronian, but only relatively or approximately so in contrast with Jonson. "The Ciceronian style," as Croll has pointed out, "cannot be reproduced in English, or indeed in any modern language. The ligatures of its comprehensive period are not found in the syntax of an uninflected tongue; and the artifices necessary to supply their function must produce either fantastic distortion or insufferable bombast." ("Attic Prose," *Schelling Anniversary Papers*, p. 134.)

18. Citations from Jonson throughout are to the edition of C. H. Herford and Percy and Evelyn Simpson, 11 vols. (Oxford, 1925–1952). The following abbreviations are used in the present chapter:

> *Disc.: Timber, or Discoveries*
> *CR: Cynthia's Revels*
> *EMO: Every Man out of his Humour*
> *Poet.: Poetaster*
> *SW: Epicene, or The Silent Woman*
> *BF: Bartholomew Fair*
> *NNW: News from the New World Discovered in the Moon*
> *Pan: Pan's Anniversary*
> *King's Ent.: The King's Entertainment in Passing to His Coronation*
> *Chlor.: Chloridia*

19. Croll, "Baroque Style," p. 433.

20. The transference of language from the printed page to the

speaking voices of actors in a theater involves, necessarily, many accommodations. Most of these, however, occur on the level of phonology, and hence are properly analyzable only by microlinguistic techniques, including scrutiny of phonetic sequences, stresses, pitch, juncture, and the like. Even for a contemporary text, it is doubtful whether such an analysis would produce very satisfactory results. George L. Trager and Henry Lee Smith, Jr. (*An Outline of English Structure*, Studies in Linguistics, Occasional Papers 3 [Norman, Oklahoma, 1951], pp. 50–51) list at least eight different ways of saying "How do they study?" where the variations are confined entirely to pitch, stress, internal juncture and terminal juncture, and even so are not exhaustive. When we deal with such far more complex utterances as Jonson's sentences, when we take into account the problems of declamation in a theater whose declamatory techniques are at best only half understood, in a language three hundred years old whose phonology has been only fragmentarily reconstructed, we are facing a set of variables so formidable as to make any meaningful phonological appraisal a will-o'-the-wisp. One must, then, renounce formal discussion of this problem and confine oneself to repeating truisms, such as the fact that a good playwright somehow contrives to make his dialogue speakable, that — as actors know — an intricate sentence of Congreve's can be pronounced more trippingly on the tongue than a simpler one from William Archer's translation of Ibsen, because the former was written by a master of theatrical speech and the latter was not.

In Jonson's case, one can of course point to certain details of phonetic realism — his growing tendency to substitute the "-s" ending of third person singular verbs for the more literary "-eth" inflection, his use of clipped forms (as he would have thought them) such as "'hem" for "them" — and to his employment, on a massive scale, of modish phrases and cant terms that he would have scorned to use in his own person. But in sentence structure, if it can be separated from the rest, significant differences between the stage prose and the non-dramatic prose are few, partly because of the very nature of the baroque rhetoric to which Jonson was committed. What Jonson does, in fact, as this chapter is trying to show, is to take syntactic strategies normal in his critical prose and use them in the theater for specifically theatrical purposes, for characterization and effects of realism and satire.

I should like here to thank my former colleague James Sledd for turning the gimlet eye of a trained linguist on an earlier version of this chapter. In so doing, he rescued it from many errors. What errors it now contains have been perpetrated since he read it.

21. *The Senecan Amble*, p. 145, p. 156, n. 1.
22. *The Advancement of Learning*, Everyman ed., p. 24.
23. *The Senecan Amble*, pp. 89, 115, 118, 120, 184, and *passim*.
24. Croll, "Baroque Style," p. 437.
25. "Baroque Style," p. 443.
26. "Baroque Style," p. 447.
27. *Miscellaneous Criticism*, ed. Thomas Middleton Raysor (Cambridge, Mass., 1936), p. 217.
28. "English Prose Style," in *Miscellaneous Essays* (London, 1892), p. 7.
29. Montaigne, "Du repentir," *Essais*, ed. Albert Thibaudet, Bibliothèque de la Pléiade (Paris, 1958), p. 899.
30. See note 23 above.
31. "Baroque Style," p. 452.
32. For the "possessive as antecedent of a relative pronoun," a peculiarity of Elizabethan syntax in general, see A. C. Partridge, *Studies in the Syntax of Ben Jonson's Plays* (Cambridge, 1953), pp. 46–47, and for the (baroque) use of "a common relative with different case functions," p. 70. Jonson's own *English Grammar* (Herford and Simpson, VIII, 453–553), it might be added, is, disappointingly, of little help. The section on syntax (pp. 528ff.) devotes itself mainly to combinations required by idiom (agreement of noun and verb, position of article and noun, etc.) and a few minor variations. It deals only hastily and perfunctorily with connectives, and it ignores (as do other grammars, for that matter) the whole area of the "probable" and "possible" in syntax, of acutest interest to stylistic study.
33. The fact that these lines form part of a long excerpt borrowed almost intact from John Hoskins does not invalidate them as evidence of Jonsonian style. It is, in fact, remarkable how smoothly the extract from Hoskins (itself an adaptation of Lipsius) fits into Jonson's own prose. On Hoskins, and the borrowings in the *Discoveries*, see the *Directions for Speech and Style*, ed. Hoyt H. Hudson (Princeton, 1935).
34. Here, as in the quotation above from *Disc.* 1404–07, I have restored the Folio reading. Herford and Simpson correct "hither. Also" to "hither also," and "serv'd" to "serve." The original reading in both cases strikes me as thoroughly Jonsonian. While certainty in such matters is impossible — Jonson *may* have intended "serve" — I trust that the evidence of this chapter as a whole will suffice to leave the benefit of the doubt with the text as it actually stands. It seems as rash to force Jonson's grammar to conform to modern practice as it was for earlier editors of Shakespeare to correct Shakespeare when

he followed a plural subject with a singular verb or took other liberties later regarded as unorthodox. For tense shift as a characteristic
of baroque poetry see Lowry Nelson, Jr., "Góngora and Milton:
Toward a Definition of the Baroque," *Comparative Literature*, VI
(1954), 53–63.

35. The fact that other writers do the same thing in similar circumstances leads one to suspect a special convention at work. See, for
example, Dekker, *The Magnificent Entertainment*, lines 67–76, 175–
179, 309–312, 456–465, 497–500, 831–845, in *The Dramatic Works*, ed.
Fredson Bowers, 3 vols. (Cambridge, 1953–1959), II, 253–303; Middleton, *The Triumphs of Truth* and *Civitatis Amor* in *Works*, ed. A. H.
Bullen, 8 vols. (Boston, 1886), VII, 239, 284–285, etc.; and Carew,
Coelum Britannicum, in *Poems*, ed. Rhodes Dunlap (Oxford, 1949),
pp. 154, 168, 176.

36. *A History of English Prose Rhythm* (London, 1912), p. 205.

37. It is uncertain how far this view would have to be modified if
one were convinced, with Ralph S. Walker, *Ben Jonson's Timber or
Discoveries* (Syracuse, 1953), pp. 1–13, that Jonson's editor, rather
than Jonson, was responsible for the haphazard grouping of the *Discoveries*, and that even such disorder as may have existed in the
manuscript merely reflected the incomplete state in which Jonson
left it. The method of composition in either case remains the same:
that of the gradual accretion of discrete fragments. And Digby's
cavalier editorial practice would seem to reflect the general feeling
of the time about what constituted a "work," or a publishable unit
of writing. It is at least arguable that had Jonson himself confronted
publication, he might have been guided by his own motto, *tanquam
explorator*, and left the fragments in something like their present
tentative, exploratory form.

38. *Shakespearean Criticism*, ed. Thomas Middleton Raysor, 2 vols.
(Cambridge, Mass., 1930), I, 49.

39. *La femme silencieuse* (with *Je ne vous aime pas*), Editions de
la Nouvelle Revue Française (Paris: Librairie Gallimard, 1926).

40. The treatment would be similar in another modern version,
proposed but not, apparently, executed, by a Mr. Elmer Harris, a
dramatist. Mr. Harris would introduce "love-passages between Epicoene and the two puppets, La-Foole and Daw," so as to provoke
mutual jealousy and thus motivate the quarrel between them. The
Ladies Collegiate, too, "must be motivated" (Gayley, *Representative
English Comedies*, II, 120–121). "Motivate! Motivate!" seems to be
the rallying cry of the adapters of Jonson. What cannot be "motivated," or made to produce further action, is discarded as "irrelevant."

This would be the place to speak of Stefan Zweig's adaptation of

Epicene into a libretto, *Die schweigsame Frau*, for Richard Strauss (1935), if that were relevant. But it is not relevant, Zweig having altered the plot so radically as to make comparison purposeless. He has, of course, "motivated" his own new plot at every point, "explained" Morose's hatred of noise in terms of a traumatic naval battle, and so forth.

41. *Ben Jonson: Selected Works* (New York, 1938), p. 25.

42. Page 30.

43. Eric Bentley, *In Search of Theater* (New York, 1954), p. 147.

44. Spitzer, *Linguistics and Literary History*, p. 11.

Chapter III. Rhetoric's Tinkling Bell

1. "Paradoxe sur le comédien," *Oeuvres*, ed. André Billy, Bibliothèque de la Pléiade (Paris, 1951), p. 1040.

2. First acted in 1597–98, but not published until 1609. See Herford and Simpson, I, 305–307; E. K. Chambers, *The Elizabethan Stage*, 4 vols. (Oxford, 1923), III, 357–358; and J. B. Leishman, ed., *The Three Parnassus Plays (1598–1601)* (London, 1949), p. 83, n. 8. John J. Enck, "*The Case Is Altered*: Initial Comedy of Humours," *Studies in Philology*, L (1952), 195–214, delivers a useful corrective to the indiscriminate application of the term "romantic" to this play.

3. J. M. Nosworthy, "*The Case Is Altered*," *Journal of English and Germanic Philology*, LI (1952), 61–70, points out resemblances between Onion's speeches in I.vii and those of the Abingdon servingmen in *The Two Angry Women of Abingdon* to support the contention that Henry Porter collaborated with Jonson on this play. The evidence is not wholly convincing; in any case, the ascription of I.vii to Porter does not substantially affect the present discussion.

4. A dissenter on this point is J. B. Leishman, ed., *Parnassus Plays*, p. 83, n. 8.

5. Entered in the Stationers' Register on August 4, 1600, and published in quarto in 1601. Described both on the Folio title page and in a postscript to the Folio text as having been "first Acted, in the yeere 1598." See Herford and Simpson, I, 331, and III, 297, 403, and Chambers, III, 359–360.

6. A point made earlier in Alexander H. Sackton, *Rhetoric as a Dramatic Language in Ben Jonson* (New York, 1948), p. 61.

7. Entered in the Stationers' Register on April 8, 1600, and published twice in quarto the same year. See Herford and Simpson, I, 373–374, and Chambers, II, 360–363.

8. Oscar James Campbell, *Comicall Satyre and Shakespeare's Troilus*

and Cressida (San Marino, California, 1938), p. 71. On the relation between Carlo's similes and the jests of Charles the Fryer of Chester (reported by Nashe in *Pierce Penniless*) see Charles Read Baskervill, *English Elements in Jonson's Early Comedy*, University of Texas Studies in English, I (Austin, 1911), pp. 174–180.

9. *Works*, ed. Bullen, II, 267.

10. Most of the key words in Fallace's rhapsody are attempts to imitate the jargon of the court. "Fine," as an approbative epithet, is "a courtly affectation gone vulgar" (Arthur H. King, *The Language of Satirized Characters in Poëtaster*, Lund Studies in English, X [Lund, 1941], p. 38); "neat" illustrates the courtly word used in a pseudo-courtly sense (pp. 46–47); and "sweet" is affected when used vaguely in the sense of "pleasing in general" (p. 184). The same is doubtless true of "cleanly," "daintily," and "comely."

11. Strictly speaking, Fastidious' floridities belong to the language of "complement" (or, as we would spell it, "compliment"), a mannered style characterized by magniloquence, hyperbole, and surplus (King, p. 64), while Fallace is aiming at "courtly" speech. King distinguishes as follows: " 'Courtly' is a socio-stylistic, 'complement' a stylistic, term. Courtly speech may be colloquial but not pedantic; complement may be pedantic but not colloquial" (p. xxix). For an analysis of the vocabulary of compliment, with many examples, see King, pp. 64–84, and for the word "complement" itself, as used by Jonsonian characters, pp. 66–68.

Two other studies of Jonson's language should be mentioned: Joshua H. Neumann, "Notes on Ben Jonson's English," *Publications of the Modern Language Association*, LIV (1939), 736–763, and Esko V. Pennanen, *Chapters on the Language in Ben Jonson's Dramatic Works*, Annales Universitatis Turkuensis, Series B, XXXIX (Turku, Finland, 1951). The former discusses Jonson's vocabulary and his contributions to modern English; the latter analyzes, among other things, the language of affectation in the plays: neologisms, coined derivatives, phrasal verbs, and the like.

12. Acted at Blackfriars early in 1601, entered in the Stationers' Register on May 23, and published the same year in quarto. See Herford and Simpson, I, 393–396, and Chambers, III, 363–364. There is no agreement as to the priority of the Quarto or Folio text. Henry De Vocht (*Comments on the Text of Ben Jonson's Cynthias Revels*, Materials for the Study of the Old English Drama, New Series, XXI [Louvain, 1950]) discusses the matter minutely and launches a full-scale attack on the authoritativeness of the Folio.

13. Alexander H. Sackton, "The Paradoxical Encomium in Eliza-

bethan Drama," *University of Texas Studies in English*, XXVIII (Austin, 1949), p. 95, suggests further concerning this speech that "the praise of a city or its rulers, its buildings such as hospitals and churches, and its streets were all conventional subjects in the tradition of the rhetorical encomium. It is partly their conventionality which makes the speech comic." Likenesses between this scene and others in *Cynthia's Revels* and scenes in the academic play of *Timon* were demonstrated in Baskervill, *English Elements*, pp. 268–272, but it is not certain which play was written first.

14. *Miscellaneous Criticism*, ed. Raysor, p. 47.

15. Performed in 1601, entered in the Stationers' Register the same year, and published in 1602. See Herford and Simpson, I, 415, and Chambers, III, 364–366.

16. Pp. 108–166. It is perhaps King's lexicographical bias that makes him find Tucca's vocabulary more striking than his syntax; for me it is the reverse.

17. "It is generally held that Marston helped Dekker with the play, in spite of the single name on the title-page" (Chambers, III, 293).

18. King, p. 108, proposes a common source, i.e., the speech of Captain Hannam himself, for the linguistic traits shared by the two Tuccas, because "Dekker knew what Captain Hannam's speech was like, but probably had no text of *Poëtaster* to work on (*Satiro-mastix* was entered on the Stationers' Register before *Poëtaster* . . .)." But Dekker himself says that he copied Jonson: "*Ist not as lawfull then for mee to imitate* Horace, as Horace Hannam?" (*Satiromastix*, "To the World," lines 34–35).

19. *Dramatic Works of Dekker*, ed. Bowers, I, 342–343, 378.

20. *Selected Essays*, rev. ed. (New York, 1950), p. 128.

21. *Comedies*, ed. Bonamy Dobrée, World's Classics (London, 1944), pp. 245–246, 248.

22. Levin, ed., *Ben Jonson*, p. 6.

23. See Herford and Simpson, I, 332–335.

24. Even if one shares the extravagant opinion of Swinburne (*A Study of Ben Jonson* [London, 1889], p. 12) that this defense "is worth all Sidney's and all Shelley's treatises thrown together," one may still feel that Jonson acted wisely in cutting it from the Folio version.

Chapter IV. Things of Sense

1. First acted in 1603; entered on the Stationers' Register Nov. 2, 1604; published in quarto in 1605. See Herford and Simpson, II, 3–4, and Chambers, III, 366–368.

2. Acted in 1605 or 1606 (see afterpage to Folio text); published in quarto in 1607. See Herford and Simpson, II, 49–50.

3. First acted in 1609 by the Children of the Revels, and entered in the Stationers' Register the same year. "Quarto editions dating 1609 and 1612 have been alleged to exist; but the first extant version is that of the Folio, in 1616" (Herford and Simpson, III, 69). See also Chambers, III, 369–371, and W. W. Greg, "Was there a 1612 Quarto of *Epicene?*" *The Library*, XV (1934), 306–315.

4. Levin, "Notes on Convention," in *Perspectives of Criticism*, p. 67 (paraphrasing Victor Hugo).

5. André Malraux, *Les voix du silence* (Paris, 1951), pp. 304, 306, 309.

6. The tradition that sees in Jonson primarily a realistic writer begins with his own contemporaries, with a remark in *The Return from Parnassus*, Part II, lines 294–296: "A meere Empyrick, one that getts what he hath by obseruation, and makes onely nature priuy to what he endites" (*Parnassus Plays*, ed. Leishman, p. 244). Characteristic of more recent utterances would be the emphasis on Jonson's realism in Julian Symons, "Ben Jonson as Social Realist: *Bartholomew Fair*," *The Southern Review*, VI (1940–41), 375–386, or the reference to Jonson's "detailed, objective transcripts of life" in Marco Mincoff, "Baroque Literature in England," *Annuaire de l'Université de Sofia*, Faculté Historico-Philologique, XLIII (1946–47), 56.

7. On these ancestral beasts, see Baskervill, *English Elements*, *passim*, with its account of the native sources on which Jonson drew.

8. Interestingly, it was Jonson who first coined the word "graphic" and brought it into the language (Neumann, "Ben Jonson's English," p. 761).

9. *Les voix du silence*, p. 459.

10. See Crane, *Shakespeare's Prose*, p. 101.

11. In my article, "Ovid, Juvenal, and *The Silent Woman*," *Publications of the Modern Language Association*, LXXI (1956), 213–224.

12. For a psychoanalytic discussion of this ambivalence and an extremely harsh verdict on Jonson for his neuroticism, see Edmund Wilson, "Morose Ben Jonson," *The Triple Thinkers*, rev. ed. (New York, 1948), p. 221 and *passim*. A much more amiable essay by H. R. Hays ("Satire and Identification: An Introduction to Ben Jonson," *Kenyon Review*, XIX [1957], 267–283) regards the neuroticism as a source of insight, and quite properly shifts the emphasis from Jonson's own psychic disturbances to the dramatic creations in which he objectified them.

13. Levin, ed., *Ben Jonson*, p. 30; John J. Enck, *Jonson and the Comic Truth* (Madison, 1957), pp. 136, 142, 143, 147.

14. Harry Levin, *The Overreacher: A Study of Christopher Mar-*

lowe (Cambridge, Mass., 1952), p. 22, applies this term to Marlowe.

15. Enck, *Jonson and the Comic Truth*, p. 208.

16. To avoid confusion, the modern spelling, "compliment," is adopted here, but the word is to be understood in its Elizabethan and linguistic sense.

17. *Language of Satirized Characters*, pp. 70–80.

18. E. K. Chambers (*The Mediaeval Stage*, 2 vols [Oxford, 1903], I, 375, n. 3) mentions a fourteenth-century "Société des Foux" founded on the lines of a chivalric order.

19. *Comedies*, ed. Dobrée, p. 142.

20. Jonson's own addition to a passage translated from Heinsius. See Maurice Castelain, ed., *Discoveries* (Paris, 1906), p. 135.

21. *Works*, ed. Ronald B. McKerrow, 5 vols. (London, 1910), I, 213.

22. Enck, *Jonson and the Comic Truth*, p. 139.

23. It is worth noticing, in connection with the wintriness of the language, that when Jonson adapted Libanius' Sixth Declamation for his own purposes in *Epicene*, he translated several water and flood metaphors to describe the inundating effects of feminine gabble, but carefully excluded three references to fire. Libanius' Morosus complains that when he answered his wife, he only fanned the flames of her loquacity, that when he quoted Euripides in an attempt to silence her, he only set her tongue the more ablaze, and that when he resorted to force and gagged her, he found he had thrown fire on fire (*Libanii Sophistae Praeludia Oratoria* . . . , trans. Federicus Morellus [Paris, 1606], Sigs. 2C5v, 2D2v, 2D3). Jonson's avoidance of this trope, whether conscious or not, suggests the consistency with which he maintained the frosty climate of his play.

See Aurelia Henry, ed., *Epicoene*, Yale Studies in English, XXXI (New York, 1906), pp. xxviii ff., for a discussion of the edition of Libanius cited above, and the suggestion, based on verbal similarities, that Jonson used the Latin translation rather than the Greek original.

24. A chapter on *Epicene* in Edward B. Partridge, *The Broken Compass: A Study of the Major Comedies of Ben Jonson* (New York, 1958), pp. 161–177, analyzes the motif of sexual ambiguity very skillfully. See also Enck, *Jonson and the Comic Truth*, pp. 139–140, 148–149, and some remarks of my own on the same theme, as it appears in *Volpone*, in "The Double Plot in *Volpone*," *Modern Philology*, LI (1953), 83–92.

25. John J. Enck, "Ben Jonson's Imagery," unpubl. diss. (Harvard, 1950), p. 286.

26. Applying criteria proposed for Shakespeare by C. L. Barber (*Shakespeare's Festive Comedy* [Princeton, 1959], p. 8), one may say

that *Epicene* shows Jonson moving away from satiric toward saturnalian comedy: "The butts in the festive plays consistently exhibit their unnaturalness by being kill-joys. . . . Pleasure thus becomes the touchstone for judgment of what bars it or is incapable of it." With qualifications, this applies to Morose, who marries not for his own pleasure at all, but in order to thwart the pleasure of others, and whose "incapability" is a cardinal trait.

27. Oscar James Campbell ("The Relation of *Epicoene* to Aretino's *Il Marescalco*," *Publications of the Modern Language Association*, XLVI [1931], 752–762) makes out an extremely convincing case, which could even be extended. Unconvincing, on the other hand, is the case for Machiavelli's *Clizia* argued in Daniel C. Boughner, "*Clizia* and *Epicoene*," *Philological Quarterly*, XIX (1940), 89–91. Except for old age and crotchetiness, which they share with hundreds of other comic characters, there is nothing important in common between Morose and Machiavelli's "vecchio tutto pieno d'amore."

28. *Essays*, ed. W. P. Ker, 2 vols. (Oxford, 1926), I, 86–88ff.

29. *Essays*, ed. Ker, I, 174; I, 140.

30. Frye, *Anatomy of Criticism*, pp. 163–171.

31. To Charles Mills Gayley's assertion that "Morose is, in one aspect or another, reproduced in the Surly of *Sir Courtly Nice*, the Manly of *The Plain Dealer*, the Sullen of *The Beaux Strategem*, and the Croaker of *The Good-Natured Man*" (*Representative English Comedies*, II, 128), one can respond only with dumfounded amazement. With the doubtful exception of Manly, none of these characters bears sufficient trace of Morose — in voice, gesture, or function — to warrant a split second's consideration. If any Restoration character can claim descent from Morose, it is Heartwell, the titular hero of Congreve's *Old Batchelor*. Heartwell, like Morose an elderly misogynist, like Morose makes a reckless marriage. Too late he finds himself wedded to a trollop. His young friends, the wits, after making him a public laughing-stock, reveal that the marriage was a hoax. Heartwell's torments are plainly modeled on those of Morose. See especially *The Old Batchelor*, V.xiii, and for some striking verbal parallels, cp. *The Old Batchelor*, V.xiii.40–50 and 68–70 with (respectively) *SW* II.ii.43–47 and IV.iv.8–11.

Chapter V. Flesh and Blood

1. First acted in 1610, according to the title page in the Folio; published in quarto in 1612. See Herford and Simpson, II, 87–88, and Chambers, III, 371–372.

2. Harry Levin, "Jonson's Metempsychosis," *Philological Quarterly*, XXII (1943), 288; Enck, *Jonson and the Comic Truth*, p. 193.

3. First acted on October 31, 1614 (see Induction, lines 64–71), and published in folio in 1631 together with *The Staple of News* and *The Devil is an Ass*. See Herford and Simpson, II, 131. Charles Read Baskervill ("Some Parallels to *Bartholomew Fair*," *Modern Philology*, VI [1908–09], 109–127) discusses possible sources for scattered details, especially the pseudo-Shakespearean play of *Sir Thomas More*, on which see also Herford and Simpson, X, 167–170. C. F. Tucker Brooke (ed., *The Shakespeare Apocrypha* [Oxford, 1908], p. xxxiii) debates the possible influence of the anonymous play *The Puritan*.

4. John Addington Symonds, *Ben Jonson* (New York, 1886), p. 112.

5. Brome's *The Weeding of the Covent-Garden, or the Middlesex-Justice of Peace* (1658), in *Five New Playes* (London, 1659), Wing 4872, contains at least three major characters modeled closely on three in *Bartholomew Fair*. Brome is described on the title page as "An Ingenious Servant, and Imitator of his Master, that famously Renowned Poet *Ben. Johnson*."

Resemblances between *Covent-Garden Weeded* and *Bartholomew Fair* were listed in E. Koeppel, *Ben Jonson's Wirkung auf zeitgenössische Dramatiker und andere Studien* (Heidelberg, 1906), pp. 171–176, and again in Mina Kerr, *The Influence of Ben Jonson on English Comedy 1598–1642* (New York, 1912), pp. 69–72. A few footnotes below will document these similarities in slightly more detail.

Brome's Gabriel is copied from Jonson's Busy, and there is frequent duplication of Busy's stylistic tricks. For the appositions see Gabriel, " 'Tis mighty headie, mighty headie," sig. [2]E7v, where Brome smudges the effect by not varying the adverb.

6. *The Anatomy of Abuses*, ed. Frederick J. Furnivall, New Shakspere Society (London, 1877–1879), p. 156.

7. Cp. *Covent-Garden Weeded*, sigs. [2]B4v–B5: "But truly I vvas looking at that Image; that painted idolatrous image yonder, as I take it," and [2]D8: ". . . by your own right hand you might have smote him, smote him with great force, yea, smote him unto the earth." Busy does not anaphorize verbs.

8. Norton R. Tempest, *The Rhythm of English Prose* (Cambridge, 1930), p. 49.

9. Cp. *Covent-Garden Weeded*, sig. [2]F3: "*I* may not forbear, *I* am moved for to smite him; yea, vvith often stripes to smite him; my zealous wrath is kindled, and he shall flie before me."

10. Cp. *Covent-Garden Weeded*, sig. [2]Dv: "O prophane tinkling the cymbals of Satan, that tickle the eare with vanity, to lift up the

mind to lewdnesse. Mine eares shall be that of the Adder against the Song of the Serpent."

11. On the *clausulae* see Morris W. Croll, "The Cadence of English Oratorical Prose," *Studies in Philology*, XVI (1919), 1–55, and Tempest, *The Rhythm of English Prose*, pp. 74–82. For the "native English cadence" see Croll, pp. 41–42, and Tempest, pp. 82–103.

12. *Works* (London, 1603), STC 19647, sig. E6v.

13. *The Whole Treatise of the Cases of Conscience, Distinguished into Three Books* (London, 1608), STC 19670, sig. 2H4.

14. *Anatomy of Abuses*, p. 68.

15. *A Second and Third Blast of Retrait from Plaies and Theaters* (*1580*), in W. C. Hazlitt, ed., *The English Drama and Stage under the Tudor and Stuart Princes* (London, 1869), p. 140.

16. Quoted in H. Hensley Henson, *Studies in English Religion in the Seventeenth Century* (London, 1903), p. 182.

17. For Perkins' contribution to Ramism in England, specifically in his treatise on preaching, see Wilbur Samuel Howell, *Logic and Rhetoric in England, 1500–1700* (Princeton, 1956), p. 206.

18. Sig. P2v. The "question" (see Busy in I.vi.57) becomes a more or less technical term in the literature of casuistry.

19. Dryden recognized very well the extent to which artistic tampering forbade literal realism, and stated the difference (one difference, at any rate) with his usual lucidity: ". . . he does so raise his matter in that prose, as to render it delightful; which he could never have performed, had he only said or done those very things, that are daily spoken or practised in the fair: for then the fair itself would be as full of pleasure to an ingenious person as the play, which we manifestly see it is not. But he hath made an excellent Lazar of it; the copy is of price, though the original be vile" (*Essays*, ed. Ker, I, 114–115).

20. Several of Overdo's rhetorical schemes are catalogued in Sackton, *Rhetoric as a Dramatic Language in Ben Jonson*, pp. 154–155.

21. *The Rhetoric of Aristotle*, trans. Richard Claverhouse Jebb, ed. John Edwin Sandys (Cambridge, 1909), pp. 68ff. Cicero, of course, makes similar recommendations, that the orator demonstrate his "dignitas," his "liberalitas," etc. (*De partitione oratoria*, viii.28, in *De oratore*, ed. E. W. Sutton and H. Rackham, Loeb Classical Library [Cambridge, Mass., 1942], II, 332). One might find a rough model for the whole of Overdo's oration in *De partitione oratoria* 27–60, *ibid.*, II, 330–356.

22. Carroll Storrs Alden, ed., *Bartholomew Fair*, Yale Studies in English, XXV (New York, 1904), p. 180.

23. One wonders, incidentally, what Jonson's royal patron thought

of this scene. James I's *Counterblaste to Tobacco* (ed. Edward Arber, English Reprints [London, 1895]) published anonymously in 1604 but acknowledged and included among the king's collected works in 1610, fulminates against the "filthie abuse" in language so similar to Overdo's as to make the latter sound almost like deliberate parody. For James, tobacco has a "venemous facultie" and a "hatefull smell" (p. 103); its use is a "vile custome" (p. 109) and a "filthie noueltie" (p. 112); it is "a branche of the sinne of drunkennesse" (p. 109), stirring up lascivious appetites. Its effects on the human organism are disastrous: "Smoke becomes a kitchin far better then a Dining chamber, and yet it makes a kitchin also oftentimes in the inward parts of men, soiling and infecting them, with an vnctuous and oily kinde of Soote, as hath bene found in some great *Tobacco* takers, that after their death were opened" (p. 111). Smoking, concludes the king, after an account of its villainous effects on the commonwealth, is "a custome lothsome to the eye, hatefull to the Nose, harmefull to the braine, dangerous to the Lungs, and in the blacke stinking fume thereof, neerest resembling the horrible Stigian smoke of the pit that is bottomelesse" (p. 112).

24. *Satires* I.iii.19–37, in *Satires, Epistles and Ars Poetica*, ed. H. Rushton Fairclough, Loeb Classical Library (Cambridge, Mass., 1926), p. 34.

25. At least, it is not enough to preserve a *magistrate* from folly. "*Wise*, is rather the Attribute of a Prince, then *learned*, or *good*. The learned man profits others, rather then himselfe: the good man, rather himselfe then others: But the Prince commands others, and doth himselfe" (*Disc.* 1003–06). Reading "magistrate" for "prince," we can apply the statement to Overdo.

26. Chambers, *Elizabethan Stage*, I, 269–307.

27. Quoted from Andreas Gerhard Hyperius, *The Practise of preaching*, Englished by Iohn Ludham (London, 1577), fol. 9r–9v, in Howell, *Logic and Rhetoric*, p. 112.

28. Brome may have grasped this connection dimly himself. See *Covent-Garden Weeded*, sig. [2]B2 (Cockbrain): "the spark of impiety," "the egge of a mischief."

29. It is diverting to discover that Stephen Gosson, a playwright of a very different stripe, one suspects, from Jonson, also wrote a play about Catiline, but instead of later turning it to a jape, pointed to it in his subsequent diatribes against the theater as one of the rare plays that did not defile the ears of the hearers: ". . . some of their playes are without rebuke. . . . The Black Smiths Daughter, and Catilins Conspiracies. . . . The last because it is knowen to be a pig of mine owne Sowe, I will speake the lesse of it; onely giving you to under-

stand that the whole mark which I shot at in that woorke was to showe the rewarde of traytors in Catiline, and the necessary government of learned men in the person of Cicero, which foresees every danger that is likely to happen, and forstalles it continually ere it take effect" (*The School of Abuse* (*1579*), Shakespeare Society [London, 1841], pp. 29–30).

30. See Herford and Simpson, II, 142, and the relevant passage in the *Conversations*, lines 295–305 (Herford and Simpson, I, 140–141).

31. Crosswill, in *Covent-Garden Weeded*, is Brome's typically inept and sentimentalized version of Wasp. But again, Brome is assiduous in copying the stylistic quirks of the Jonsonian original. See sig. [2] C8: "Uds precious *I* minde nothing, *I* am so crost in mind that *I* can minde nothing, nor *I* will minde nothing, dee see"; and [2]F7v: "It does not please me, nor thou pleasest me, nor any thing pleases me."

32. Cp. *Covent-Garden Weeded* (Crosswill): "But I will be obeyed in my own way, dee see" (sig. [2]B2v), "I'll make your heart ake else, dee see" ([2]B4v), "Let him look to't. Dee see" ([2]B5), etc.

33. Alden, ed., *Bartholomew Fair*, p. 172, where sixty-eight occurrences of the word are instanced.

34. See Baskervill, *English Elements*, pp. 43–44, and Enck, *Jonson and the Comic Truth*, p. 190.

35. *Gulliver's Travels, A Tale of a Tub, Battle of the Books, etc.*, ed. William Alfred Eddy (New York, 1933), pp. 494, 497.

36. W[illiam] Gifford, ed., *The Works of Ben Jonson*, rev. F. Cunningham, 9 vols. (London, 1875), IV, 509.

37. Levin, ed., *Ben Jonson*, p. 21.

38. Troubleall's slogan reinforces one of the common reproofs against Puritanism, which the Puritans were forced to refute with indignation. "I haue heard them reason," exclaims Stubbes, "that mutuall coition betwixt man and woman is not so offensiue before God; For . . . doth not the Lord (say they) (as it were with a stimule or prick, by his mandat, saing *crescite* & *multiplicamini* & *replete terram*: increase, multiplie & fill the earth,) stirre them vp to the same?" (*Anatomy of Abuses*, p. 90).

For Ray L. Heffner, Jr. ("Unifying Symbols in the Comedy of Ben Jonson," *English Stage Comedy*, ed. W. K. Wimsatt, Jr., English Institute Essays, 1954 [New York, 1955]), "The central theme" of *Bartholomew Fair* "is the problem of what 'warrant' men have or pretend to have for their actions," and Troubleall's lunacy, hence, a "fantastic caricature of the widespread and not unnatural human craving for clearly defined authority," becomes "the most significant unifying device in the play" (pp. 89–90).

39. Enck, "Ben Jonson's Imagery," pp. 349–350.

40. Juvenal, I, 7–14, 85–86; Persius, Prologue, and I, *passim* — in *Juvenal and Persius*, ed. G. G. Ramsey, Loeb Classical Library (Cambridge, Mass., 1940), pp. 2, 8, 310.

41. X.iv.8 — *Epigrams*, ed. Walter C. A. Ker, Loeb Classical Library (Cambridge, Mass., 1920), II, 154.

42. *Works*, ed. McKerrow, III, 195–201.

43. *Non-Dramatic Works*, ed. Alexander B. Grosart, Huth Library, 5 vols. (London, 1885), II, 101.

44. Perhaps it is part of a larger pattern common to comedy as a genre. In comedy, "even the gods . . . are bourgeois — Dionysus in the *Frogs*, Heracles in the *Birds*, Hermes in the *Plutus*" (Albert Cook, *The Dark Voyage and the Golden Mean* [Cambridge, Mass., 1949], p. 48).

45. Stubbes, *Anatomy of Abuses*, p. 137.

46. *Elizabethan Critical Essays*, ed. G. Gregory Smith, 2 vols. (London, 1904), I, 76.

47. *Ibid.*, I, 176, 199.

48. *An Apology for Actors* (1612), facs. ed. Richard H. Perkinson (New York, 1941), sig. F4.

49. ". . . sometimes they [the puppets] were signalled out for ridicule as a 'ridiculous idle childish invention' [Nashe]; sometimes for attack, along with minstrels and interludes, as 'ministers of vain pleasures, enchanting men's ears with poisoned songs,' that 'with idle and effeminate pastimes corrupt noble wits' [Geoffrey Fenton], but often they were ignored: puppets are not specified by name in any of the Vagrancy Acts, nor in the manifestos forbidding resort to all places of common assembly during times of plague" (George Speaight, *The History of the English Puppet Theatre* [London, 1955], p. 69).

50. E.g., Maurice Castelain, *Ben Jonson l'homme et l'oeuvre* (Paris, 1907), p. 381.

51. Stubbes, *Anatomy of Abuses*, p. 143; John Northbrooke, *A Treatise against Dicing, Dancing, Plays, and Interludes* (*1577*), ed. J[ohn] P[ayne] C[ollier], Shakespeare Society (London, 1843), p. 99; Gosson, *Plays Confuted in Five Actions*, in Hazlitt, ed., *The English Drama and Stage*, pp. 170–177.

Chapter VI. Painting, Carpentry, and Prose

1. L. C. Knights, *Drama and Society in the Age of Jonson* (London, 1937).

2. Of the standard studies of the masque, Rudolph Brotanek, *Die englische Maskenspiele* (Vienna, 1902), and Paul Reyher, *Les masques*

anglaises (Paris, 1909), are still useful. The richest discussions of the background in festival and folk drama are those of E. K. Chambers in *The Mediaeval Stage*, I, 89–419, particularly the chapter entitled "Masks and Misrule," and in *The Elizabethan Stage*, I, 106–212, on masques and pageantry. Mary Sullivan, *The Court Masques of James I* (New York, 1913), deals mainly with political aspects such as the disputes for precedency among the foreign ambassadors. A concise essay with bibliography by Percy Simpson appears in *Shakespeare's England*, 2 vols. (Oxford, 1916), II, 311–333. Enid Welsford, *The Court Masque* (Cambridge, 1927), contains an excellent account of the background and continental analogues of the masque, but is somewhat disappointing in its treatment of the climactic Stuart period. The most exhaustive survey of masque staging, copiously illustrated, is that of Allardyce Nicoll, *Stuart Masques and the Renaissance Stage* (London, 1937). Finally, the notes to the masques in Herford and Simpson (X, 386–710) are thickly provided with extracts from contemporary records.

3. *Anatomy of Criticism* (Princeton University Press, 1957), pp. 287–288. (The *auto* takes its name from the *auto sacramentale*, or religious festival play, of Calderón.)

4. *The Mediaeval Stage*, I, 391, 400.

5. Allan H. Gilbert, "The Function of the Masques in *Cynthia's Revels*," *Philological Quarterly*, XXII (1943), 211–213; Ernest Talbert, "The Interpretation of Jonson's Courtly Spectacles," *Publications of the Modern Language Association*, LXI (1946), 454–473; Allan H. Gilbert, *The Symbolic Persons in the Masques of Ben Jonson* (Durham, 1948), pp. 25–26.

6. See Dolora Cunningham, "The Jonsonian Masque as a Literary Form," *ELH*, XXII (1955), 115–121.

7. It may be well to call attention to the ambiguities in the terms "masque" and "antimasque." The first, in its strictest sense, refers to the dances performed by the masquers (entry, main, and going out; measures and revels), the second to the grotesque caper introduced as contrast. Jonson's definition implies as much, but Jonson speaks not only of a "*Daunce*" but of a "shew," which may be taken to include any songs, spoken dialogue, and stage effects that accompany the dance. There is a further complication in the fact that "masque" may mean either the entire spectacle or only that part of it distinct from the antimasque.

8. See the careful analysis of D. J. Gordon ("*Hymenaei*: Ben Jonson's Masque of Union," in *Journal of the Warburg and Courtauld Institutes*, VIII [1945], 107–145), especially of the political aspects of the entertainment (pp. 120–128); "*Hymenaei* is not only a formal

wedding masque; *Hymenaei* is a dramatic and symbolic representation of the Union of the Kingdoms as it was conceived in the propaganda issued by men who had the approval of the king himself" (p. 127).

For a fascinating study of microcosmic symbolism in the sixteenth-century Italian court theater, especially with respect to theater construction and stage design, see Richard Bernheimer, "Theatrum Mundi," *Art Bulletin*, XXXVIII (1956), 225–247. The more familiar literary aspects of the theme are treated in Jean Jacquot, " 'Le théâtre du monde' de Shakespeare à Calderón," *Revue de Littérature Comparée*, XXXI (1957), 341–372.

9. *The Elizabethan Stage*, I, 194.

10. Frye, *Anatomy of Criticism*, p. 286.

11. A more particular circumstance that may have hastened the drift toward comedy was the queen's sickness and her withdrawal from masquing. She danced for the last time in 1611 (Chambers, *The Elizabethan Stage*, I, 174), after which the splendors of the "queen's masque" became, obviously, impossible.

12. "Rediscovered" because comic prose is frequent enough in the country entertainments of the previous reign. In Lyly alone, the contention between a gardener and a mole-catcher at Theobalds, the speeches of Pan and two nymphs at Bisham, of the rustics at Sudeley, the bailiff and the dairymaid at Harefield, the Porter, the Pilgrim, and the Angler at Cowdray, are all composed in a winningly colloquial and fresh vein of Euphuism. Lyly also anticipates some of Jonson's themes. The fortunetelling episode at Harefield suggests Jonson's fortunetelling gypsies; the letters of greeting to the queen from her loyal subjects abroad, in the entertainment at Rycote, reminds one of Jonson's use of Welsh and Irish types in his masques. See Lyly, *Works*, ed. Bond, I, 417–504.

13. Compare, for example, with Robin's account of his disguises and misadventures (*Love Rest.* 87–125), the complaint of Capriccio in Chapman's *Masque of the Middle Temple and Lincoln's Inn* 18–22: "A man must be a second Proteus, and turn himself into all shapes, like Ulysses, to wind through the straits of this pinching vale of misery. I have turned myself into a tailor, a man, a gentleman, a nobleman, a worthy man; but had never the wit to turn myself into an alderman" (*Comedies*, ed. Thomas Marc Parrott [London, 1914], p. 447). As late as 1633, changes were being rung on this theme. See Shirley, *The Triumph of Peace*, in *Dramatic Works and Poems*, ed. William Gifford and Alexander Dyce, 6 vols. (London, 1833), VI, 280–281, where the wives of tradesmen connected with the preparation of the masque clamor for admission.

14. *Works*, ed. Percival Vivian (Oxford, 1909), p. 90. Campion, it may be added, was a conservative, and the prose in his only masque with prose in it, *The Entertainment at Cawsome House* (1613), is far more Lylian than Jonsonian.

15. Edgar Hill Duncan ("The Alchemy in Jonson's *Mercury Vindicated*," *Studies in Philology*, XXXIX [1942], 625–637) distinguishes accurately between Jonson's use of similar materials in the present masque and in *The Alchemist*. *The Alchemist* is an attack on imposture and credulity; *Mercury Vindicated* satirizes alchemy itself and its presumption in trying to improve on nature.

16. *Aminta, favola boscareccia*, ed. Angelo Solerti (Turin, 1926), pp. 135–138.

17. See D. J. Gordon, "The Imagery of Ben Jonson's *The Masque of Blacknesse* and *The Masque of Beautie*," *Journal of the Warburg and Courtauld Institutes*, VI (1943), 129–130.

18. *Anatomy of Criticism*, p. 290.

19. I concur here with Miss Enid Welsford's interpretation, in *The Court Masque*, pp. 168–244. Miss Welsford traces the influence of the French *ballet de cour* even on Jonson as early as 1617, in *The Vision of Delight*, and to foreign pressures in general she attributes the Poet's sarcasms against antimasques in *Neptune's Triumph* (pp. 198, 203). Herford and Simpson, on the other hand, stress the disintegrating effects of the "approximation to comedy" as a path "to decay and ruin for the Masque" (II, 311).

20. The verses of invective, "To his false freind Mr. Ben Johnson," reprinted in J. Alfred Gotch, *Inigo Jones* (London, 1928), Appendix B, pp. 254–255, have nothing to say about masques or masquing.

21. See D. J. Gordon, "Poet and Architect: The Intellectual Setting of the Quarrel between Ben Jonson and Inigo Jones," *Journal of the Warburg and Courtauld Institutes*, XII (1949), 152–178.

22. "Of Maskes and Triumphs," *Essays*, ed. Geoffrey Grigson, World's Classics (London, 1937), p. 157.

23. *Works*, ed. Vivian, p. 75.

24. *The Complete Works in Verse and Prose*, ed. Alexander B. Grosart, 5 vols. (London, 1885), III, 196, 307.

25. *Le théâtre et son double* (Paris, 1938), p. 79. Artaud, conversely, regards the ephemerality of the masques as an ideal to be copied today: "Sous la poésie des textes, il y a la poésie tout court, sans forme et sans texte. Et comme l'efficacité des masques, qui servent aux opérations de magie de certaines peuplades, s'épuise; — et ces masques ne sont plus bons qu'à rejeter dans les musées — de même s'épuise l'efficacité poétique d'un texte . . ." (pp. 83–84).

26. *Comedies*, ed. Parrott, I, 444.

27. *Poems and Masks*, ed. E. K. Chambers (Oxford, 1912), pp. 87–88.

28. *Ibid.*, p. 67.

Chapter VII. Jonson and the Language of Prose Comedy

1. *On Poetry and Style*, trans. G. M. A. Grube, Library of Liberal Arts (New York, 1958), p. 9. The translations concur on this point, except that L. J. Potts, *Aristotle on the Art of Fiction* (Cambridge, 1953), p. 22, has "the very nature of the thing" rather than "nature herself" — which seems to make little difference.

2. Dedicatory Epistle to *Six premières comédies facécieuses*, in Viollet le Duc, ed., *Ancien théâtre françois*, 10 vols. (Paris, 1854–57), V, 2–3.

3. *Tutte le opere*, ed. Giuseppe Ortolani, 14 vols. (Milan, 1946), VII, 1381.

4. *Language of Satirized Characters*, pp. 162–163.

5. Harry Levin, in conversation.

6. *Plays*, ed. H. Harvey Wood, 3 vols. (Edinburgh, 1934–39).

7. Introduction to Eudora Welty, *A Curtain of Green* (New York, 1941), p. xvii.

8. *Dramatic Works*, ed. H. F. B. Brett-Smith, 2 vols. (Oxford, 1927), II, 190.

9. *The Verbal Icon* (Lexington, Kentucky, 1954), pp. 133–151.

10. Doubtless it is the difference between the "empiricism" of English style and the rationalism of French style that prompts James K. Feibleman to remark that "the comic writers, Congreve, Vanbrugh, Farquhar, Wycherley and others, had what Molière did not have: a keen perception of the smallest details of daily life. The British were empiricists in comedy . . . they could find the little faults, the contemporary evils, with an unerring eye" (*In Praise of Comedy* [London, 1939], p. 59).

11. *The Old Drama and the New* (London, 1923), pp. 174ff.

12. *Oeuvres complètes*, ed. Raymond Picard, Bibliothèque de la Pléiade, 2 vols. (Paris, 1950), I, 328.

13. Letter to John Dennis, "Concerning Humour in Comedy," *Comedies*, ed. Dobrée, p. 7.

14. *Essays*, ed. Ker, I, 176.

15. *Aspects of the Novel* (London, 1927), pp. 93–106.

Index

Index

INDEX